W. Du Buse pin.

A HISTORY OF DEVONPORT

View of Plymouth, the Sound, Stonehouse and Mt Edgcumbe from beyond Stoke. c1680 watercolour by W Du Buse artist (City of Plymouth Museum & Art Gallery)

British Library Cataloguing in Publication Data

Chris Robinson
History of Devonport
A catalogue record for this book is available from the British Library

ISBN 978 - 0 - 9543480 - 9 - 0

Written and illustrated by Chris Robinson
Lay Out and Design Chris Robinson

First published 2010

Published by
Pen & Ink Publishing
34 New Street, Barbican
Plymouth PL1 2NA
Tel: 01752 705337/228120
Fax: 01752 770001
www.chrisrobinson.co.uk

Printed and bound in Great Britain by
Latimer Trend & Company Ltd
Estover Close
Plymouth PL6 7PL
Devon

CONTENTS

PRORSUM·SEMPER·HONESTE

FOREWORD
Marc Gardiner

It's a bright morning in April 2010, and I'm sitting at my 10th floor window looking out over Devonport and the city beyond. On the site of the former Stores Enclave of the dock's South Yard, builders teem about the scaffolding as the regeneration gathers pace and we begin to sense once again something of the vibrancy and grandeur of old Devonport.

But this regeneration effort is not just about buildings: we've tried to capture the area's historic community spirit – well documented in this book – as we work together to improve people's lives and opportunities. Devonport has a proud history, and this pride survives amongst its people despite the problems that have hit the area in recent times, and the impact these have had on its reputation. Indeed, changing Devonport's reputation, creating a new image of the area in the eyes of those looking in from the rest of Plymouth and beyond, has been a big challenge. It's helped that Plymouth Albion has moved here and that the Brickfields and the Mount Wise cricket pitch have been handed over by the MOD: together these bring thousands of people here to play from week to week.

The replacement of substandard flats with state of the art housing, for sale as well as rent, is transforming the appearance of the area and offering attractive options to people to come and live here. I hope that this book will contribute further to the creation of a more three-dimensional – and more positive – story about Devonport.

Plymouth local historian Chris Robinson has written an in-depth, fascinating account of Devonport, from its birth in 1690 to its rapid growth during times of war and peace into a town of international significance and renown, through to its decline during the 20th century and the beginnings of recovery today. Chris' work, which is brought to life by the wealth of images and the eyewitness accounts across the ages, has taught me much I didn't know, and has corrected me on much I thought I did. Reading the more recent history, I was intrigued to begin to recognise the Devonport of my lifetime and to better understand how and why it ran into difficulty.

In closing his work, Chris questions the sustainability of recent developments, and he is right to do so. We are working hard to anchor the gains and secure the continuation of the transformation when we're gone, but there are inherent risks to this ambitious regeneration project which set out to tackle and reverse the strong forces working against the interests of Devonport people and to achieve some social justice. We cannot be complacent.

I welcome the publication of this important work, which masterfully tells the story so far as we work together to take it up from here.

Marc Gardiner

Marc Gardiner Resident & Chair
Devonport Regeneration Community Partnership
April 2010

INTRODUCTION

I have chosen to write this book in four separate guises, covering four distinct periods of time.

The beginning of our story is recounted through the persona of the first Master Shipwright of the Dockyard, Elias Waffe.

Appointed in January 1690 just months after the decision had been taken to site a new Royal Dock Yard somewhere in the neighbourhood, Elias Waffe married Mary Theede on 15 December 1691, in London. One of the first Officers at Hamoze to be housed in the splendid new terrace here, Waffe lived next door to the Commissioner of the Yard and was second only in seniority to him.

The first section of this history of Devonport is called Hamoze simply because almost all of the early maps and written references to the new development called it that. Occasionally it is referenced as the Dock at Plymouth, but in most instances where it is given an identity of its own, it is Hamoze or Hamoaze.

In the early part of 1698 Elias moved up to Portsmouth, it was just after Mary had became pregnant with their son, also Elias. However once in Portsmouth his paths continued to cross with various characters who were important players in the early days of Devonport and so it seemed logical to use his voice for this part of the story. However we have no written record of any of his observations and so the narrative, while based on actual events, is the product of artistic licence.

Edward Hoxland, meanwhile, it is who picks up the literary baton in 1796, for that was when he published *The Plymouth Dock Guide, or An Authentic Account of the Rise and Progress of that Town.*

As such it predated any published specific account of Plymouth by a lifetime – the first essays towards a full history of Plymouth appearing in the 1870s.

Wherever possible I have used Hoxland's narrative as it appeared, adapting it here and there to make it a little more accessible, I have also added in elements of other contemporary texts, most notably Britton and Brayley's *The Beauties of England* published in 1801. The extensive section on Dock (Devonport) in the Devon volume was written anonymously:

'For the miscellaneous remarks on the present and recent state of society in Dock, we are indebted to a very intelligent inhabitant, whose habits of observation, and long residence in the town, have rendered him fully competent to describe its manners.'

Not surprisingly, the arrestingly frank comments by this unidentified writer are somewhat less glowing than Hoxland's rather gentle soft-sell observations; after all, Hoxland was writing to promote his book, his business and the town in which he worked; Britton and Brayley's project, meanwhile, was written to give readers a flavour, both in words and pictures, of different parts of the country. Interestingly enough, however, a similar tone pervades George Lipscomb's 1799 account of his *Journey into Cornwall through the counties of Southampton, Wilts, Dorset, Somerset and Devon, interspersed with remarks, Moral, Historical, Literary and Political,* one or two extracts from which I have also included.

Henry Whitfeld, on the other hand, was, in the 1890s, the editor of the *Devonport Independent*, and as such he waged a campaign, through the paper and through pamphlets like 'The Curse of Devonport' and 'The Boy at the Back of Morice Square' against the squalid conditions in the town, the blame for which he not unreasonably laid at the feet of the St Aubyn estate who then owned much of the town.

In 1899 Whitfeld published *Plymouth and Devonport in Times of War and Peace,* a weighty tome, couched in purple prose and packed with anecdotal excerpts from old newspapers.

Picking up where Whitfeld left off, I have endeavoured to provide an overview of Devonport in the twentieth century, with considerable assistance, during the Second World War years, from Pat Twyford, another newspaper man, and Ron Radford, a Devonport resident.

Until relatively recently the Devonport story had not been as happy as it might have been, however there is genuine optimism across the community today and I only wish it would be possible to see how everything stands at the end of this century. However, that will be the task of someone yet to be born.

Chris Robinson *Summer 2010*

HISTORY OF DEVONPORT

Chris Robinson
with maps and engravings
colour-washed by
Rob Warren

This publication was funded by Devonport Regeneration Community Partnership which is part of the Department for Communities and Local Government's 10 year New Deal for Communities (NDC) programme.

1690-91 Jno. Paige

In this Gentleman's Mayoralty happened nothing memorable, but that the dock in Ham hoas was begun, & that the 2d Sept at the end of it, a Storm drove our Grand fleet then on ye Coast into this Harbour, where the Coronation of ninety gunns was Sunk and men drowned except 14, and the Harwich of 74 Gunns Lost under Mt Edgcomb.

Russel In the Brittannia Admiral of the Red, Killigrew In the duke of ye Blew. here was also ye Sovereign, &c.

View of Plymouth from Mount Edgcumbe, watercolour by W. DuBusc c.1680 (© Plymouth City Museum & Art Gallery)

Hamoze *Elias Waffe*

Setting the Scene

On 18 January 1690 I had the great honour to be appointed the first Master Shipwright of His Majesty's Dockyard at Plymouth. However, you should not be deceived into thinking that I arrived to take on a fully working yard – nothing could be further from the truth.
Mr Dummer, the Assistant Surveyor of the Navy, whom the Admiralty had sent out to find a suitable site for a new naval dockyard, the previous year, was still looking favourably on the Cattewater as a possible location. Consequently, my role was to help prepare the way for the establishment of a new dockyard: what materials we would need to have on the site; which buildings, what number of men. At the same time that my position was advertised the Navy Board were also seeking a Master Attendant, a Master Caulker and Storekeeper.
At that stage the Navy were not looking for much more than a dry dock that they could use to repair ships; ships that were in the area but not easily able to make it up to Portsmouth. To that end Mr Dummer had also considered Dartmouth a possibility, but eventually settled on Plymouth. Nevertheless, the modest nature of the project he had been charged with still had him thinking in terms of the Cattewater, even though, less than two weeks before I was appointed, the Admiralty had reported that, after meeting the King, in court, 'at the Robes', *'His Majesty resolved that he would have a dry dock built of stone at Ham Oze in the Port of Plymouth'* and to that end they had requested that the Navy Board get on with the job.
As the forces of fate were to have it, it wasn't until November 1690 that Mr Dummer finally decided against the location and work actually began on turning the Hamoze site into a real dockyard.
By that time both the people and Parliament were clamouring for some sort of action in the wake of the French naval victory (26 July 1689) at Beachy Head and the enemy's subsequent bombardment of Teignmouth. There was genuine concern that the French, who now seemed to have command of the English Channel, might be planning an invasion to restore King James and his Popish ways to the English throne.
So it was that the scale of the new Plymouth dockyard grew. At first just a few storehouses were added – for ship's stores – principally to relieve the pressure on the victualling facilities that the Lord Protector, Cromwell, had set up overlooking the Cattewater on the side of Lambhay Hill.

The Civil War

The introduction of victualling facilities there had done much to enhance the town of Plymouth after the dark days of the Civil War. Some of the residents can still recall those difficult years and the triumphant reception that was afforded Cromwell and Sir Thomas Fairfax in March 1644 when they came into the town just two weeks after the Cornish Army had surrendered and some two months after the last Royalist troops had marched away from the siege of Plymouth.

'300 pieces of ordnance were discharged to welcome them thither.' The two great Parliamentarian leaders were entertained as richly as was possible in a town that had been under siege since November 1642. Not surprisingly the population had reduced during the long years of confinement, so too had the levels of business and trade, thus the long-awaited Parliamentarian success brought the prospect of increased prosperity.

Cromwell and Fairfax went up onto Plymouth Hoe and visited the fort erected there in Drake's time, some fifty years earlier – an undoubted improvement on the old castle that overlooked Sutton Harbour. The Roundhead generals also made a tour of the semi-circle of works outside the town wall, such as it was, and Fairfax took the opportunity to make Colonel Edgcumbe an offer for the surrender of Mount Edgcumbe House. Edgcumbe was promised that his house would not be garrisoned and he could continue to enjoy the use of it with his personal safety and that of his possessions, guaranteed. He agreed and handed over 30 pieces of ordnance and stores of ammunition. Mount Wise House, overlooking Mount Edgcumbe, had been occupied by the Parliamentarians during that time. Odd as it may now seem, until we began work on the dockyard at Hamoze, Mount Wise House was the only building of consequence in this area. It was erected, and named, a hundred years ago (in 1591) by Sir Thomas Wise in respectful imitation of his neighbour Richard Edgcumbe, who had had Edgcumbe House built some forty years before that.

View of Mt Edgcumbe, by Gerard Edema (1652-1700) oil on canvas (© Plymouth City Museum & Art Gallery) *Prior to its development the estate was covered with brake and abounded in partridges; no roads or thoroughfares intersected it; and the approaches were merely beaten tracks.*

The Wise family evidently acquired the Stoke Damerel estate through marriage, back in 1428, but for many years chose to remain in the family seat at Sydenham, near Launceston, rather than move here where the manor house then was at Keyham (Keame) a little to the north of our site.

Unlike Mount Edgcumbe House, Mount Wise House commanded spectacular views of Plymouth Sound. However the estate around it is largely featureless, lacking the trees and planting that give any area its varieties of shape and colour and vista. Nevertheless Sir Thomas Wise's son, also Thomas, lived here, after his father's death, and together with Mary, his wife, had eight children. Of these children, it was young Edward Wise who inherited the estate after his father, Thomas died, aged forty.

Edward, who was just ten years old when the siege of Plymouth started, had a difficult few years as, not only was Mount Wise occupied by Cromwell's men, but they also established a garrison at the ancestral home, Sydenham, and did extensive damage to that property.

Thus it came to pass that Edward sold Mount Wise House, and the rest of the Manor of Stoke Damerel, to William Morice for £11,050 in 1667 – Wise wanted to raise funds for re-building Sydenham House, near Launceston.

Morice was then in his mid-sixties, he had been a Devon MP since 1648, but was one of the 230 or so MPs who were excluded in the Purge instigated by Colonel Thomas Pride's men later that year. This was the event that ultimately precipitated the execution of King Charles less than a month later.

Two years after that Morice was appointed High Sheriff of Devon and in 1654 he took his seat in the Parliament of the Protectorate: he also served in subsequent Parliaments under Lord Protector Cromwell.

Had the Cromwell's son Richard enjoyed the support of the Army, William Morice's subsequent career may have been much different – along with that of countless others – for it was his role in the Restoration that saw Sheriff Morice knighted and appointed Secretary for State.

View of Mt Edgcumbe, by Gerard Edema (1652-1700) oil on canvas (© Plymouth City Museum & Art Gallery)
The mansion at Mount Wise was surrounded by a few fields which yielded food for the family in possession.

Sir William Morice

Restoration of the Monarchy

Although it is not that long ago it is worth recalling that Richard Cromwell was removed from power by the Army just seven months after succeeding his father. Led by Fleetwood, who was swiftly styled Lord General, Commander-in-Chief, and General John Lambert, who became Major-General of All Forces in England and Scotland, the Army then attempted, through their 'Committee of Safety' to do battle with the Governor of Scotland, and another Devon man, George Monck.

Monck's motives were, at the time, a little unclear, but the end result was that Lambert's army, having not been drawn into armed conflict, became disenchanted and, as they were not receiving regular payments, started to slink away. General Monck was thus able to take London without spilling any blood

General Monck

Having courted both Parliament and, secretly, the exiled Charles Stuart, Monck became the principal architect of the terms and conditions (the Declaration of Breda) under which our Country again became a Monarchy.

April 1661 Coronation of Charles II, Monck is behind the King.

The King lost little time in conferring a knighthood on Monck whom he also made Master of the Horse in the King's Household and Duke of Albermarle, Earl of Torrington. Fleetwood, meanwhile, was relieved of his command and, for his part in the affair, General Lambert was sent to the Tower of London at the beginning of March 1660. Escaping from his imprisonment the following month, Lambert made one last attempt to rekindle the Civil War, but was recaptured and subsequently incarcerated in a much more secure place of detention - Drake's Island - and there he was to remain until his death not that many years ago (1684).

Sir William Morice, it will not surprise you to learn, was a relative of General Monck and a key member of the team that the King assembled around him, becoming a Privy Councillor as well as (in June 1660) the first ever Secretary of State for the Northern Department - a position he held until his resignation in 1668. Sir William was, for most of that time, a Lord of the Treasury, and was almost certainly - I don't know if it was recorded - present at the laying of the foundation stone for the Royal Citadel, commissioned by King Charles, on Plymouth Hoe.

Together with the new Victualling Yard that Cromwell had instigated, this new major fortification helped to make Plymouth an increasingly important port for the country and doubtless had some influence over Mr Dummer's arguments in favour of the town for a Dockyard being sited here rather than at Dartmouth. With guns pointing out over the Sound and the town (the King was clearly anxious that the people of Plymouth should not resist the Royalist cause again) the Citadel provided protection for ships heading either for Sutton Harbour or the Cattewater, in one direction, and the Tamar and the Hamoze, in the other.

Mr Dummer was also shrewd enough to point out that, while the approach to the new yard at Hamoze was by no means straightforward, the fact that it was difficult and needed skillful piloting, counted in its favour, on the grounds that it would be even more difficult for the enemy to make the same journey and thus our ships would have a distinct advantage.

Up until the time we began working on establishing the new yard no reliable survey of the Sound, and the rivers pouring into it, had been undertaken. However, the situation was very swiftly remedied.

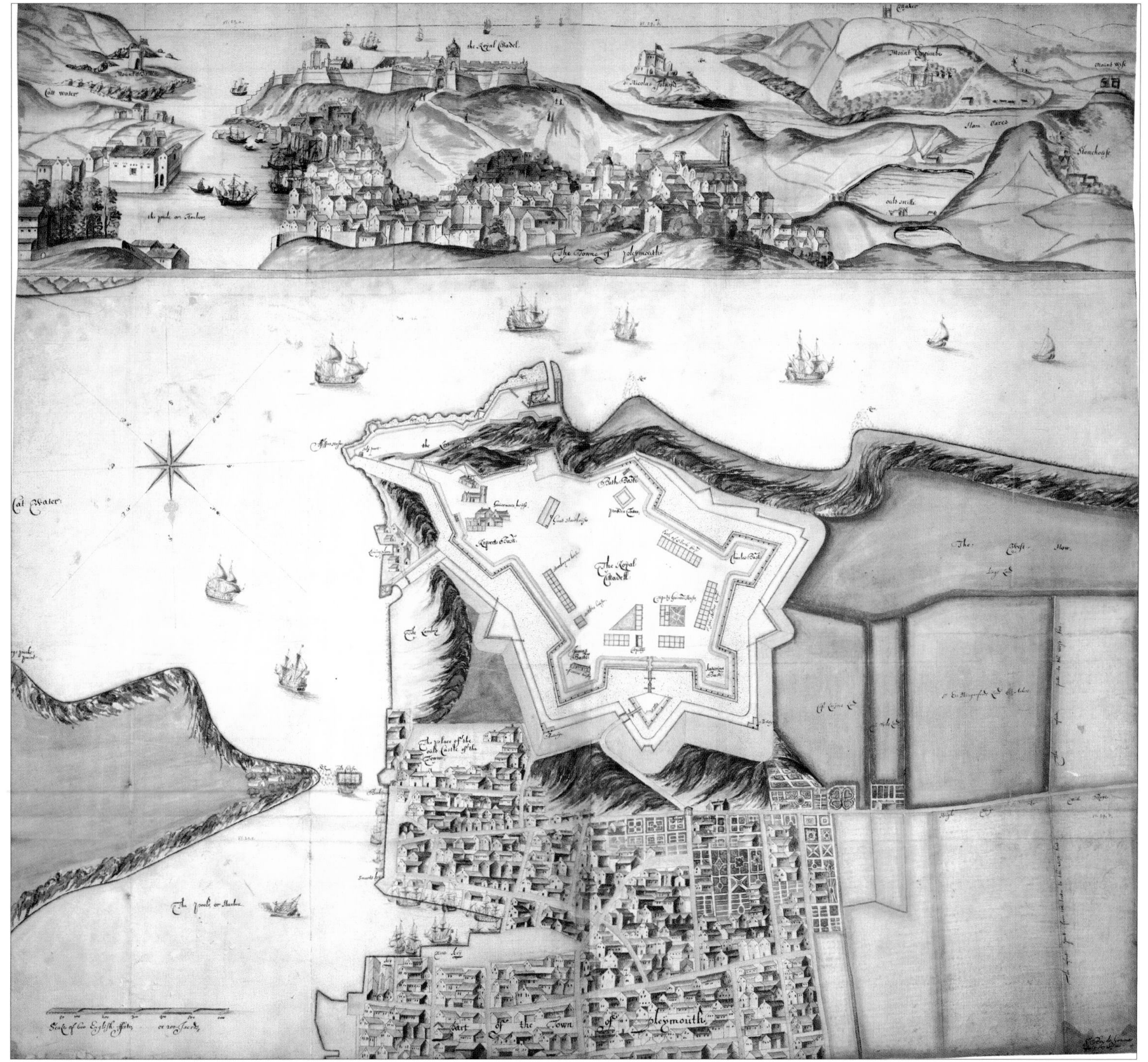

Decorative plan and perspective of Plymouth and the Citadel by the architect of the Citadel, Sir Bernard de Gomme. (National Maritme Museum)

Sir William Morice

Meanwhile, to return to the tale of our Lord of the Manor: Sir William Morice's main use to the restored monarchy was in Parliament, and as an MP he represented Plymouth in the House of Commons from 1660 through to his death in December 1676. Thirteen years later, his son, also Sir William Morice, entered the House of Commons as the MP for Newport (Morice senior had also represented that constituency at one point); Sir William's spell in Parliament, however, was to be short-lived as he died in office the following year. A particularly tragic feature of this situation was that his own son, another William, had died the previous year (1688) aged 28, all of which meant that the Lord of the Manor when we started creating a new dockyard for His Majesty on part of that land, was Sir William junior's only son from his second marriage, nine-year-old Nicholas Morice.

Of course, in the turbulent times since the Restoration of the Monarchy there has been further unprecedented change with regard to the ruler of our nation, as in the same year that the second Sir William Morice died, His Majesty, King James, was blessed with a son, thereby guaranteeing, in the eyes of many, Catholic succession. Parliament had already, unsuccessfully, tried to block any situation whereby any more Catholics might bear the English crown (in 1679) and this new arrival undoubtedly worried a great many of our citizens. A number of James' Protestant opponents secretly wrote to William of Orange, in the Netherlands.

In driving Louis XVI's French troops out of Holland, William firmly established himself as a champion of Protestantism. Like James II, William is also a grandson of Charles I, his mother being Charles' daughter Mary. Born in November 1650 William was keen, as his father had been, to cement Anglo-Dutch relations and on his 27th birthday he married his cousin, Mary, the daughter of James, Duke of York, who was destined to become King James II.

Diplomatically of course this was a good move, but truth be told, observers of the event found it to be most odd. Royal marriages often do produce strange matches, but seldom has a bride been so visibly upset.

Accounts suggest that the young Mary (she was but fifteen at the time) cried throughout the proceedings, proceedings which she had attended wearing funereal black attire. Standing an inch short of six-feet, the bride, in addition to being so much younger was also somewhat taller - a good four inches - than her groom. The union, however, has held firm and, following the requests for them to come over here in 1688, the Royal couple arrived at Torbay at the beginning of November with some fifty warships, 200 transport vessels carrying about 15,000 troops and 4,000 horses. After landing the Prince, and several thousand English and Scots troops, then in Dutch service, the fleet then swung around here and moored at Plymouth.

The Governor of Town, John Grenville, Earl of Bath, although long a friend of the Stuart kings, surrendered the Citadel and arrested the Commander of the Regiment in the garrison - the Earl of Huntingdon.

Sir John Grenville

Like Sir William Morice, Sir John Grenville is a cousin of General Monck and as a faithful servant of Charles I he was knighted by the King during the first Civil War in August 1643. It was the month the young nobleman celebrated his fifteenth birthday, and the gesture followed the Royalist capture of Bristol. Sir John's father, Sir Bevil Grenville had been killed the previous year at the battle of Lansdown and Sir Bevil's men instantly mounted the young heir on his father's horse and swore their allegiance to him.

Wounded and unconscious after the second Battle of Newbury in 1644, Sir John was found lying among the dead. He was, however, rescued and the following year he was appointed a Gentleman of the Bedchamber of Prince Charles (who was but a year or two his senior). The two became close friends and at the conclusion of the Civil War, Sir John accompanied Prince Charles to the Scilly Isles, then Jersey and France. After Parliament had ordered the execution of King Charles, the Prince appointed Sir John Governor of the Scillies, and, over the next couple of years, from bases in Tresco and St Mary's, Sir John raised funds for running the Royal Court in exile, by directing Royal privateers against both English and Dutch merchant vessels in the Channel.

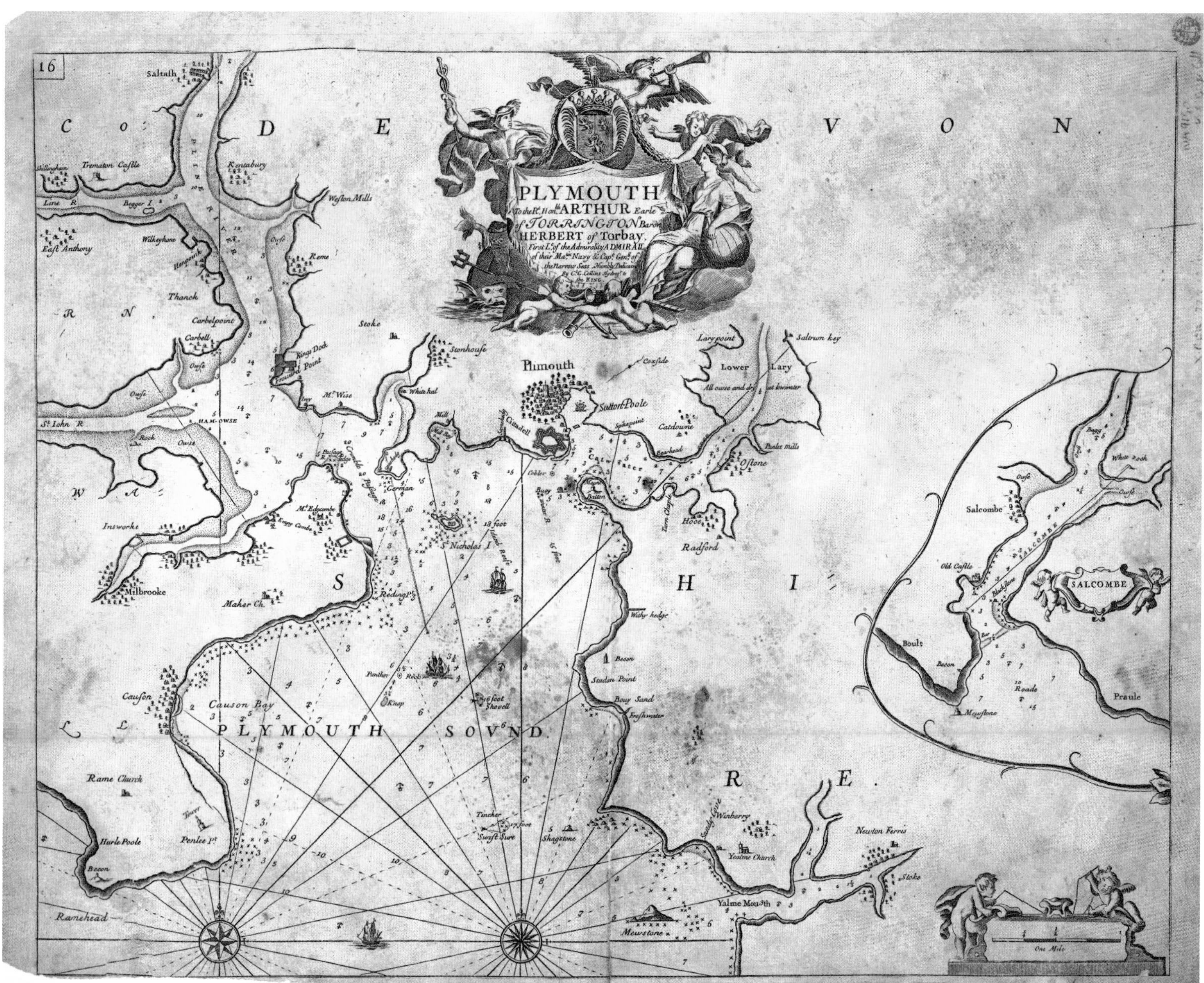

1693: The first detailed survey of Plymouth Sound with the King's Dock marked.

Forced to surrender in May 1651, and then briefly held prisoner here in Plymouth, Sir John was given the choice of either joining Prince Charles in exile or remaining in England.

He chose the second path and throughout the Protectorate worked stealthily as Charles' leading representative.

In 1654 he was associated with the Action Party, who had plotted to seize Pendennis Castle and Plymouth, and he was duly arrested the following February in the wake of an early uprising of south-western Royalists.

Four years later he was under suspicion again but was released on parole. By this time however Sir John had already set the wheels in motion for the Restoration of the Monarchy.

Sir John's first contact with his second cousin, General Monck, in this affair, was relayed via the General's brother, Nicholas, who Sir John had appointed as the incumbent of the Grenville family church on the Kilkhampton estate.

The clandestine passing of messages carried on for almost two years before a secret meeting was arranged in St James's Palace in March of 1660. It was at that meeting that Monck pledged allegiance to Charles. Sir John then made his way to Brussels where he personally informed the King-in-waiting of Monck's support and the terms by which the Restoration would be acceptable to Parliament. Thus it was that the aforementioned 'Declaration of Breda' was delivered to the House on 1 May.

Once installed as King, Charles lost little time in rewarding those who had been of great service to him, and for Sir John that meant he effectively became the most powerful man in Devon and Cornwall as he became Earl of Bath, Lord Lieutenant of Cornwall, Governor of Plymouth, and Warden of the Stannaries.

Six years later the stonemason responsible for chiselling out the wording on the foundation stone of the King's Royal Citadel upon the Hoe recorded the simple legend 'John, Earl of Bath 1666'. Little could anyone then have anticipated that some twenty years or so later, Sir John, having been present at Charles's death and last-minute conversion to Catholicism, would have a part to play in another bloodless coup affecting the governance of our country.

Having no legitimate issue (it is said that he sired at least nine children), Charles was succeeded by his brother James and the latter's flagrant affiliation to the Roman Catholic Church did not sit happily with many people up and down the country, particularly in Plymouth where there was already a greater degree of religious toleration that in most English towns. Thus, when William and Mary arrived in Plymouth they not only received a tumultuous reception but the people of Plymouth lost little time declaring their allegiance to them.

William and Mary

Sir John arrested the Loyalist Earl of Huntingdon, Commander of the Garrison, and surrendered the Citadel to the Royal couple. Plymouth thus became the first town in England to proclaim the new King and Queen, as the Town Clerk recorded in official records:

'God wrought a wonderful deliverance in these Kingdoms in rescuing us from Popery and Slavery ...'

Thus it was early in 1689 that Parliament, following James's flight to France, offered William and Mary the throne as joint monarchs. In so doing they were required by Parliament to accept a 'Declaration of Rights' a document which both restricted the power of the monarchy and affirmed certain rights relating to the power of Parliament. Let us hope that it heralds a greater degree of stability in the running of the country.

William and Mary take the throne as joint monarchs.

The Enterprise Begins

It will not surprise many readers to learn that the new king was a little more keen to build up the Navy than his predecessor had been. Of course much of this was to do with the fact that our old adversaries, the French, saw fresh opportunities for mischief, as support for James gave them the excuse to battle in the name of France and Catholicism.

Louis XIV had already started building a great new dockyard at Brest, in 1688, and Richelieu's fifty-year-old harbour at Cherbourg had recently been heavily fortified by Vauban.

Mr Dummer was very familiar with the work of Sebastien le Prestre de Vauban, having observed it first hand, and in some detail, in Toulon when he went on his two-year, fact-finding tour of the Mediterranean a few years ago (1682).

Sponsored by the Navy, Mr Dummer's instructions were signed by the Secretary to the Admiralty Board, Mr Samuel Pepys, and, under their terms, he was instructed to: *'collect what useful observations should arise to him, in his enquiries through the several foreign ports, appearances of land, or ought else that might conduce to our service.'*

In other words it was effectively a two-year reconnaissance trip - an extended spying mission - and by the end of it few men in the world could have had such a good working knowledge of contemporary ships and shipbuilding, docks and dockyards and the ports and harbours in which they had been established.

Remarkably, the journey almost faltered in Plymouth Sound. Mr Dummer had travelled down from Deal on the *Woolwich*, skippered by Captain Holding who was taking the Moorish Ambassador back to Tangier (the Ambassador had been in our country for about six months). However, while the *Woolwich* sat at anchor in the Sound, the Ambassador's retainers tried to mutiny - they were not successful. Happily the ship sailed on to Tangier, but Captain Holding died and was buried there and Lieutenant Rigby took command.

The *Woolwich* then sailed into the Mediterranean; their journey took them south of Sardinia and Sicily, across the Ionian Sea and to the Greek Islands of Cephalonia and Zante, then back through the Straits of Messina to Naples and Livorno where Mr Dummer left

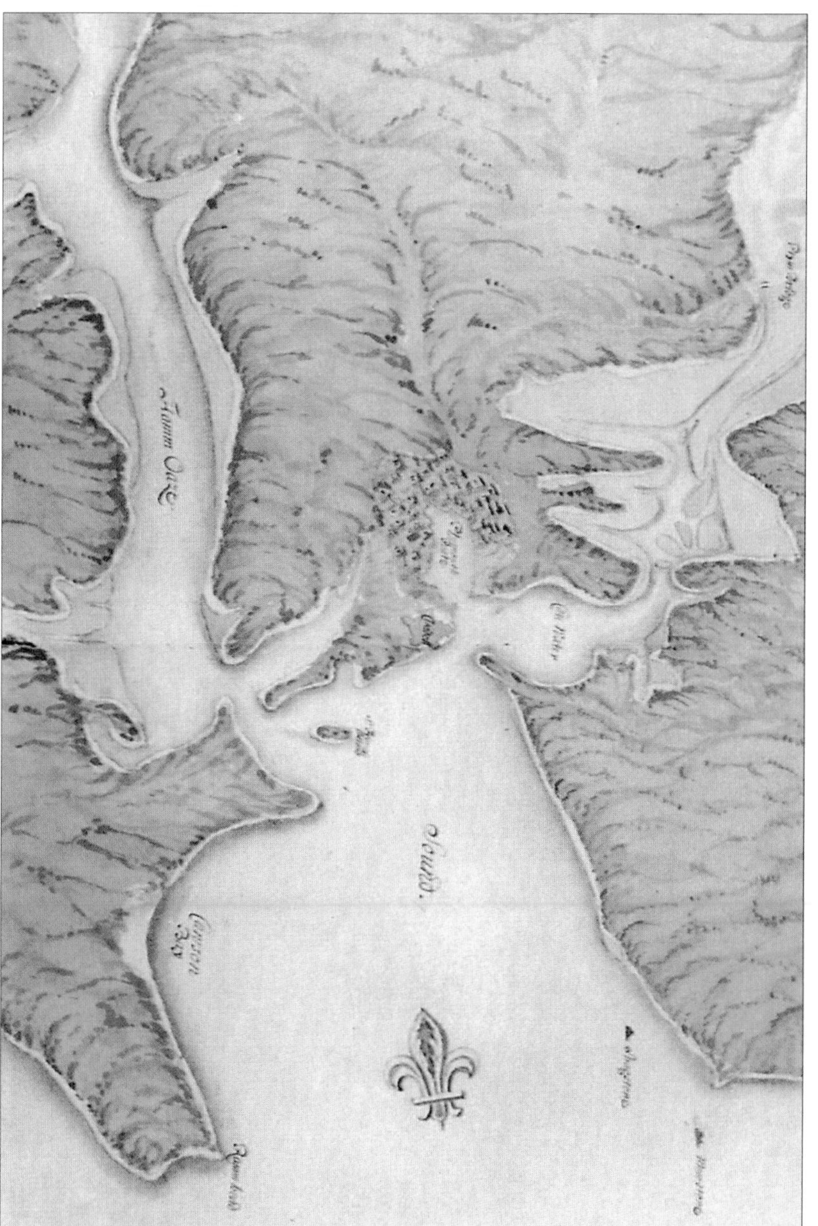

August 1682. Dummer's copy of Jerome Roch's 'Plain or Plott of Plymouth Sound Ham Oaze and Catt water' (The British Library Board - King's MS 40 f.8)

Dummer: At anchor in Plymouth Sound (The British Library Board - King's MS)

the ship. But he didn't stop drawing and making detailed notes and measurements about anything and everything, particularly about all those things that would be helpful to anyone wanting to create a new dockyard.

One feature that made a big impact on his thinking was the way in Toulon that ordnance was actually manufactured within the naval arsenal, rather than the separate site arrangement that was standard in England.

Mr Dummer also observed in his fine perspective illustrations the shape and size of storehouses, accommodation blocks, docks, quays, magazines and ships. And there were plenty of ships to look at.

At Toulon, where he was in April 1683, he found his presence there coincided with that of the French Fleet, some fifty ships of various shapes and sizes.

Getting on board to have a look around was seldom a problem. So many people were keen to have a look around these fighting ships that as long as you got a note from a 'special officer' they *'with much readiness permit you to go on board.'*

But it wasn't just fighting ships that Mr Dummer concerned himself with. From Genoa to Gibraltar, Cadiz to Constantinople, he also looked at fishing boats and cargo boats, of varying shapes and sizes, recording their proportions, from side view and their *'geometric designs'*, managing to create through a series of cross sections a model of each vessel that could be pulled into shape by a piece of string running through each section.

All in all it was a most remarkable body of work and it placed Mr Dummer as one of the leading shipwrights of our time, although Pepys himself favoured his own protégé Thomas Deane, thinking Mr Dummer to be too much of a *'philosopher draughtsman'* and not enough of a *'practical shipwright'*.

However, one undoubted practical suggestion to come out of Mr Dummer's efforts was the innovative notion that ships of a certain size should be built to a standard, thereby simplifying the ordering of stores and materials to be used in the construction process: considerations that were all the more pertinent as an order for thirty new ships was placed by the Navy. Not that the first few vessels that I was charged with building at Hamoze fell into that category.

The First Ships Are Built

Our first two launches were quite modest affairs; a pair of advice boats, the *Postboy* and the *Messenger*, both of them, as their names suggest, designed to move around the seas quickly bearing messages or dispatches or, alternatively, to bring back early intelligence of enemy positions or dispositions.

Each had a crew of some 40 men, carried four guns, and was around fifty feet long. As I recall they were both added to the Naval Fleet on 3 April 1694. Somewhat unfortunately the *Postboy's* career was all too brief as she was taken by a French privateer five months later and carried off to Dunkirk.

As the yard was far from being ready by the time we started working on our first major project, we had to hire Mr Fint's commercial boat yard to build the 48-gun *Anglesea*. She was launched a fortnight after the other two and had a full complement of 260 men. It was a proud moment and just days after *Postboy's* capture we learned that the *Anglesea*, under Captain William Prowther, had taken the privateer, *St Louis* after just an hour's sea battle. An auspicious start for our first man-of-war and a great encouragement for our men who were already working on our next major project, the *Lyme*, a fifth-rate man-of-war, that would, when operational, have a complement of 135 men. Again the new dock was not quite ready when work began and we had to hire Mr Fint's yard once more.

It was not an ideal arrangement and when we received a new Navy Warrant on 28 March 1695 – just a week or two before launching the *Lyme* – we were delighted at the prospect of being able to build a ship of similar proportions entirely within our new Dockyard. Having personally overseen all these projects it was an especially proud moment when, the *Looe* was added to the Navy in the summer of 1696.

Imagine our disappointment when, the following April, news filtered back from Ireland that she had been lost after striking a rock near Baltimore. Happily all the crew were saved, but the *Looe* sank without trace and almost 400 tons of wood was lost.

I am not always sure how aware country people are of the cost of such losses, but to build a ship like the *Looe* typically requires around 1,200 loads of timber and when one considers that you only tend to get two loads from any one tree and further that around thirty trees of such stature tend to cover an acre of ground, then to build something like the *Lyme* or the *Looe* requires the felling of some twenty acres of forest. Meanwhile, something on the scale of a first-rate man-of-war would account for five times that amount of timber: say a hundred acres of trees, trees that to have achieved reasonable growth must have been growing for maybe eighty to a hundred years. The financial implications are enormous, particularly when it is generally not possible to source timber locally and the cost of carrying timber by cart to any port for transportation is huge. These sums are all the more sharply focussed when a ship is lost.

Of course it is not just the Navy who suffer in this way as merchant ships are equally susceptible to danger on the high seas, and with the prospect of ever more shipping using the port it further increased need to address the problem of the notorious Eddystone Reef.

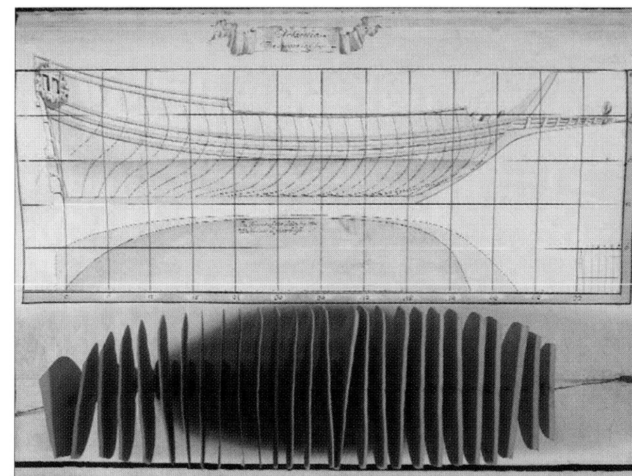

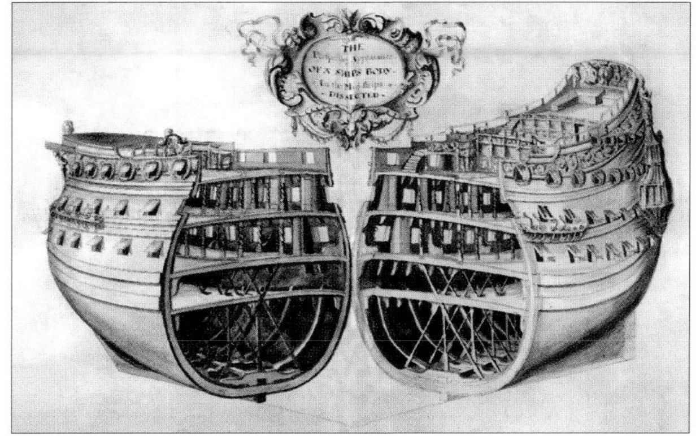

Edmund Dummer sketches. Top: A Saettia. Middle: A Saettia. Bottom: 'The perspective Appearance of a Ships Body – in the Mid-ships Dissected'. (The British Library Board - MS 40 f.181 & MS 40 f.182)

The Eddystone Reef

For many years captains and shipowners had been beseeching the masters of Trinity House to tackle the prickly problem of the red rocks of the Eddystone. In 1665, around the time that work was due to commence on the Royal Citadel, Sir John Coryton (who had sought licences in Dartmouth, Torbay and Rame Head) submitted a petition to them, but nothing happened.
Trinity House noted the request and commented that, though desirable, it '*could hardly be accomplished*'.
Then, two years after my appointment as Master Shipwright at Hamoaze, Mr Walter Whitfield reached an agreement with Trinity House, who still deeming the task impossible agreed generous terms. Over the next two summers, 1693 and 1694, Mr Whitfield undertook repeated trials on the reef, only to come to the same conclusion. Nevertheless he did not want to walk away from the challenge without finding someone to pick up the gauntlet. It is at that point that the colourful Mr Henry Winstanley enters our story.

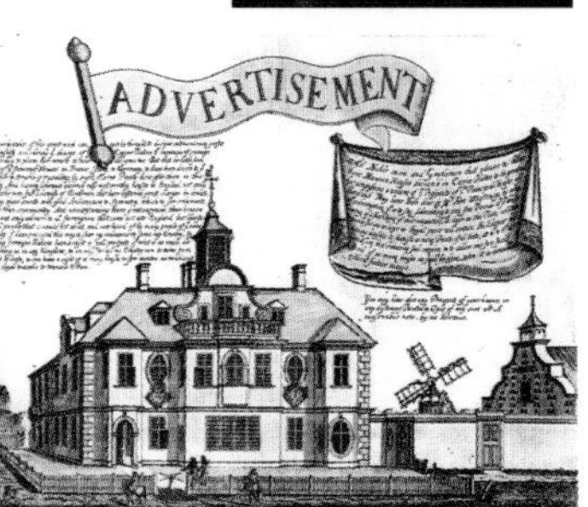

Top: *Winstanley a self-portrait*
Bottom: *The house in Littlebury.*

A former Clerk of the Works to Charles II, Charles Winstanley had made a considerable reputation – and fortune – for himself in London with a series of inventions, contraptions and illustrations produced to advertise his many attractions; among them his house in Littlebury, Essex. Entered via a turnstile, the house had a weather vane above a small central tower and a windmill which pumped water in his garden. Visitors paid a shilling to see his various mechanical and hydraulic installations, his illusory mirrors and his collection of interesting prints and cards, many of them drawn by himself. He also has a 'Mathematical Water Theatre', known as 'Winstanley's Water Works', in Piccadillly which drew large crowds.
For the reef, Mr Winstanley planned an octagonal tower of Cornish granite and wood, anchored with twelve great iron stanchions driven into the rock. The light itself to be provided by candles in a glass-lantern room at the top of the structure. Work began on 14 July 1696.
The difficulties faced were enormous; there were only really a few months in the summer when work on the reef could be carried out and even the journey to get out onto the reef could take many hours. There would be days when it was impossible to land men; days when it could take up to eight hours to get there, leaving only time for an hour or so's work, and days when after a four-to-six hour journey would result in maybe two or three hours work being done – and that was a good day!
Back in Plymouth Mr Winstanley would often encounter those who were only too happy to tell him that it simply could not be done and at the end of that first summer all they had managed was to drive the dozen stanchions into the rock.
Undaunted, Winstanley felt that they had made a good start. He had learnt many lessons already and everybody, but everybody was starting to talk about the enterprise.
Clearly this was going to be of enormous benefit to the country as a whole and the yard here at Hamoze, which was already responsible for a substantial increase in the amount of shipping needing to negotiate the treacherous rocky outcrop.
The potential benefit to enemy shipping was not to be underestimated either. One amusing incident that Mr Winstanley likes to recall, now that he is safely returned from it, was that while working on the foundation for the structure, in June the following summer, he was captured by a French privateer.
Ordinarily the Admiralty had been affording Winstanley and his men the protection and cover of a warship, the *Terrible*, but on this fateful day it had failed to appear and the sight of another warship was initially greeted with indifference by the men at work, until they realised it was a French vessel.
On Winstanley being triumphantly presented to the French King, Louis XIV berated his officers and announced that *'France is at war with England, not with humanity'*. Mr Winstanley was showered with personal gifts from the King and immediately returned to these shores.
As it transpired, Winstanley's light was not completed until November 1698, by which time I had moved to Portsmouth where Commissioner Greenhill had gone three years earlier – my wife had become pregnant and I wished to move nearer to home so I applied to become Master Shipwright there.
Nevertheless I am given to understand that there have been no ships wrecked on the reef since the light was lit.

Mr Winstanley's light stood some 120ft high and was 24ft in diameter, it was erected on a plinth of stonework strengthened by iron bands.
'An Airry or open Gallery' constructed of wood surmounted this, 'with the convenience to crane up goods and let the Sea pass through in time of storms'.
A large flag flew from the look-out post and various cranes and pulleys protruded, along with a contraption for casting down stones 'to defend the landing place in times of need'.
With the exception of the weather vane and the decorative candlesticks, all these flamboyant protrusions could be brought inside the structure when necessary, and generally the appearance of the lighthouse was altogether more streamlined that it is seen represented here.
In 1698, indicentally, three days before Christmas, Mr Winstanley was presented with a solid silver condiment set modelled on his light, in Plymouth's Guildhall by grateful merchants and citizens. It became his most prized possession.

The lighthouse, which was given to the shakes from the beginning, suffered weather damage during that first winter, and the light was often obscured by spray breaking over the top of the tower. Mr Winstanley therefore had it rebuilt in summer of 1699, on a larger scale, with extra stonework and even more elaborate decoration.
As you might imagine, Mr Winstanley's achievement brought him an even greater degree of fame than that which he already enjoyed and prints of the wondrous, life-saving structure quickly proved popular. Most were copies or adaptations of either Mr Winstanley's own engravings, or those of other artists who visited the reef, pior to Mr Winstanley's later refinements on the reef.
Even the King commissioned an image of the Light House and one Thomas Barton was charged with the task.
His Majesty was delighted with the result and had the work displayed at Kensington and ere long requested a second, larger, piece, together with draughts of several of His Majesty's warships. This was eventually delivered to him at Hampton Court.

Top left: *The Winstanley Lighthouse by Peter Monamy (1681-1749) (© Plymouth City Museum & Art Gallery)*
Bottom: *The First Eddystone Lighthouse by Unknown Artist: oil on panel (© Plymouth City Museum & Art Gallery)*

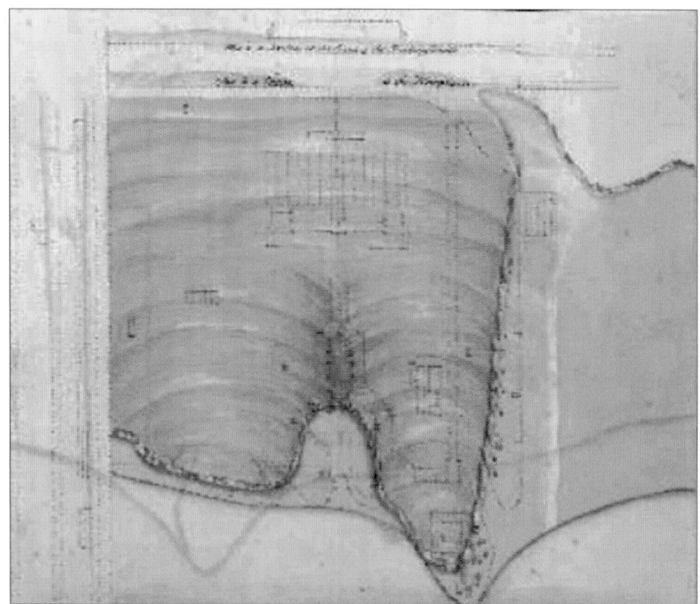

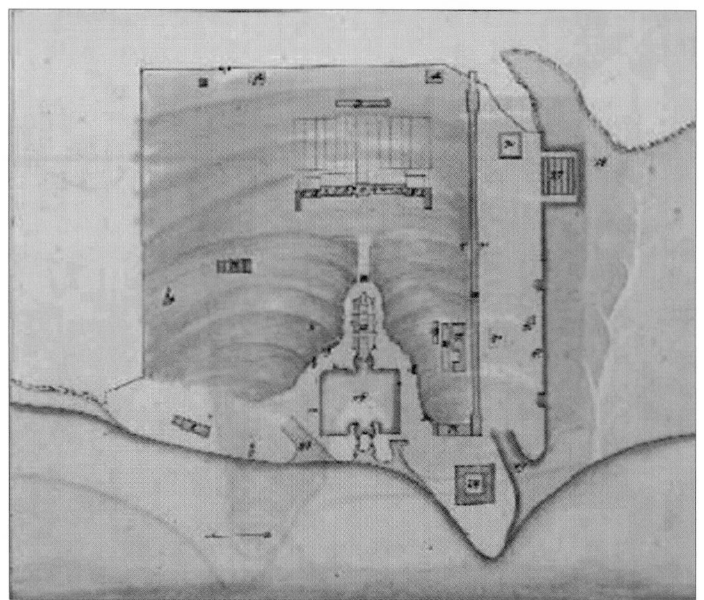

Dummer's illustrations of Point Froward before, with plans lightly added and below *after the construction work had been done. (The British Library Board - King's MS f.130) The original site comprised a field in the occupation of Mr Doidge, containing the well to which his name was later given, a field in the occupation of Sir Nicholas Morice and a third within the barton of Mount Wise itself.*

The New Docks

By this time we had already experienced a number of teething troubles of our own.

From the very beginning there had been problems with the lock gates, problems that, notwithstanding Mr Dummer's best efforts proved difficult to resolve. In December of 1692 Mr Dummer had written to our first Commissioner, Captain Greenhill, who had then been in post just a year, to say that he had shown his designs to *'the best judges I can find in town'* and gained their approval. However, such approval did not help the gates to work any better and they still were in need of adaptation when Captain St Lo arrived in March 1695 to take over from Captain Greenhill. The new Commissioner was a little less understanding of these early problems than his predecessor had been. He was also somewhat unhappy with what he described as the *'tottering condition'* of the rope house and tar house, both of which, like everything else then in the yard, had been recently built. Commissioner St Lo also expressed his concerns over the dry dock which, he maintained, had become a veritable wet dock.

Mr Dummer, who by now was Surveyor of the Navy, wrote back later that year (1697) anticipating that a second pair of gates could be put in place quite quickly as long as the Commissioner let those whose job it was get on with the work, rather than interfere all the time. Part of the problem was that Mr Dummer's design involved a double gate, rather than a three-leaf, single-gate affair of the kind previously used in our dockyards. The advantages were evident, in that the double gate was easier and quicker to open and shut, as it required just a handful of men to operate it, rather than 50-70 for the three-leaf gates. However, it wasn't until 1700 that the gates, having been re-hung, were successfully closed.

Setting up the new Dockyard at Hamoze had been a great and exciting challenge, but not without its fair share of difficulties. Mr Dummer's original brief had been to locate a suitable site for the creation of a single dry dock, *'for cruising ships only.'* Certainly that was the scale of operation I was anticipating when I was appointed. However the ever more real threat from the French, with the exiled James II hovering in the wings, prompted the King to step up spending on the Navy.

In 1689 the annual vote had been under £1.2 million but, five years later, this figure had more than doubled as had the actual number of sailors in the Navy – the figure had risen from 22,332 to 47,710. Meanwhile the original estimates for the extended version of the new facility at Hamoze had been a little over £23,000 in 1692, but by the time I left (in 1698) that figure had almost tripled. Mr Dummer, I suspect, was always aware of the implications involved but maintained that he had never wanted the true picture to be known in case it put the Navy Board off going ahead with the new Dockyard.

It is perhaps worth remembering that it was in 1692 that Sir John Tippetts, the Surveyor of the Navy had died, and Mr Dummer, as his Assistant, had succeeded him. It is an exceedingly responsible and well-rewarded post – £500 per year. Furthermore, knowing Mr Dummer as I do, I am in little doubt that he was keen to put into practice some of the ideas he had worked up utilising the great knowledge he had amassed of other docks and dockyards.

Certainly it would appear that our new dock, once the King had insisted that it should be able to take first-rate warships, is the first anywhere in Europe to have been designed as a stepped stone dock – the French had something similar at Rochefort Dock, La Rochelle, but it was not so solid. The advantages over previous dock design are quite significant; it is quicker and easier to drain and fill, less shoring is required to hold a ship in place and it's much easier to work on the hull.

However, it was not easy to achieve a bonding between the stone sides and timber plank floor and there was leakage caused by the consequent buckling of the timber, which led to difficulties with the main contractor and stonemason, Robert Waters, who Mr Dummer had brought down from Portsmouth to oversee the stonework on the new dock.

Undoubtedly this was a big undertaking for anyone and Mr Waters was bound to encounter problems on so large and novel a venture; equally of course you would expect Mr Dummer to blame anyone but himself for any problems arising from his designs. The situation had already become quite difficult in 1696. Mr Waters was accused variously of using inferior materials, of employing incompetent subcontractors and of cutting corners to reduce costs; however against this the Admiralty were notoriously slow to settle some of the their accounts and by the time I left to go to Portsmouth a couple of years later, Mr Waters was in danger of being arrested almost every day, such were the amounts that he in turn owed.

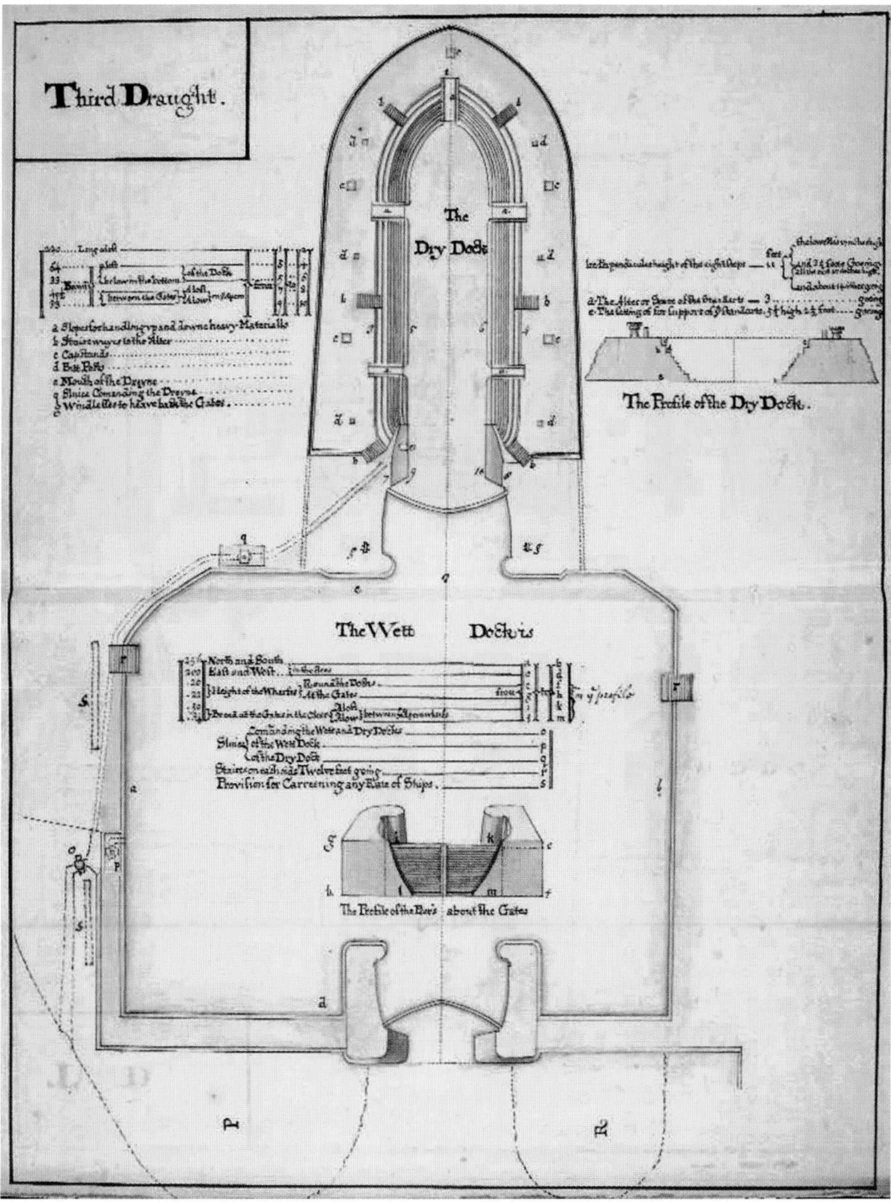

Dummer's third draught of the Dock and Wet Dock. (The British Library Board - Lansdowne MS 847 f.45)

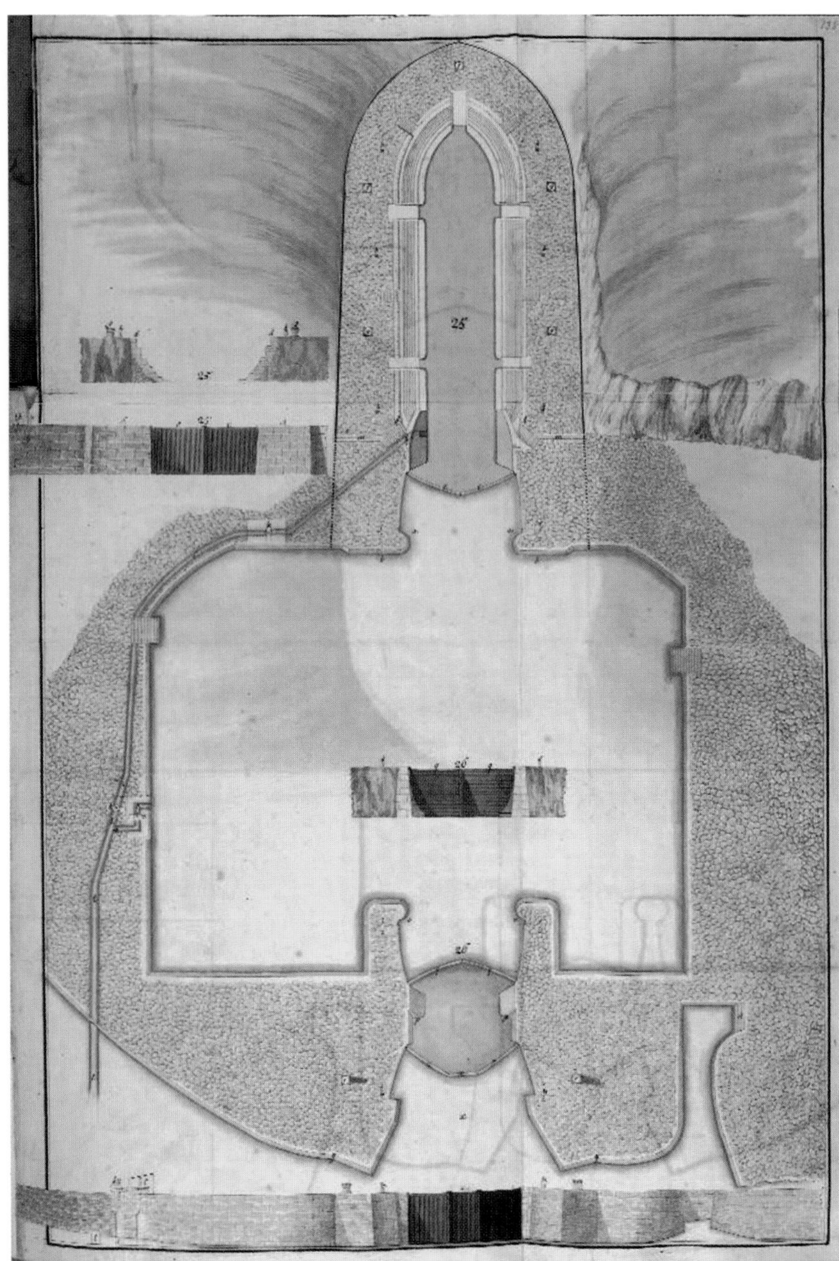

Dry dock top and wet dock below, Dummer's plan and section.
(The British Library Board - King's MS 43 f.138)

Financial Difficulties

Some of those to whom he owed money were arrested – for owing sums of fifteen to twenty pounds – a situation that seems unjust when they were waiting on payments of more than £100 from Waters. Further perspective is given to the issue when you consider that the combined cost of the new wet and dry docks were over £26,000 and most of that work was undertaken by Waters.

Sadly such financial problems had been with us since the beginning; even before his elevation to Commissioner, Mr Greenhill, as the Navy Agent here, had been forced to remind the Navy Board, in the summer of 1691, that pay for the men was in arrears. As you might imagine the situation was aggravated by the fact that so many of the men who were first employed here had been brought down from other existing dockyards, mainly from the Thames and Portsmouth, and therefore had no history with local traders, who, quite understandably, were not overly anxious to grant credit to strangers.

Still the wages were not forthcoming however, and in the August Mr Greenhill used money intended for paying contractors, to pay the men outstanding back pay for the last two months of the previous year. By February 1693 the problem had got even worse and pay was more than a year adrift.

Small wonder that some of the men supplemented their earnings by running brandy shops (increasingly popular as the tax on ale and beer had increased), or by doing jobs on the side for ship's commanders or even taking work outside the yard. Or, more simply, by pilfering material from the yard, particularly cordage and tallow – rope and candle wax – and selling it for ready money outside.

It was partly to avoid this situation that Mr Dummer had been keen to set the new Dock up at Point Froward, as there was no ready market for such stolen goods nearby, unlike in the Cattewater, or even further up the river at Saltash, both of which were difficult to secure against embezzlement. Of course it will not have escaped the attention of some that the opportunities for the Officers themselves to abuse the system are even greater and while it is not my place to make comments on individuals, it is interesting to note that the first Clerk of the Cheque at Hamoze, Mr John Addis, the man whose signature is required before any payments can be made, has built up a large personal property portfolio – privately, he owns dozens of houses.

The Dockyard takes Shape

Notwithstanding all these, behind-the-scenes goings on, the speed with which our site went from being an unspoilt, natural inlet to one of His Majesty's more substantial dockyards was breathtaking, as Mr Dummer's own sketch from 1698 shews.

As you can see the creation of the new dock necessitated tidal land being raised in order to provide dry land around the limits of the wet dock. A certain amount of this material was the spoil created by excavating the dock site which, together with further shifting of matter, allowed us to create additional flat surfaces on which we built the Great Smith's House, to the North of the dock and the enormous, four-storey (including loft and basement) Great Storehouse, to the South.

The Smith's House, with its seven great fires, was deliberately set apart from the rest, as you would expect when the rest of the site was home to so many valuable and highly-flammable materials.

The Great Store, it has been suggested, bears similarities to a storehouse in Amsterdam that was built forty years ago, and while I am not familiar with that building I do know that our impressive structure, which measures sixty feet square, is capable of holding stores for about forty of their Majesties' ships at any one time.

The original plans for the Officer's quarters, incidentally, were that it should have been for a two-storey terrace and it is claimed that the third, or upper storey, was done on the orders of Commissioner Greenhill 'against the opinion' of Mr Dummer.

It will be noticed that my residence was immediately alongside that of the Commissioner, so it is perhaps best that I do not offer a comment on this situation. That said, it remains true that the Terrace is one of the most impressive the world has seen and all who see it are hard-pressed to think of anywhere where there is a better example of such a long block designed to appear as an architectural whole.

The design is a little influenced by French and Dutch quarters with a debt perhaps to Robert Hooke. In this country, the important thing

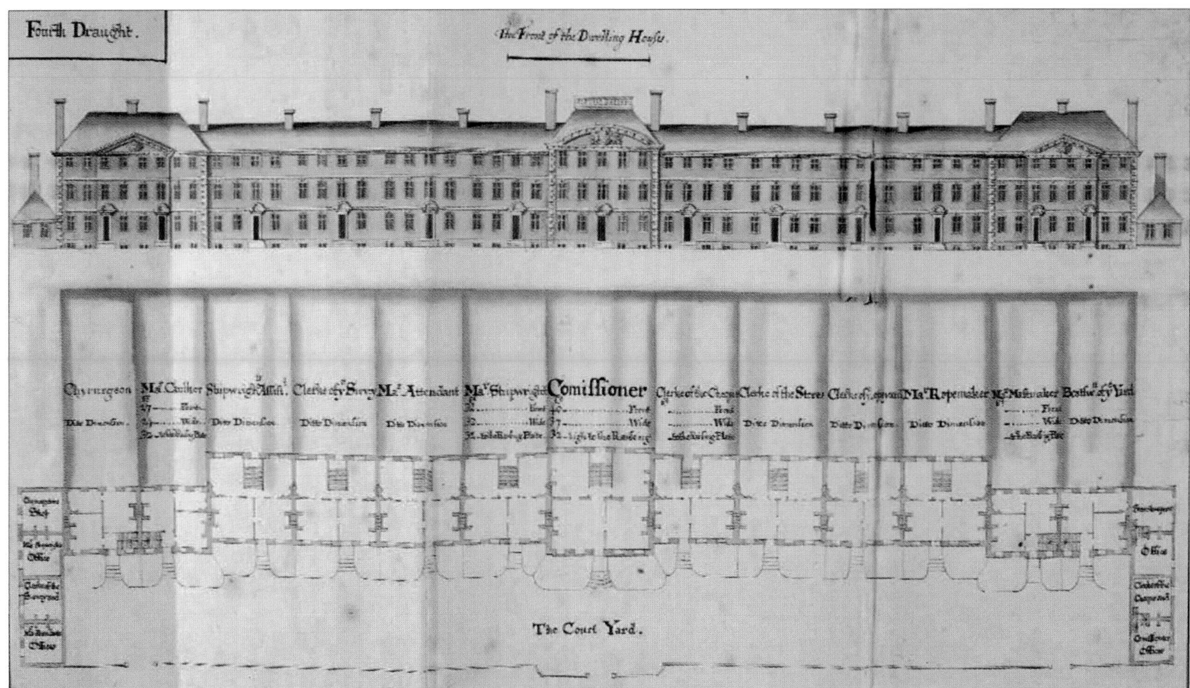

The front elevation of the dwelling houses: the Dock Yard Commissioner lived in the double-fronted middle property the rest were occupied as follows: Chyrurgeon (i.e. surgeon); Master Caulker; Shipwright's Assistant; Master Attendant; Master Shipwright, Commissioner; Clerk of the Cheque; Clerk of the Stores; Clerk of the Rope Yard; Master Ropemaker; Master Mastmaker; Boatswain of the Yard. The smaller buildings at either end running down the sides of the Court Yard, were office for the various Officers of the Yard. (The British Library Board - Lansdowne MS. 847, f.46)

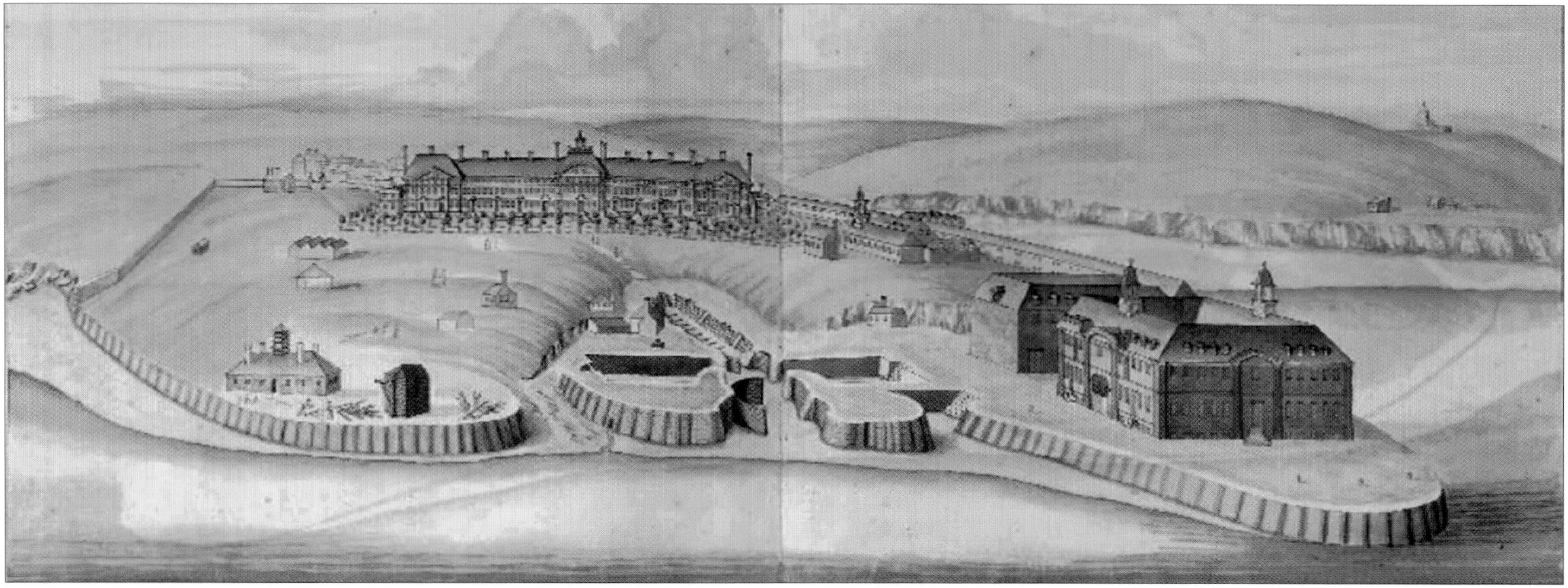

Top: *Dummer's view of the fledgling dockyard. (The British Library Board -)*
Above: *Abraham Storck, The earlier storehouse built in Amsterdam.*

however, for those of us in residence, is that each property has its own privy as well as its own porch, brewhouse, washhouse and garden.

Mr Dummer's notion was that by giving the Terrace so commanding a position over the working dock yard, the officers would be able to better monitor the work being done. To that end the Foreman of the Yard was housed in a cabin hard by the gates between the dry dock and the wet dock.

As to the other buildings as you see them in Mr Dummer's sketch, one or two of the minor structures had followed proposals Commissioner St Lo made on my behalf towards the end of 1696, namely; a shed for repairing boats, a shop for the bricklayer, another for the painter, a house for treenails and wedges, a pitch-house and a tar-house for the sailmaker.

Of the other major structures, the construction of the Rope House was by no means as straight forward as it might have been. There was a problem with the quality of the bricks that had been made on site and consequently a large part of the ropewalk wall had to be pulled down and re-erected. Running up behind the Great Store and scheduled to be over 1,056 ft long, the Rope House was another building to appear on what had been substantially tidal land – not all of it though, and the problem was, the last 40 feet of the building intruded onto land that we did not initially have any title over. Indeed it wasn't until the summer of 1698 that the Navy Board was able to authorise completion of the Rope House.

For those unfamiliar with such matters, incidentally, it may surprise many to learn that in order to fully rig a first-rate man of war a good twenty-five to thirty miles of rope is required. Add to this the fact that a good rope may give up to five years of working life it is easy to see the importance of this building and the neighbouring Hemp House – the large building behind the Great Store. It also did not escape Mr Dummer that hemp was one of the most valuable commodities in the yard and the location of this building had as much to do with internal security and the avoidance of pilferage as it did logistics.

Located alongside the Rope House, almost reaching out to the original tip of Point Froward, are the Tarred Yarn House, the Rigging House and the Tap House; out of sight, on the other side of this great long building are the Saw Pits and the Mast Houses.

It was Mr Dummer's notion that everything should be easily accessible on one site and that movement between the various stores and working areas should be cut to a minimum. Furthermore the less manhandling that was required for any raw material or item of stores, the less opportunity there would be for embezzlement and abuse.

Such was all very well for the materials, but for the men such convenience was not readily available in the first few years and in my time at Hamoze, most of the men working here were housed in hulks – old warships that had been stripped of sail and other non-essential serviceable parts, and moored close by.

Housing the Workforce

The Admiralty appeared to be in no hurry to provide proper houses on the land and it was a few years before buildings did start to appear outside the Dock Yard walls – as you can see there are a few shewn here outside the Gates, to the left of the Officer's Terrace and within a year or two of Mr Dummer completing this sketch, more houses and shops and the like started to appear on the slope alongside the northern wall of the yard. The beach at the bottom of this slope lent itself to landing small boats and this became the natural route for many men living off-shore or anywhere else a short row away. The first hut was constructed there of wood and the area soon became known as North Corner. The cottage was the first of a series facing west; isolated buildings became rows, and irregular streets were fashioned. It was to here that market traders would come as well, most notably from Saltash and other points on the Tamar.

Of course I left Hamoze in 1698 when Mr Dummer came down to produce his view of the Yard, however I was in Portsmouth when he called there as part of his mission to Survey and Describe 'the Principal Harbours with their Accommodations & Conveniences for Erecting Moaring Secureing and refitting the Navy Royall of England'.

In truth it was a remarkable document as it included an inventory of every dwelling house and office in Their Majesties' Dockyards. A Surveyor of the Navy Mr Dummer instructed the Clerks of the Survey *'to carefully set down what belongs to their Majesties in every room ... how it is furnished and fitted'.*

Mr Dummer's concern was that all too often when Officers move on they have a tendency to take certain essential items with them – *'furnace locks, lead locks, hinges, chimney pieces, hearths, and other things belonging to their Majesties'* causing every house to be fitted up again as a new Officer moves in.

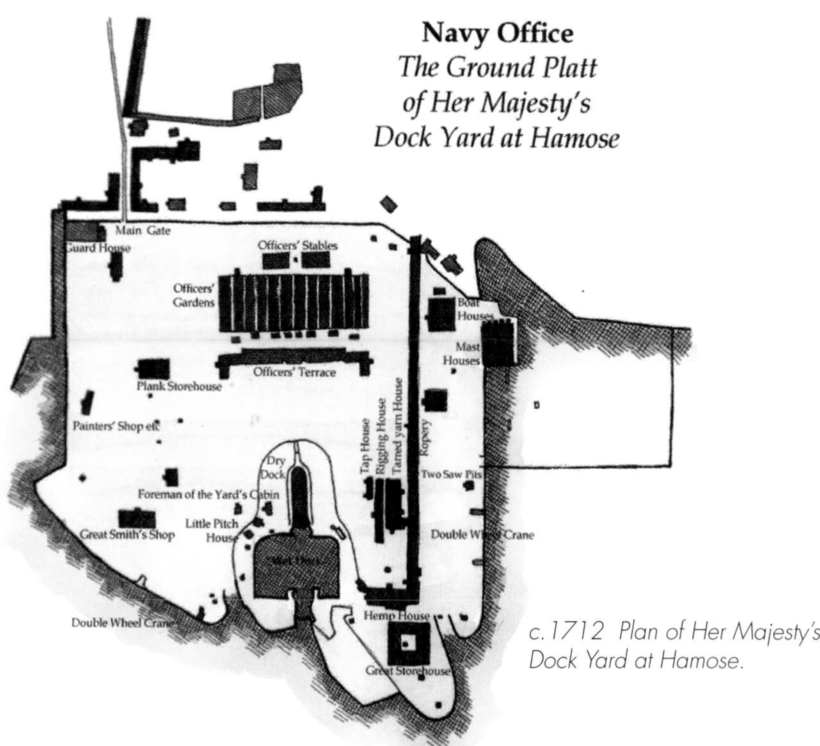

c.1712 Plan of Her Majesty's Dock Yard at Hamose.

Mr Dummer's Downfall

Such 'irregularities' have long been a problem and not just in the Royal Navy and sadly Mr Dummer himself was involved in some unpleasantness in Portsmouth where he became embroiled in a dispute with a contractor, Mr Fitch, over the workmanship and costs of work on a dry dock there. The case began at the end of 1696, but was still ongoing when I moved to Portsmouth two years later, by which time Sir Christopher Wren, Surveyor of the King's Works, had inspected the work himself. In the end the Court decided that the works were indeed defective and Mr Dummer issued instructions for their remedy, however it was also found that Mr Fitch was still owed money for other contract work he had done before he had been thrown off the site, almost £11,000.

The matter did not end there, however, as Mr Fitch, eager for revenge, alleged that Mr Dummer had suggested to him - Mr Fitch - that if he were to give Mr Dummer a gift of £100 and help him with the sale of timber in Plymouth, then Mr Fitch may find himself awarded a handsome Naval contract.

It was by no means a simple case but Mr Dummer took great pains to point out that he had offered thirty years' loyal service to the crown while the work and reputation of the vengeful Fitch had been clearly compromised.

In the end, the case was eventually found in Mr Dummer's favour, but Mr Dummer's appointment as Surveyor of the Navy was not renewed. A few years later, in 1702, the enterprising Mr Dummer broke into completely new territory and started up mail service between Plymouth and the West Indies, he also started to build his own ships.

Bigger Boats are Built

Which brings me back to the Royal Dock at Plymouth and the last two ships I oversaw before moving to Portsmouth. The first was the *Germoon Prize*, which like the first two boats we built here, was an advice boat, but a little larger than the other two and rated a sixth-rate warship with a useful complement of guns.

Captured from the French four years before she came here to be rebuilt in the summer of 1696, she had been engaged in useful service gaining intelligence for the Admiralty running up and down the coast of France.

The rebuilding did not take too long and it is perhaps worth noting that possibly as much as a third of all the work done in the Royal Dockyards is currently this type of reconstruction work. Once a Master Shipwright has deemed there to be too much decayed timber for ordinary repairs or the Master Caulker has decided that the annual caulking and tarring will no longer stay all leaks, then a ship, if it is thought still to be economical, is rebuilt.

In the most extreme cases this can involve taking the ship apart completely and reconstructing a 'new' one using as much of the old timbers, etc., as possible, quite often this would lead to the vessel being given a new name, but not so with the *Germoon* which was very quickly back in the water.

Having received the Warrant to work on her 'forthwith' in May, she was back in service under the command of Captain Smith before the end of September.

Sadly, as a post-script to this little story, I learned, when I was in Portsmouth some four years later, that the *Germoon* had been lost in the Caribbean: she was overset while being careened at Puerto Bello in the summer of 1700. Imagine my dismay therefore when, just a couple of months later, I was given news of the *Carlisle*, the last and the largest of my undertakings at Hamoze.

Notwithstanding the *Anglesea*, which was put together on Mr Fint's Yard, the *Carlisle* was the biggest ship produced in my time at his Majesties' new yard. At 709 tons she was also almost 100 tons bigger than the Anglesea anyway and certainly longer and wider.

Commissioned by Captain Francis Dove, the *Carlisle* was 'added to the Navy' on 16 May 1698 and was designed to replace another fourth-rate vessel of the same name, which had been launched five years earlier at Deptford. This *Carlisle*, the first known to the Navy, had been wrecked in 1696.

Meanwhile, our new *Carlisle* spent most of her first year or so on convoy duties, however in September 1698, she was moored up in the Downs. Captain Dove was ashore, but most of the crew were on board when there was an explosion. No-one knows what caused it, but the *Carlisle* and all who were on board at the time were lost - it was a dreadful tragedy.

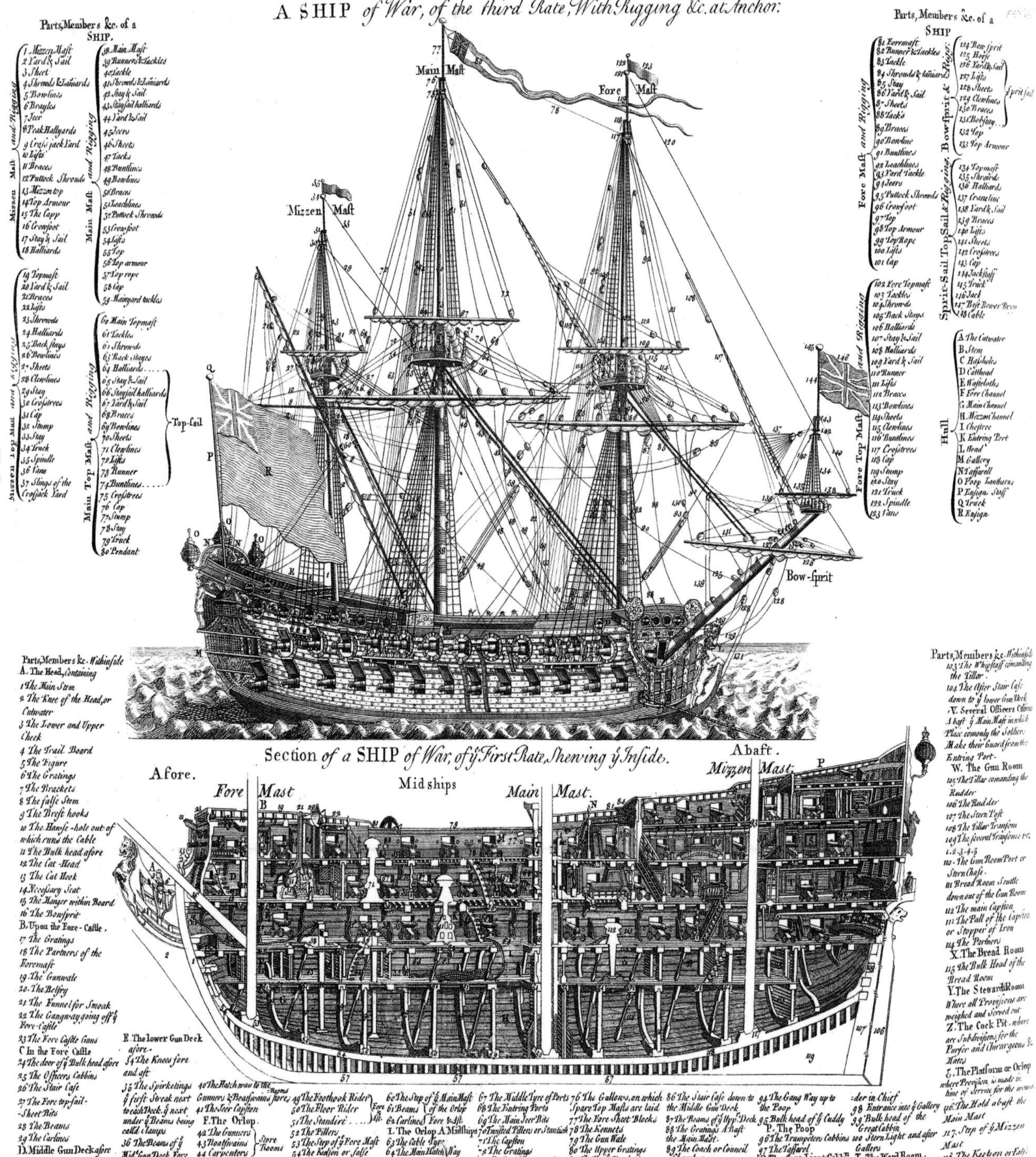

Ship plans showing the rigging for a third-rate war ship, top, and bottom, the cross section of a first-rate man of war.

Furthermore, when news arrived the following year, 1701, of the loss in the Atlantic of the *Messenger,* it meant that none of those first five ships we worked on at Hamoze (with the exception of the two put together at Mr Fint's yard), are now still afloat.
As the launch of any ship is, for the Master Shipwright, like the birth of a child it will be easy to see how wistfully I look back now on our early achievements at Hamoze.
I wish my successor, Thomas Podd, who came down to Hamoze from Harwich, a more enviable record.
Undoubtedly he started his tenure on a much surer footing than I had; by the time I left Hamoze the Yard was almost fully functional, it had become a recognised feature on the landscape and the people of Plymouth were looking upon the whole enterprise in a more favourable light.

On Local Opinion

There had, inevitably, been mixed feelings at first; raising the profile of the area in this way undoubtedly increased the level of enemy interest and potential threat to the town, it also meant competition for the available workforce and for stores; and it meant a much greater likelihood of local men being pressed into Naval service. Such a fear was arguably borne out by the 'recruitment' figures between 1693–1696 when some 1,300 Devon men were pressed, 500 more than any other maritime county and several times more than most of them.
However, it didn't take long for local men to realise the employment potential, and the commercial contract supply opportunities that come with a major Royal Naval Dockyard. Neither was it difficult for outsiders to see the impact for themselves as the number of men working in the Yard rose from a little over 50 when work began on the docks themselves to somewhere in the region of 500 when the first of two transport boats was launched in August 1702.
A smallish vessel designed to pick up timber and other materials from around the country, and then bring such items swiftly back to the Dockyard, this was the *Hamoaze* and her working twin, the *Plymouth*, was launched two years later.

On Local Travel

Reaching Plymouth any way other than via the sea is not especially easy, not even from Hamoze, as even that journey involves a long walk via the Millbridge which crosses Stonehouse Creek at a point just beyond the parish church of Stoke Damerel. The lanes on the Plymouth side of the creek are narrow and not always reckoned to be that safe after dusk.
The roads generally in this part of the world are difficult and for the most part remarkable for their steepness and certainly not suitable for wheeled carriages of any kind – indeed, travel any distance from any of the local ports and I very much doubt you'll see a wheeled carriage anywhere in the county. What is more you take your life in your hands if you travel across the county lanes on anything but a horse familiar with the local terrain.
And yet, cross-country carriage of nearly every kind is done on the backs of horses, although very occasionally you might see an ox pulling a sledge hither or thither. But hay, corn, straw, fuel (generally wood apart from Plymouth which has a supply of Newcastle coal), stones, dung, lime, etc., are carried on horseback.
Hay, corn, straw, faggots, and other relatively light items are loaded between crooks formed of willow poles about seven or eight feet long and joined in pairs with cross bars about eighteen inches to two feet long. Two pairs of these crooks are slung across the horse's back, some four or five feet from each other, and then loaded up, the load sitting a foot or more off the horse's back.
Heavier articles are carried on shorter crooks: dung, sand and building materials are carried in 'pots' or very strong panniers tied together above the saddle; while lime is usually carried in narrow bags – two or three of them thrown across a wooden pack-saddle.
Plymouth itself is quite a wealthy town and the housing there is of a good standard, stone being almost everywhere abundant; timbers from broken ships provide seasoned building material and slates are procurable at a small expense. The availability of such commodities was useful in establishing our new facility at Hamoze and one noble

lady traveller passing through in my time was minded to observe that already it '*looks like a little town. The buildings are so many, and all of marble with fine slate on the roofs, and a little distance it makes all the houses show as if they were covered with snow and glisters in the sun, which adds to their beauty* (Celia Fiennes - Through England On A Side Saddle 1695).'

A rare sight in Devon: The roads of the county are generally poor, like the rest of the country they are dependent on the efforts in each parish of an overseer of highways. These men are appointed from among the parishioners but are not paid, furthermore when they deem that work is required - to fill ruts or potholes with earth or stones, then the labour is provided by other parishioners, all of whom are required by law to provide six days' labour each year towards this work. As you might imagine this 'statute labour' is not popular with people and as a consequence roads suffer from decay and neglect. With the ever-increasing demand for roads to take wheeled carriages so the problem has been exacerbated and in recent years the permitted width of waggon wheels has been increased from four to nine inches with the prospect of a five pound fine or a month in prison for those caught contravening these regulations. The more narrow the wheel the more easily damaging scars can be cut in the surface of the road.

On Food, Drink and Employment

Plymouth also has a first-class fish market, long esteemed the first in the Island for the abundance, variety and excellency of its sea fish. The public corn mills are usually supplied with water from the leat introduced by Drake, the poor take their own corn to the mills. The basic food of most working people, around and about, is barley bread, skim-milk cheese and potatoes. Most of the potatoes consumed locally come from Moretonhampstead some thirty miles away, while cherries, pears, strawberries and walnuts are principally obtained from Bere Ferrers.

The main beverage is cider, or during a scarcity of this, beer; the liquors are a base kind of spirit drawn from the sediment of cider ... and of course smuggled French brandy.

Within the Service itself, beer is more a staple feature, especially at sea and standard issue for all men is a gallon a day, water being deemed a poor alternative. And while many men may fear impressment into the Service for some it does offer, in theory, an income that perhaps exceeds what they might make in rural parts where many families are very hard pressed.

There are labourers in places who appear to be little more than drunken, idle fellows, but in truth are forced to be honestly dishonest. They argue, not unreasonably, that a poor man cannot look after a family on only six shillings a week or fifteen pounds a year. Locally servants are even more poorly paid, their yearly wages of the order of six to eight pounds a year for men and little more than half of that for women. Under these circumstances it is easy to see why the children of paupers in rural areas, especially boys aged just seven or eight, are sent to farmers as apprentices until they are well into their twenties!

And we are not talking of a small section of society here, it has been estimated that around a quarter of the English population currently live as 'cottagers and paupers' on such low incomes - that is around 1,300,000 out of a total of 5,500,00 people.

The figures have been drawn up by a Mr Gregory King who estimates that almost two-thirds of the population subsist on wages below the poverty level, which Mr King puts at forty pounds a year. Taking the farming figures together with the fact that many Cornish miners were earning an average of just ten pounds a year when the Dockyard

reached operational standards, it is easy to see how attitudes to our development at Hamoze were quick to mellow.
It wasn't just about the opportunities for employment but also it opened up new markets for produce too.
With wages above tuppence an hour for a ten-hour day, our shipwrights, if they work extra tides or nights (when they are on double time) could earn two or three times that amount quite comfortably, although it still clearly leaves them below what Mr King deems sufficient for an adequate living, it is still considerably better than what is on offer in some other parts of this neighbourhood.
Not all men working in the yard are shipwrights of course, but they are the largest group, by some distance, accounting for over a third of our workforce, a further 20% are general labourers, around 10% work in the ropery, with the rest mainly riggers, caulkers and sawyers.
Clearly numbers grew quite spectacularly during our first few years, and continued to grow after I left, however Parliament's decision in the early part of 1699 to make severe cuts in the defence budget, had some impact, not least of which was the sudden increase in the number of ex-servicemen now looking for work.
It was no secret that the King was unhappy with this decision, he felt it left the nation 'too exposed', he was also doubtless fearful for his own safety after the exposure of a couple of Jacobite plots to take his life.

On Monarchy and Religion

The Jacobites, supporters of the exiled James II (the term comes from the Latin Jacobus, meaning James), are always bound to create a degree of uncertainty, uncertainty compounded by the general mutterings of insurgent Catholics up and down the country.
Incidentally, on the subject of religion it is interesting to note in Plymouth generally there is a greater degree of religious freedom than there is to be found in many towns and ports across England. The Toleration Act, granting freedom of worship to Nonconformists who have taken the Oaths of Allegiance and Supremacy (of the King not the Pope) was well-received down here by the Baptists, Congregationalists and others.

Incidentally, throughout my time at Hamoze the principal place of worship for all was the nearby church of Stoke Damerel, and it wasn't until 1700 that the Yard had a chapel of its own. The new facility, I am given to understand, is called St Lo's in honour of Commissioner George St Lo, after whom the new four-gun yacht launched at Hamoze that same year, was also named.

George St Lo

The Act of Settlement more recently passed (1701) was even more forthright in its anti-Catholic stance and ensured that any successor to the throne must be Anglican: a situation that was put to the test earlier than anticipated when fifty-two-year-old King William died (in March 1702) as a result of a fall from his horse, after his mount had stumbled on a molehill.
He has been succeeded by his thirty-seven-year-old sister-in-law Princess Anne (who is also his first cousin), who after eighteen pregnancies, is still without an heir (only five of the confinements have resulted in a live birth and tragically both sons and all three daughters have since died).
Curiously enough, within weeks of Queen Anne's succession, the country was again at war, this time over the question of the succession of the Spanish throne. Their king – Charles II – had died in 1700 without leaving an heir, but, under the terms of his will, he bequeathed the crown to Louis XIV's grandson, Philip of Anjou, who duly became the king of Spain. The worry here, however, and in most of Europe was that France, through Philip, might try to annex the Spanish empire. Thus it was that, joined with the United Provinces, Prussia, Austria, Scotland and most of the other states of the Holy Roman Empire, we found ourselves at war again.
France had exacerbated the situation by recognising James II's son, also James, as King of England, following the death of his father the previous year.
Whatever the political ramifications of the situation, it meant that there was a renewed sense of urgency in all of the Royal Dockyards. Commissioner St Lo left Hamoze early in 1703 for Chatham and was replaced, albeit briefly by Captain William Wright.

1703: The Great Storm

Captain Wright's appointment commenced on 1 May 1703 and in the event his tenure of office lasted less than a year, but what a time it was. As the winter of 1703 approached the country was visited by one of the worst storms it has ever known. Many of our ships were returning from fighting in the Mediterranean, when a series of gales swept the country. Locally, Mr Winstanley was in residence in his lighthouse, effecting some refinements and having already expressed a wish that should a great storm ever blow up he would be there on the reef to see what effect it would have on his creation.

It all began on a late Wednesday afternoon in November – it had started out as fine day for the time of year, but around four o'clock a brisk gale blew up and intensified as the evening wore on. The following day the wind dropped somewhat but by Friday it had gained in strength and blew with renewed force, reaching its most destructive heights between midnight and daybreak of Saturday 27 November.

So bad was it that many thought the end of the world had come, and for some, indeed, it had. The Eddystone Lighthouse was swept off the rocks and Mr Winstanley and six colleagues were lost off the reef.

Elsewhere off the coast the fleet, under the command of Sir Cloudesley Shovel, were in two sections, some, with the Admiral were anchored near Gunfleet, Essex, and managed to ride out the storm with little damage, the others, however, were off the Downs, that four-mile wide channel that lies between the treacherous Goodwin Sands and Deal off the Kentish coast and there but a few escaped; seven major warships were destroyed along with several other smaller vessels – nothing was left of them. All told some 1,500 officers and men were lost – a fifth of the seamen of the sovereign fleet.

At Bristol such a volume of water was pushed up the Severn that the water rose some ten feet above any known high tide levels. Portsmouth looked as though it had been sacked by enemy forces. There were losses at Chatham, Harwich, Spithead.

Outside of the Navy hundreds of merchant craft were lost, on the Thames around 700 ships were rocked together in the Pool of London. And not only ships were lost, but so too were many of the oak trees needed to replace them; 17,000 trees were lost in Kent alone; in the New Forest some 4,000 oaks came crashing down, as did some 400 windmills. Across the south coast more than 8,000 lives were lost as roofs, chimneys,

Destruction of the Eddystone Lighthouse. From Chambers' Book of Days, Vol II, 1864

Referring to the loss of the Light in his book – *The Storm* – published in 1704 Mr Defoe wrote: *'At night it was standing, and in the morning all the upper part from the Gallery was blown down, and all the people in it perished, and by a particular misfortune, Mr Winstanley, the contriver of it, a person whose loss is very much regretted by such as knew him, as a very useful man to this country. The loss of the light house is also a considerable damage, as 'tis very doubtful whether it will be ever attempted again, and as it was a great security to the sailors, many a good ship having been lost there in former times.*

It was very remarkable, that, as we are inform'd, at the same time the light house was blown down, the model of it in Mr Winstanley's house at Littlebury in Essex, above 200 miles from the Light House, fell down, and was broken to pieces.'

Monamy Storm (detail - National Maritime Museum)

In Plymouth the devastation was widespread. The Friary Green, Old Tree Slip, and other points were strewn with wreckage, and two sons of Mr Collier met a tragic fate as they watched the mountainous waves rolling into the harbour. They had stationed themselves behind the Old Fish House, the whilom military store on the Barbican which had so long served to break the rush of the waters into Sutton Pool. A huge bore suddenly swept towards the ruins, carried them away with the two victims, and the lads were last seen on the crest of the surf beyond the possibility of rescue.

walls and complete houses were laid waste in the violence. Even the Queen was forced to take shelter in a cellar at St James Palace, as chimneys fell and part of the roof caved in.

As the sun rose that Saturday there was but a temporary respite as during the course of Sunday and Monday the tempest returned, such that on the Tuesday many were reluctant to go to bed. However, the following day the hurricane abated, gradually winding down, and away. By four o'clock, the very hour at which it had begun the previous week, the nightmare vanished and calm returned.

Many claimed that the visitation had been God's way of expressing his anger at the 'crying sins of the nation', our lack of progress in our fight with the French, and the Queen and Parliament decreed that a day (19 January 1704) be set aside for fasting to beseech God to forbear sending another even greater storm.

The tragedy was widely covered in various newspapers that have appeared across the country in recent years and Mr Defoe, a writer, published a book, simply called *The Storm* based on the information people sent him after he had placed an appeal in many of these journals.

'No pen could describe it, nor tongue express it, nor thought conceive it unless by one in the extremity of it.'

Counting the Cost

In material terms the losses sustained across the country were almost unquantifiable, but figures of £200,000 were estimated in Bristol and over £1,000,000 in London, where all the churches, many of them only recently rebuilt after the Great Fire, suffered some damage.

For a while the price of building materials to patch, repair and rebuild, increased five-or six-fold, and bricklayers' wages rose in proportion. Some losses were easier to rectify than others, and after five years of no wrecks on the Eddystone Reef, the question of replacing Winstanley's Light became most pressing. Cynics suggested that no-one would be foolhardy enough to try again, Winstanley, as it transpires, had still been several thousand pounds out of pocket when the storm hit.

However, just two days after Winstanley's light was swept away, a merchant vessel, the *Winchelsea*, returning from Virginia laden with tobacco, not knowing that the light had gone, struck the reef and was torn apart. The ship, her cargo and all but two of her crew were lost. The urgent need for a replacement light could not have been more graphically put.

Trinity House themselves were not prepared to underwrite the venture and so it happened that the lease was acquired by Captain Lovett. Under the terms of an Act of Parliament, Lovett was granted permission, for a period of 99 years, to levy a toll of a penny per ton of cargo, inward and outward bound, from all ships passing the to-be-built Eddystone Light.

A New Light

To design his light Lovett appointed a Cornish-born silk merchant who had his business in London – John Rudyerd. Mr Rudyerd had, by all accounts, been born into a large and 'roguish' family, from whom he had run away to Plymouth as a boy.

In Plymouth he found work as a servant and before long had endeared himself sufficiently to his master, to persuade the latter to send him to school to be properly educated. It was an opportunity that young Mr Rudyerd took full advantage of and after finishing his schooling his former master helped set him up in business. Moving later to London, Mr Rudyerd became very successful and continued to maintain an interest in learning.

Clearly his enquiring mind impressed Captain Lovett and, once charged with the task, Mr Rudyerd decided to seek out the views of two of my peers, Master Shipwrights from the Royal Dockyard at Woolwich, Mr Smith and Mr Northcott.

The new light was designed to be watertight and seaworthy as a ship would be. To give it flexibility and strength it was given a smooth wooden skin and a stone core for ballast to better resist the wind and waves. A conical, rather than a ten-sided shape as Winstanley had used, was also employed to present less of a flat surface to the elements and a large wooden mast was laid up through the very spine of the structure.

Finding the conditions no more favourable than Winstanley had, Mr Rudyerd started work on the reef in the summer of 1706, exactly ten years after Mr Winstanley had begun his great enterprise.

As you might expect there were still men around locally who had worked on that project and Mr Rudyerd was only too happy to call on their services. Once again the Navy provided a degree of cover and by the summer of 1708 work was in such a state of fowardness that a light was once again lit upon the rocks although it wasn't until the following year that the work was actually completed.

Although not quite as tall as Mr Winstanley's edifice, the new lighthouse is altogether less fussy and more simple; it stands a little over seventy feet tall and has four rooms, a store, a living room, bedroom and a kitchen, the ceiling of which supports the lantern.

Let us hope that his achievement is an altogether more enduring one, although, without that storm, it is possible that Mr Winstanley, and his light, might still be with us.

Above: Rudyerd's light c1708

Further Developments in the Yard

King's Dock, an early view. (Cyberheritage)

By this time, as you might imagine, there had been many developments at Hamoze itself: a small gunwharf and storehouse had been established below Mount Wise and across from Stonehouse; houses had started to appear hard by the Dock Yard gates, and along the North Corner; Thomas Podd had moved on as Master Shipwright and came to join me at Portsmouth – we worked together on the *Royal Katherine* which was launched in 1703. Thomas's successor, Benjamin Rosewall, had also moved on and John Lock was now ensconced alongside the Commissioner, Captain William Wright.

Commissioner Wright is now in his second spell at Hamoze, having been in post but briefly between May 1703 and February 1704. After that Captain Greenhill, who you may recall arrived as the first Commissioner at Hamoze more than twelve years earlier, returned for a four-year spell of office.

Apart from servicing ships of the line, there was little major building work carried out in the Dock Yard throughout much of this period, although arguably the biggest project to date was executed as the 64-gun, third-rate *Rupert* was rebuilt and launched.

Originally a Harwich ship launched back in 1666, the *Rupert* was brought to Hamoze before I left in 1697 and work began on taking her to pieces. In the event, the rebuilding was overseen by me, then Master Podd and Benjamin Rosewall who completed the job in October 1703. At a little over 900 tons she was the biggest warship that the new yard had yet worked on.

Within days of *Rupert* taking to the open sea the Admiralty placed an order for the Yard's next major construction, a 60-gun fourth-rate vessel destined to be marginally bigger than the *Rupert*, and to be known as the *York*. There was, however, a rider to the contract, in that the Admiralty insisted that any work on the *York* should not be allowed to interfere with any refit work being done at Hamoze.

In the wake of the Great Storm that struck the following month, it clearly became a matter of some priority for all the Royal Dock Yards to do what they could to make sure that all the survivors of that calamity be checked for their seaworthiness.

However, the losses themselves meant that the Navy was depleted and with the war across the Channel progressing well, it meant there was an ever greater demand for new warships. Thus it was that, more than a year before the *York* was ready, an order was made, in March 1705, for another fourth-rate warship to be built at Hamoze.

John Lock had been appointed Master Shipwright just four weeks before that, so he had his hands full from his very first day. The *York* was launched in April 1706 and the second of those warships, the *Plymouth*, followed in May 1708, by which time the *Phoenix* was in for a rebuild.

Sir Cloudesley Shovel's Disaster

Part of the ill-fated fleet commanded by Sir Cloudesley Shovel that had run into problems in Scilly Isles, the *Phoenix* had been seriously damaged having run aground, but was able to float free ending up in Hamoze in March 1708 when she was paid off. This rebuild wasn't actually done in the Yard however, rather it was carried out in the commercial premises of Mr Jos Bingham.

The *Phoenix* and all aboard her, had been extremely fortunate. Sir Cloudesley Shovel, Commander In Chief of the British Fleets, had been returning, in heavy weather, with the fleet, to England from the Mediterranean, on 22 October 1707 when his ship, the *Association*, struck rocks just off the Isles of Scilly. Tragically so too did the *Eagle*, the *Romney* and the *Firebrand*. The *Phoenix*, the *Lenox* and *La Valeur* had become detached from the main body of the fleet, but they too were driven in amongst the rocks of the Scillies.

Happily the *Phoenix* managed to break free, but the crew of another vessel, the *St George*, had the heartbreaking experience of watching the Admiral''s ship go down in just a few minutes. All 800 men on board were lost. By the time the other wrecked vessels had been accounted for, hundreds more men had been lost.

The tragedy caused great consternation across the country, particularly in the naval ports where so many of the men had families.

It appears that the Admiral and his navigators were convinced that they were off Ushant, that island off the north-westernmost tip of France that marks the southern entrance to the English Channel, when in fact, they were off the northern entrance to the Channel - at the Isles of Scilly.

The accident says much about the parlous state of our navigational equipment, although a rumour for some time persisted that one able seaman had tried to suggest to his officers that they were off-course; it is said that he was about to be swung from the yardarm for his insolence when the ship went down.

Sir Cloudesley's body was washed ashore, at Porthellick Cove the following day and brought into Plymouth on board the *Salisbury*. From there it was taken up to the Citadel where he was attended by the recently retired local surgeon, Dr James Yonge, who personally oversaw the embalming of the Admiral's corpse, prior to it being conveyed to London where it was interred at Westminster Abbey at the Queen's cost.

Left: *Cloudesley Shovell.* Right: *James Yonge.* *(nb: It later emerged that Sir Cloudesley had somehow managed to survive the wrecking of his ship and was still conscious when he was swept up on St Mary's. Raising an arm to gain the attention of a local woman, she was attracted by the priceless emerald ring he had on his hand. Thereupon she beat out what life was left in him and bit off the ring-bearing finger. The story only came to light years later when the woman, on her deathbed, confessed it to a clergyman and produced the stolen jewellery. The ring was subsequently returned to the Admiral's heirs.)*

Sir Cloudesley Shovell's ship the Association *foundering off the Scilly rocks, with the* Eagle, Romney *and* Firebrand. *22 October 1707.*

Samuel and Nathianel Buck 1735. His Majesty's new Dockyard takes shape.

Plymouth Dock *Edward Hoxland*

By 1710 the number of men working in the Dock Yard had more than doubled since Elias Waffe had left to go to Portsmouth a little over a decade earlier. There were now some seven hundred and forty-one men on the books, of whom 270 were shipwrights, 165 were labourers, 71 worked in the ropeyard, 48 were riggers, another 29 were caulkers and there were a dozen sawyers.

The scale of the operation put it well beyond the bounds of anything that had previously been seen in the area and meant there was plenty of employment for complementary tradesmen and merchants as just to feed, clothe and house such a large workforce required quite significant resources. The Naval victualling arrangements in Plymouth were consolidated in 1705 with a new Victualling Office at Lambhay, although the bakehouse at Coxside was kept in service, but a more significant development took place just north of the Dock Yard a few years later, in 1718 when negotiations opened between the Board of Ordnance and Sir Nicholas Morice to lease land upon which a new Gun Wharf with attendant storehouses could be sited.

The move followed the failure to agree terms with Mr Edgcumbe over extending the existing facility below Mount Wise; it seems that Mr Edgcumbe wasn't interested in selling or leasing any of this land there, stating that it would require an Act of Parliament to make him do so.

Meanwhile, Sir Nicholas Morice *'the greatest Jew in these parts'* was himself reluctant to sell land for less than six times its normal price and so, just as the Admiralty had been forced to lease the Dock Yard site, once again they were compelled to lease land for the new Gun Wharf. By this time, a substantial residential and commercial development had sprung up along the northern wall of the Dock Yard, so the Gun Wharf had to be set a short distance further up the river.

Colonel Christian Lilly, the Senior Officer for the Plymouth district, produced an estimate for the work, which came out a little under £17,000. William Cowley, a stonemason from London, was awarded the contract for the bulk of the construction work, towards the end of 1720, and, soon afterwards, Abraham Curtis had the carpentry and joinery contract.

Colonel Lilly oversaw the early work and in all likelihood was responsible for the layout and design of the storehouses and main terrace, although the influence of Sir John Vanbrugh, who was then Comptroller of the King's Works, is evident throughout and there doubtless would have been some input from Lilly's draughtsman, Schutze, as well.

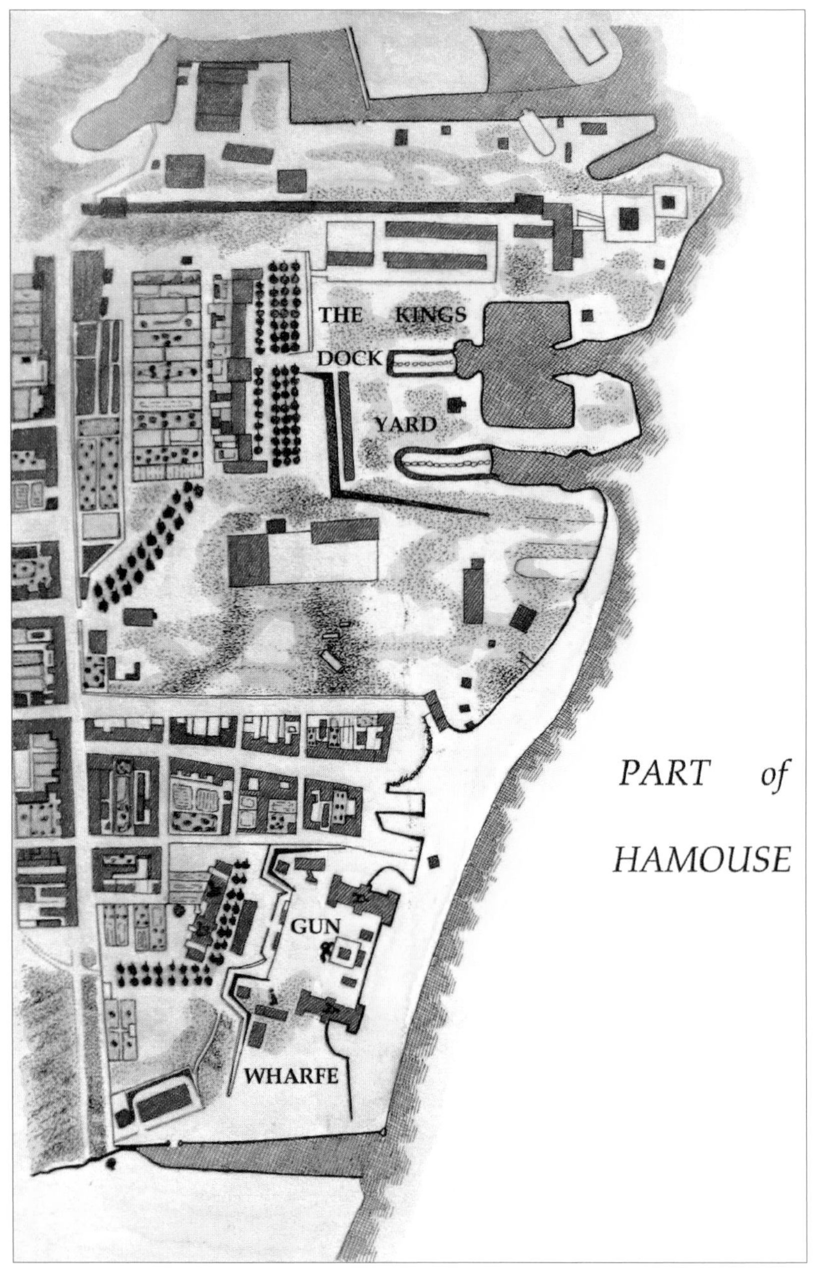

With a brief that saw him responsible for all Ordnance property from Portland down to the Isles of Scilly, Colonel Lilly was not on hand for all the new workings though and it has been suggested that Mr Andrew Jelfe, a surveyor for the Board of Ordnance, who was appointed Overseer and Clerk of the Works on the new development in January 1720, may have designed the Yard entrance, the guard houses and a number of the labourer's houses.

Just as the Officer's Terrace had a commanding view of the Dock Yard, so also was the Gun Wharf arranged, the imposing officer's terrace here although not quite as long, was equally as high. Seven sets of grates, coppers, stoves and sink were fitted in the well-appointed block, with *'fourteen holes and covers to seats in the Bogg Houses'* at the back.

The wharf itself was symmetrically set out with a semi-circular basin at either end and a great storehouse alongside each basin at right angles to the waterline. Along the length of the wharf itself sat two treadwheel cranes and and a small powder magazine. Gun barrels were stored in an open space behind and there was also a limekiln and forge for the armourer.

Within four years the yard was already partly operational and the character and appearance of this new town had been transformed again. As that celebrated writer, Mr Daniel Defoe was to comment in his *Tour Through Great Britain* at the time (1724): *'It is, in short, now become as complete an arsenal or yard for building and fitting men-of-war as any the Government are masters of, and perhaps much more convenient than some of them, though not so large.'*

He continued: *'The building of these things, with the addition of ropewalks and mast-yards, etc., has brought with it an abundance of trades-people and workmen to the place, so they began by little and little to build houses on the lands, adjacent, til at length there appeared a very handsome street, spacious and large, and as well inhabited; and so many houses are since added that it is become a considerable town, and must of consequence in time draw abundance of people from Plymouth itself.'*

As for Plymouth itself, Mr Defoe ventured to suggest that *'it is, and will always be a very considerable town, while that excellent harbour makes it such a general port for the receiving all the fleets of merchant's ships for the southward (as from Spain, Italy, the West Indies etc.), who generally make it the first port to put in at for refreshment or safety, from either weather or enemies.'*

Samuel and Nathianel Buck 1735. His Majesty's new Dockyard takes shape.

Samuel and Nathianel Buck 1735. Plymouth, Mount Batten, Mount Edgcumbe and West Stonehouse

'The town is populous and wealthy, having, as above, several considerable merchants and abundance of wealthy shopkeepers whose trade depends upon supplying to seafaring people that upon so many occasions put into port. As for the gentlemen – I mean those that are such by family and birth and way of living – it cannot be expected to find many such in a town merely depending on trade, shipping, and seafaring business: yet I found here some men of value (persons of liberal education, general knowledge, and excellent behaviour) whose society obliges me to say that a gentleman might find very agreeable company in Plymouth.'

Although it is difficult to be accurate about such matters it would seem reasonable to suggest that the population of Plymouth around this time was approximately 8,000 persons, while Plymouth Dock, which, less than forty years earlier, numbered little more than a handful, had grown to almost 3,000, making it already bigger than the long-established community of Stonehouse that sits between the two other townships.

Saltash

Next greatest in importance, and size, locally was Saltash. This *'little, poor, shattered town' was also visited by Mr Defoe who made the crossing by ferry;*
'The Tamar here is very wide, and the ferry-boats, bad; so that I thought myself well escaped when I got safe on shore in Cornwall.'

'Saltash,' he wrote, *'seems to be the ruins of a larger place; and we saw many houses, as it were, falling down, and I doubt not but the mice and rats have abandoned many more, as they say they will when they are likely to fall. Yet this town is governed by a mayor and aldermen, has many privileges and sends members to Parliament, takes toll of all vessels that pass the river, and has the sole oyster-fishing in the whole river, which is considerable.*

This town has a kind of jurisdiction upon the River Tamar down to the mouth of the port, so that they claim anchorage of all small ships that enter the river; their coroner sits upon all dead bodies that are found drowned in the river and the like, but they make not much profit of them.

There is a good market here, and that is the best thing to be said of the town; it is also very much increased since the number of the inhabitants are increased at the new town, as I mentioned as near the dock at the mouth of the Hamoaze, for those people choose rather to go to Saltash to market by water than to walk to Plymouth by land for their provisions. Because, first, as they go in the town boat, the same

The ferry crossing to Saltash.

boat brings home what they buy, so that it is much less trouble; second, because provisions are bought much cheaper at Saltash than at Plymouth. This I say, is like to be very great advantage to the town of Saltash, and may in time put a new face of wealth upon the place.'

The Continued Growth of Dock

Hindsight is a wondrous thing and writing now at some seventy years distance from Mr Defoe's observations we can see how little prevailing opinion anticipated the continued rise of our community. Plymouth Dock today has surpassed all of its near neighbours in terms of population and prosperity. While Plymouth has doubled in size since Mr Defoe was here in 1724, Plymouth Dock, today, in 1796, has grown almost eightfold, such that with over 20,000 persons living here it is now bigger than Plymouth and even the County town, Exeter. The latter, while undoubtedly possessing more history than Plymouth or Dock, has been slow in adopting improvements – notably paving and the cleaning of streets – consequently it has an unsavoury odour and apart from the one great street that runs through it, east to west, the rest is little more than a collection of dirty lanes. The streets are not flagged, neither are they cleaned as frequently as in other parts of the kingdom. It is a similar story in Plymouth where the streets in general are narrow and not as clean as those of Dock.

The streets of Dock, being more recently laid out, are wider and more imposing and paved with a species of marble which is very common in the quarries of Mount Wise and about Mount Stone (beyond the Long Room at Stonehouse). In the more public streets, where there is any slope, the stones are extremely white, showing a variety of veins after heavy rain.

The improvement and maintenance of the streets are, together with the running of the workhouse, under the direction of the Commissioners appointed by an Act of Parliament some fifteen years ago (and in turn just fifteen years after the first street paving in London itself). I am pleased to say that the paving is gradually being extended to the extreme parts of the town and to the lesser streets.

But to return to Mr Defoe's thought that an increase in the size of Dock would speedily result in improved circumstances for Saltash, it wasn't long after his visit that regular markets were being held here, in Fore Street, in a temporary wood-shambles near the Dock Yard gates.

The New Market

Then, about thirty years ago, the big pond to the south of Fore Street and a little outside the Dock Yard wall, was filled up and converted to a market site in a very commodious manner.

Now, plentiful supplies of every kind of provisions are poured into the market three times a week – Tuesdays, Thursdays, and Saturdays – and are a matter of astonishment to all strangers to these parts.

Butcher's meat, in general, is a penny per pound cheaper than anywhere west of Bristol, and the quantities of fish, fowl and poultry which are sold here are almost incredible. The prices of some of the choicest fish has increased a little because it can now be transported to distant markets more easily but the quantity remaining is usually abundant and reasonably cheap. The John Dories are as good as you will find anywhere, while in the mackerel and pilchard season the quantities available exceed all description short of actually seeing it for yourself.

The other benefit of all this activity here is the great influx of ready money which in turn helps support an ever-increasing number of men and boats employed in the fishery, and thus affords the maintenance of many families.

Of course the main work in the town is the Dock Yard. With some 2,500 men currently employed there, it is no wonder that the town has grown so large, so quickly.

One Street after Another

After initial developments stretching out either side of the original main thoroughfares into the town - Fore Street for those arriving by foot and North Corner for those coming in by boat - the town gradually expanded to the south. Princes Street, King Street and Queen Street were among the earliest developments to follow, with the beginnings of Granby Street appearing soon after that.

By 1730 there were but one or two houses on the east side of what is now the town square, but nothing to the north and the place where Marlborough Street now stands was a pasture or meadow.

The back lane running in line with Fore Street to the south, the one we now call Cherry Garden Street, was then just called Back Street and on its south side it ran as far as the present St Aubyn Street.

Running south off Fore Street, Catherine Street, Stafford's Hill and Dock Wall with the Crosslanes, were laid out next and then, running down from the corner of the ponds where the market was created, Duke Street appeared, at an angle that broke away from the grid- like pattern that hitherto had been followed.

Undoubtedly one of the main considerations behind the rapid expansion to the south of Fore Street around this time was the construction of a bridge across the lower part of Stonehouse Creek.

Connections to Plymouth and Stonehouse

Prior to that time the access into Dock from Stonehouse had not been a particularly easy one. There was a footpath along the edge of the marsh above Millbay that led down to a ferry-crossing which was operated by a pilot who would guide his boat across the creek by pulling on ropes laid across the water. Because of the very narrowness of the avenues and approaches to and from the said ferry, and other obstructions, the route could only be used by those on foot.

The crossing was difficult by day and rather desolate and dreary by night. Most who chose to go from one town to the other after sunset would generally wait until a little group had collected, sufficiently strong to dissuade potential attackers.

Some pedestrians forded the creek, while others went round by way of Millbridge, this being the usual route for those travelling with pack horses. Here again, however, precautions were often necessary and traders travelling between Plymouth and Dock with treasure and merchandise would supply each man with a set of pistols in the event of an encounter with a highwayman. The opening of the bridge greatly improved the traffic between Plymouth and Dock and allowed for easier access for wheeled transport.

Lord Edgcumbe and Sir John St Aubyn, the two landowners either side of the creek, applied for an Act of Parliament to enable them to bridge the crossing almost thirty years ago (1767).

The Stoke Damerel estate had come into the hands of Sir John St Aubyn, of Clowance, through his marriage, in 1725, to Catherine Morice. Catherine was the daughter of Sir William Morice and the estate had passed to her on the death of her brother, also Sir William Morice, when he died in 1749 (some of the other estates incidentally had passed to Catherine's sister, Barbara (who in turn had married Sir John Molesworth).

As well as inheriting the manor of Stoke Damerel there was the not insubstantial matter of some £10,000 in cash, conveyed in the form of 80,000 half-crown pieces, which were transported almost the whole length of Cornwall, from Werrington to Clowance, in two carts.

Meanwhile, East Stonehouse, along with West Stonehouse, Cremyll and Maker, has been in the hands of the Edgcumbe family since Sir Piers Edgcumbe married Joan Durnford some three hundred years ago (1493). Sir Piers obtained a licence to empark part of his new estate and soon afterwards his son, Richard, had a new family seat - the present Mount Edgcumbe house - built and the family moved down from Cothele.

The desirability of improving access between East Stonehouse and Dock became all the more urgent after the completion of the Royal Naval Hospital in 1762. Hospital provision here had long been needed but the Navy Board were anxious to monitor the success of their new hospital facility at Portsmouth (Haslar) before beginning a similarly ambitious project here.

Thus it was that it wasn't until 1756, three years after Haslar had opened, that the Commissioners for the Sick and Wounded purchased a site in this area.

This site, No Place Field, which had belonged to Mr Henry Tolcher, was ultimately deemed to be too small, however, and so it came to pass, two years later, that a number of fields further down the creek,

Sir John St Aubyn

the seaward side of the Millbridge, were purchased from the Edgcumbe estate. It would appear, incidentally, that the Navy Board's preference for building on the south side of the creek was largely determined by the reluctance of the St Aubyn estate to do anything other than lease the land on the north side of the creek.

However, while a waterside location meant that it was easy to convey sick and wounded servicemen by boat straight from warships to the hospital gates, it did mean that, for land-based personnel an improved link between Stonehouse and Dock was now a priority.

John Smeaton, who had been in the area some ten years earlier working on his replacement for Rudyerd's Eddystone Lighthouse (which had burned down in December 1755), was the engineer selected to produce designs for the bridge, which he duly did in the summer of 1767.

William Payne's view of the Royal Naval Hospital and Stonehouse Creek from Tavistock Road (West Country Studies Library)

The Royal Naval Hospital, Stonehouse had been preceded by a hospital ship, Canterbury, which was paid off in November 1762.

John Smeaton.

Mr Smeaton's Bridge

Mr Smeaton has built a number of bridges around the country and we are fortunate that he was prepared to come back down here as it was unusual for him to work this far from the Great North Road between Edinburgh and London. Originally from Leeds, his family home was in Scotland. Furthermore, when working here in Stonehouse on his lighthouse, some villains poisoned Mr Smeaton's dog, compelling him to place a porter on guard, armed with a musket.

We should perhaps point out that Stonehouse Bridge was one of several that Smeaton was working on simultaneously thirty years ago. Having just finished Coldstream Bridge over the River Tweed when he produced his designs for Stonehouse Creek, he was also working on Perth Bridge over the River Tay, the Newark Viaduct over the River Trent and a couple of canals (at Ripon, and the Forth and Clyde).

For those too young to remember, we should perhaps remind our readers that this was a revolutionary time for travelling as the Turnpike Act of just a few years earlier (1760) had led to rapid transformation in the quality of our roads. All over the country landowners started to substantially improve stretches of public highway crossing their estates in return for the right to put up toll gates and charge travellers in order that they might get a return on their investment ... and of course, in the long term, to make a profit. Most charge a penny for a person on horseback or threepence for a coach, maybe sixpence for a heavily laden cart and a shilling for a wagon.

The Parliamentary Act obtained by Lord Edgcumbe and Sir John has empowered them to demand as tolls *'before any passage over the said bridge be permitted'* – for every chaise, chair or calash drawn by one horse the sum of twopence; for every cart, dray, car, sledge or other carriage drawn by one horse, mule or ass, the same amount; for every coach or chariot drawn by two horses, the sum of threepence, sixpence if there were more than two horses. The toll for pedestrians is set at one halfpenny.

As you might imagine, the construction of the bridge meant a number of changes on the Stonehouse bank, and necessitated the demolition of several buildings, but the benefits to the local inhabitants of all three local communities have been immeasurable. The benefits to Sir John St Aubyn and Lord Edgcumbe have not been inconsequential either, as by the late 1790s the tolls were paying them £2,000 a year.

Of course, much more recently Lord Edgcumbe has been involved with another major enterprise that has done much to improve access and egress to and from Dock. As I am sure you are aware, I am referring to the new ferry crossing to Torpoint which the Earl of Mount Edgcumbe has established with Reginald Pole Carew, esquire, of Anthony.

Stonehouse Bridge by William Payne (1760-1830) watercolour (© Plymouth City Museum & Art Gallery)

The Torpoint Ferry

Having committed themselves to constructing wharves, landing places and all related buildings, and to build and keep a competent number of substantial boats for the use of the said ferry, together with a sufficient number of capable and experienced ferrymen, our patrons opened the new service on 4th July, 1791.

Under the terms of the Act, provision is made that boats for foot passengers, market goods, etc., may pass to and from North Corner in the same way as they had before. While the boats for carriages, horses, cattle, sheep, hogs, and other animals now usually pass from a new hard, which has been made on the beach to the north of the town.

Passing from Fore Street, you come up King Street into the Square; which, having crossed, diagonally conducts you through the Lines to a new purpose-built road.

About 300 yards northward from the end of the new hard at high water a Passage House has been just erected for the accommodation of travellers and others who are aiming to cross the Ferry, during normal operating hours. The fare and lodgings are good and a coach sets off from here for Falmouth every Monday, Wednesday and Friday morning at six o'clock and returns the following day.

The beach here is flat, and extends westwards about 500 yards to the low-water mark, from whence the direct passage over the Tamar is not much more than half a mile.

The hours of plying across the river are from four in the morning to ten in the evening from March 25th to September 28th, and from six in the morning to eight in the evening from September 29th to March 24th.

The tolls payable are: one penny for every foot passenger; twopence for every horse; one shilling and sixpence for a two-wheel chaise with one horse; two shillings and sixpence for a coach with two horses; five shillings with four Horses; ten shillings and sixpence for a hearse (returning the same day without a corpse, and including a horse &c. and attendants); one shilling and sixpence for every cart drawn by one or two horses; five shillings for a waggon pulled by three or four horses; sixpence. for every bull, ox, or cow, and one person attending; twopence for every calf or hog and one person attending; eleven pence for every score (twenty in number) of sheep with one person attending; and proportionally for a lesser number; five pence for every score of hounds, with one person attending; sixpence for every hogshead of beer, &c., ton of goods, merchandize, coals, lime, &c.; one shilling and twopence for a bag of corn or grain, pair of hampers, pots, or crooks. All these Tolls are double on Sundays, and allow a return - always on the same day - once. Tolls for carriages always include the horses, &c.; but not the attendants, except for a hearse.

Ships in 'Ordinary'

For those unfamiliar with the sight of our great ships of war, here on this crossing you will see a great many of them laid up 'in Ordinary'. In times of peace, those vessels which are deemed surplus to requirements are taken out of commission and stripped of all their rigging, except their lower masts and the guns; meanwhile the spars, sails, cables and cordage and every requisite is marked and placed in the storehouse with the name of the ship to which they belong, so that they can be readily restored to the vessel when it needs to be prepared for action again.

It is to be observed that the guard ships are moored at sufficient distances to prevent accidents or alarms from salutes. On public firing days it is easy to avoid passing just at that time, which is always set at one o'clock. There are six such days each year; the King's and Queen's birthdays, the anniversaries of the Royal Accession and Coronation, and the 29th of May, and 5th of November.

On the Cornish side of the crossing is Torpoint, a village mostly of modern date, which is the home, for the most part, to the warrant officers and their families of the ships in ordinary. Each ship has a skeleton crew of boatswain, gunner, carpenter and cook, together with a very small number of seamen to assist them.

In less than half a mile from Torpoint is the Seat of Lord Graves, Admiral of the White. It is called Thanckes and in turn gives its name to the bay on that bit of waterline on which it sits.

Morice Town and the Hamoaze.

Morice Town

Soon after the completion of the New Passage, in 1796, on the Devon side, a house carpenter and builder of the name of Crossing, began to build on a spot nearly adjoining on the west with the ferry and on the south with the glacis of the lines surrounding Dock. The convenient situation of the housing thus began and increased the population of Dock, immediately occasioning the erection of additional buildings. The place is now growing under the name of Morice Town, to perpetuate the memory of Sir William Morice, from whom the manor descended to Sir John St Aubyn.

It now, in 1801, consists of two streets, running parallel with each other, and part of a third thoroughfare. To the west a canal has also been created, it is about 300 feet long and 90 wide and there are spacious wharfs and warehouses now being built along each side of it.

A brewery, the Tamar Brewery, the most complete and extensive in the west of England, has also been established near the Canal. Further canals and wharfs are now being considered.

The Lines

Having mentioned that the new road crosses through 'the Lines' it is perhaps appropriate at this point to talk about this most distinctive feature of Dock.

As the routes into the town became progressively easier so it was thought necessary to better protect the Government's interests; thus it was that, in 1766, power was vested in the Governor General and Members of his Majesty's Board of Ordnance to purchase such land as was thought necessary within Mount Wise and Stoke Damerel for the defence of the Dock Yard and shipping in the harbour, &c.

In this way certain meadow, pasture, and waste grounds were purchased from the lord of the manor and these, together with the Dock Yard and New Ordnance Wharf, entirely surround the town, all except for two common landing points at Mutton Cove and North Corner.

Ten years earlier, in 1756, when we joined what would come to be known as the Seven Years' War against France and French interests in North America, it had been deemed prudent to create an earthwork rampart, fronted by a ditch, all the way around Dock, from the new Gun Wharf right down to the old Gun Wharf at Mount Wise. Some thirty guns could be mounted around the lines and the work was completed by 1765, two years after the fighting had stopped and France had lost most of their colonies in North America. The French navy had also been severely weakened and once again there was no doubting the supremacy of the British Navy.

The threat reappeared however and in 1770 a special Act sanctioned the raising of fortifications and trenches around Dock and new plans were prepared by Mr Smelt, the man in charge of the Engineer's Department. After the combined French and Spanish fleets appeared in Cawsand Bay in 1779, General Dixon hastened the completion of the defences and Mr Francis Basset marched from Tehidy at the head of a thousand miners to supply the necessary labour.

There were three gates within the lines: the North Barrier, leading to Newpassage; the Stoke Barrier, leading to Tavistock; the Stonehouse Barrier, leading to Plymouth. A redoubt and block-house on Mount Pleasant commanded the lines, so that Dock was surrounded by defences.

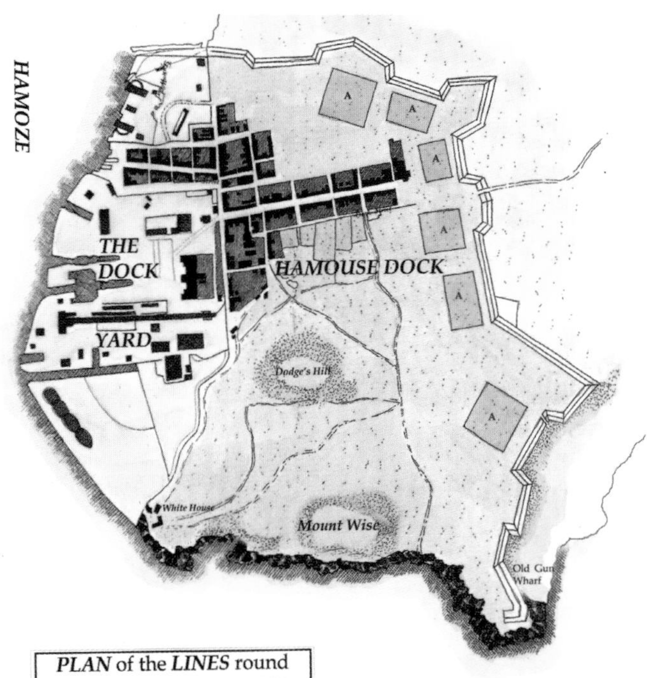

Above: *Military uniform of the day.* Left: *Plan of Plymouth Dock c1750 redrawn by James Robinson.*

The Military Barracks

At the beginning of that same period we had a sustained period of barrack building which resulted in the construction of two large blocks - Marlborough Square and George Square - each of which could accommodate four companies of men, with four lesser blocks in between - Granby, Frederick, Ligonier and Cumberland - each of which could take three companies.
The sudden influx of Army personnel had a considerable impact on the population of the town as well as the complexion of it and among the most notable recent changes has been, in the last seven or eight years, the construction of a massive wall, about twelve feet high, near the limits of the King's ground. The wall has been constructed so as to separate the barracks and parade grounds entirely from the town.

1782 Blockhouse near Dock from Mount Edgcumbe

The Ordnance Wharf

Near the north west side of the Dock Yard is the Ordnance Wharf, where a prodigious assortment of ammunition is constantly in store, as well as a great variety of arms of every description: cannons, canonades, mortars, bombs, swords and almost every other device which has been contrived by man to take away the life of man.
The Powder Magazine, a plain building of white stone, stands northward of the Dock Yard, at the water's edge.
Great precaution is taken before admitting strangers to view this repository, in which many thousand barrels of powder are constantly lodged. All persons wearing swords or spurs are obliged to leave them with a guard at the outer door, where they are furnished with a pair of clogs, lest any accident should happen from a nail which might have been used in the sole of a shoe and cause a spark.
The building however is not especially interesting, it looks rather like the cellar of a large wine merchant, full of small casks rather than large ones.
Steel conductors, for the security of the building against the effects of lightning, are placed at the angles of the building and during times of storm, an awful, but at the same time beautiful, spectacle can be observed in the playing of the electric fluid upon the wires.

Mount Wise Fort, Plymouth Dock, taken from Passage Beach. 'Most humbly inscribed to Lieut. Gen Haviland, Commander in Chief of his Majesty's forces in the Western District and Col. of the 45th Regt. by his most obliged humble servant William Hay - 1780.'

Governor's House by William Payne (1760-1830) watercolour (Westcountry Studies Library)

The Governor's House

Another major change to the landscape in the last few years has been the building of the new Governor's House on Mount Wise. Opposite to Mount Edgcumbe, of which it has a pleasant view, it also commands a vista of Drake's Island, the Sound and across Lord Boringdon's elegant mansion at Saltram.
Sir Thomas Wise's old house had been taken down some years earlier and a fort had been constructed on the site. Consisting of eight 24-pound guns with two mortars on the most elevated spot, the fort has two further batteries at a small distance on lower ground, but sufficiently commanding on the west side and three others similarly situated on the east side. Together they make a very formidable defence against any forcible attempt of hostile ships to enter the harbour.
It is perhaps worth pointing out that to get this far any hostile craft will have already had to negotiate the batteries of Easter and Wester Kings, the guns of St Nicholas Island and the Citadel, not to mention the Battery of Obelisk Point on the opposite shore and that of George's Fort within the walls of the Dock Yard.
Parliament sanctioned the building of the new Governor's House in May 1789 and the measure was pushed through by the Master General of the Ordnance, the Duke of Richmond, whose younger brother, Lord George Lennox, earlier this year (1796) became the first Governor to occupy the building. Previously the Governor of Plymouth had had his residence in the Citadel, so the move is a further indication of the growing importance of our town.
The new building consists of a central section which contains an attic storey, with two lower wings; on each side of which is a large open court enclosed with a wall, and detached offices at the each end.
In the middle of the north front is a semicircular projection; there are two coach entrances and the barrier wall is continued on the east side to the Lines. It stands just fifty to a hundred yards from the last houses to have been built in George Street which were completed eleven and twelve years ago. The houses in George Street are quite attractive properties and are altogether more substantial than many of the houses we have seen to date in Dock.
There has been plenty of other building work within the Government establishments in recent years too.

Inside The Dock Yard

The Mast House pond was only completed about four years ago; this was achieved by removing the rocks which remained to complete the wharf for launching, or for hauling up the timbers for the masts. The pond is a large piece of water enclosed from the sea by a strong wall which is at least ten feet thick and almost four hundred feet long. The surface is laid flat with large flagstones of coarse granite. Water flows into the pond through two openings which are about forty feet wide and have light wooden bridges running across them.
The new facility represented a great improvement, for previously masts had been subject to decay, having been left on the mud and exposed to the weather. Cracking from exposure to the sun is a major problem as an immense number of masts, yards, etc., are always kept in this pond. It may interest the reader to know that the main mast for a first-rate man of war measures 119 feet 8 inches in length and is 10 feet in circumference. They are made up of many pieces of balk formed to fit into each other, then rounded, and pressed together with iron hoops, driven on red hot.
The situation whereby obstacles – rocks, hills, etc., had been perceived as a problem was swiftly eliminated on the grounds that marble rock, that so much of this area is comprised, affords an ample supply of stone and lime for building. This makes the prospect of building at Dock considerably less expensive than, say, at Portsmouth.
Consequently, although little development of note was carried out in the Yard for some years – between the addition of a double dock in the 1720s and the end of the War of Austrian Succession (in 1748) – the Admiralty decided to review the facilities here.

Admiralty Visit

In 1749 Lords Anson, Barrington and Sandwich paid us a visit and observed that many of the buildings here were in a bad state of repair and in danger of falling. The Officers then in charge argued that the constant process of fitting and refitting ships during the war had left little time to tend to the fabric of the Yard itself. And indeed it was true that during the latter stages of that conflict a strong western squadron had been established here, a development that had done much to enhance, not just our reputation, but the scale of our endeavour. There were, by this time, as many men working here at Dock as there were in the biggest Yards in Chatham and Portsmouth.

However, despite making these observations there was little evidence of any urgency in addressing the problems and it wasn't until we had successfully fought another war with France (the Seven Years' War) that improvement work began.

That particular episode with the French put considerable strain on the facilities both here at Dock and at Portsmouth and before the conflict had even been concluded the Navy Board petitioned the Admiralty with a view to improving and expanding the yard. They were especially concerned about the risk of fire spreading on the crowded site (there had been a very serious fire at Portsmouth the previous year).

Thus it was that on 11 November 1761 the Admiralty Board approved a petition that paved the way for a sustained period of growth and improvement; actions which have secured for our Navy an unrivalled reputation at sea and conferred upon the country the best-equipped dock yards in the World.

On securing approval for their proposals, the Navy Board lost little time in submitting their plans; plans that entailed almost doubling the size of the Yard. However, with so much of the town now laid out, a substantial amount of preliminary work was necessary. This involved dislodging thousands of tons of rock, most of it achieved with the use of gunpowder, so that a level site could be created. Mr Dummer's great storehouse was removed and eight new storehouses, arranged around two imposing quadrangles, were proposed. A new and much longer ropery (running at right angles to the existing facility) was

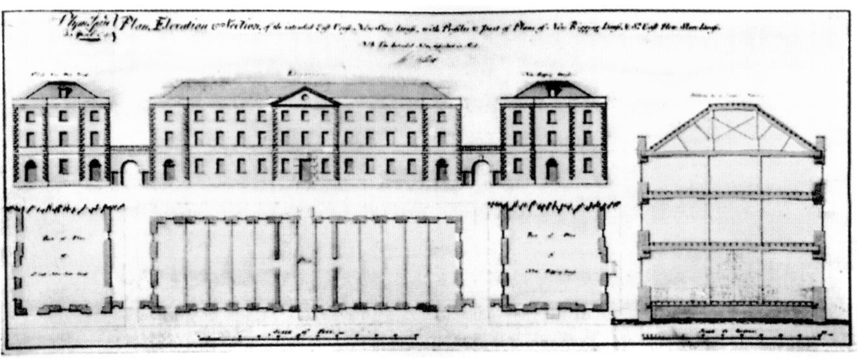

1790: Some of the storehouses that form part of the double quadrangle

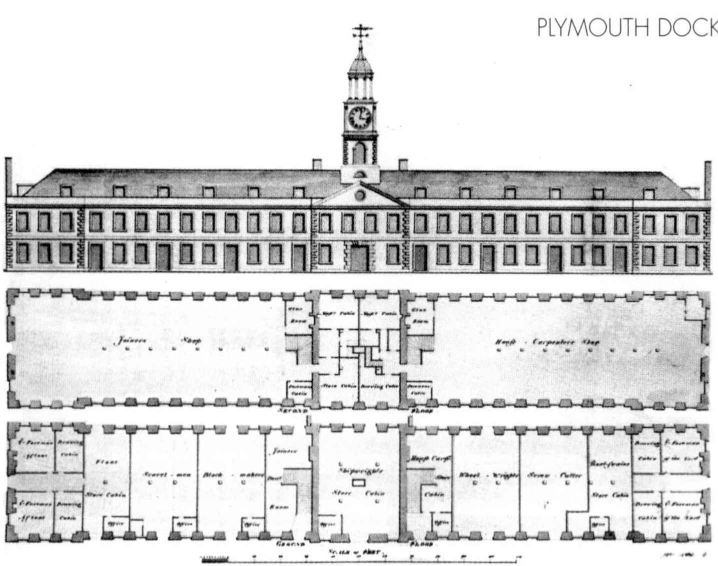

The amply proportioned Joiner's and Carpenter's shop.

also mooted, along with a new smithery, more building slips and a new dry dock.

Work on the new slips commenced right away and by 1764 they had been completed. By that stage the east and west storehouses were also under way and within another two years work had begun on a handful of other new buildings: the White Yarn House; the Tarring and Wheel House; the Black Yarn Houses; the Spinning House and the Laying House.

Seven years later most of these projects had been completed and work had started on the Laying House, the Mast Houses and Slips, the Clerk's Office and Store, the South Slip, the Master Ropemaker's House and new wharf walls.

The Rope Makers

The Master Rope Makers live in dwellings behind and parallel with the Rope Houses. The Rope Houses themselves are two lime-stone buildings which run parallel to each other. They are two stories high and have cellars below and are 1,200 feet long. In the upper storey twine is made and the yarns are prepared for the cables that are laid, or twisted together, below. The largest cables that are made for shipping are twenty-five inches in circumference and a hundred fathoms long (600 feet), they weigh a little under 120 cwt (6 tons) and are made up of over 3,000 yarns.

Extensive work around the mast pond took place during the 1770s, the North West Storehouse was also constructed at this time as were: the South Slip, the Smith's Shop and a couple of Guard Houses.

The Slip is for hauling up and graving, that is cleaning, the bottom of small vessels, such as sloops of war – cutters etc.

Beyond this is the Camber, a long canal about seventy feet wide at the upper end of which is a basin where boats sit. On the north side of the basin is the Boat House where boats are built and repaired and kept until they are needed. Here, prior to 1768 was the limit of the Dock Yard, hence everything to the south of this point is still referred to as the 'New Ground'.

The Blacksmith's Shop

It is here, south of the canal that we find the new Blacksmith's Shop. A spacious building over 200 feet square, it contains forty-eight forges. The largest anchors made here weigh five tons; they are made out of iron bars forged together and are moved in and out of the fire by cranes.

Those who are unaccustomed to places of this kind generally feel strong sensations of horror when they first enter; the clanking of the chains used to blow the bellows, the dingy countenances of the workmen, the immense fires, and, above all, the yellow glare thrown on everything by the flames shining through the dismal columns of smoke that continually fill the building, together form an unforgettable scene.

The smiths are allowed a certain amount of weak beer every day over and above their wages – the strength of the beer is increased when they are engaged on anchor work. To give the process some further idea of scale, around 10,000 sacks of coal a year may be burned in the Blacksmith's shop.

In front of the Blacksmith's shop is situated the Anchor Wharf where hundreds of anchors for ships of war are stored, all of them painted and supported in an upright position in an attempt to prevent rusting.

The Boiling House

Near this wharf we find three slips where the shipbuilding is carried out – adjoining them is the Boiling House. It is here that any planks needing to be curved are boiled in water for some considerable time and then placed, still hot, into position on the ship as it is being built, and immediately fastened. Without this process it would be impossible to bring timber of such great size into the required shape.

There is yet more perpetual boiling to be found alongside the Double Dock (so called because of its ability to deal with two battle ships at the same time).

Inside a blacksmith's shop.

The boiling here is of coal tar pitch: a bubbling, black, pungent material which is applied to the undersides of ships and to seams to render them watertight.

There are a good many odours that present themselves in the Dock Yard, few more powerful or all-pervading as that which is associated with the burning place at the head of the New Union or North New Dock which was made in the year 1789 (some twenty-seven years after the original Union Dock). The burning place is where all the old copper from ships' bottoms is brought and cleared of all the verdigris, weeds, mussels etc before it can be re-used. To do this the copper is laid out on iron bars, raised about a foot from the ground, and covered with chips and shavings, which are afterwards set fire to. The smoke is excessively nauseous, and deleterious in the extreme; yet, when the wind blows from the west, which is mostly the case here, the town is filled with it.

After a while the copper is taken out of the fire and beaten with mallets to remove the dirt and so on. This refuse used to be thrown away but recently it has been found to contain a large quantity of metallic particles and it is now sold at a reasonable price.

North of these areas we find the Plumber's, Braziers, and Armourer's shops, as well as the Bricklayer's and Stonecutter's Yards. Behind all this, the rock, having never been levelled, rises very high ... and irregularly: on it are a few sheds and storehouses.

Visiting the Yard

Overall the diversity of employments, ingenuity and manual activity, exhibited in the various departments of the Dock Yard present a very interesting spectacle to those who have not been accustomed to appreciate the effects of human industry on a grand scale. Perhaps no site is better calculated to enable a thinking person to appreciate what can be achieved through continued labour than the *'gradual growth of a few pieces of timber, into the majestic wonderful structure that encounters the winds and waves'* and forms the most complete security against invasion that Great Britain can possess.

For strangers who may wish to be better acquainted with the Yard we recommend their obtaining the company of some inhabitant of the town to procure their admission by a note to the Commissioner; whereupon a warder will be appointed to conduct them round the Yard. For those who cannot obtain such admission (and it is very rarely not granted) they can inform themselves by rowing up the harbour.

Most notable among those to inspect the Yard in recent times were their Royal Highnesses the King, Queen and the three eldest Princesses. In the summer of 1789 the Royal party travelled here in coaches, drawn by prancing teams of six horses. Troops awaited their arrival and while at Dock the Royal entourage had breakfast with the Commissioner, Captain Sir John Laforey at his house within the yard, where the Earls of Chesterfield, Howe and Chatham awaited them. The King expressed his highest satisfaction with what he had seen and Captain Laforey was soon afterwards created a Baronet and promoted to a Flag, while his son was made a Lieutenant and appointed to the command of the *Trusty*, a fifty-gun ship, for the Antigua Station - an island of which he already has large possessions. He was also appointed Governor.

Plymouth Harbour, Devon by Thomas Rowlandson (1756-1827) watercolour (© Plymouth City Museum & Art Gallery) Bequeathed by Lady Frances Ann Stevens through the Art Fund

After viewing everything in the facility and witnessing many of the operations performed here - driving bolts, twisting ropes etc. - and the opening of the large North New Dock (the largest in the Kingdom) the King then spent an hour on board the *Impregnable*, the ships in the harbour saluting all the while.

As the Royal barge was pulled to the shore, it was accompanied by a decorated cutter, rowed by six fine young women and steered by a seventh. The girls were clothed in loose white gowns with yellow cotton safeguards and black bonnets, and the shoulders of each were resplendent with sashes of purple bearing the inscription in gold 'Long Live their Majesties'.

The Royal return to Saltram was attended by a flotilla of sloops and boats; ship followed ship with salutes; and the guns boomed from Mount Edgcumbe.

The following morning there was a naval review and from a vantage point near the Mewstone the King watched one hundred battleships emerge from different parts of the harbour. A mock battle ensued concluding with a hearty rendition of Rule Britannia.

In the afternoon the King and Queen crossed to Mount Edgcumbe and as they passed by Stoke Church a new peal of eight bells was rung for the first time.

An inscription in the belfry marks the occasion and concludes thus:

'May Concord Reign Among Us as we Ring,
Pray God Preserve our Country, Church, and King,
On whose account these Bells were first rung Here
When George our King did in the West Appear.'

Only a little way behind such a visit in terms of pomp and splendour is the celebrations and gaiety surrounding the launch of the latest three-decker.

It is the eternal theme for weeks in advance, and it is no inconsiderable part of the pleasure of the townsfolk to visit, in the breakfast hour, the advance of the preparations. Every morning the new warship was surrounded by anxious hundreds, many of whom, allured by the trumpetings of fame, journeyed from the adjacent country side.

It is a continual source of delight to witness the progress of the shipwrights and the painters, and to notice the gradual disappearance of the scaffolding until the form of the vessel rises upon the view in all its symmetry, magnificence and strength.

The eve of a launch is observed as a carnival and parties are made up for the following day. Cousins from distant villages and towns pour into the area and bustle and anticipation prevail.

In a hundred festive nooks the experts discuss the dimensions and capacities of the new floating wonder and veterans recall old stories of old vessels, with lion heads and lion-hearted crews, and many an anecdote of personal encounters with one or other hero who has made a mark on one or other chapter of history.

On the eventful afternoon the gates open to a multitude of happy faces and a steady stream passes through the streets in deep and dense masses until, at last, the flow accumulates in one closely compacted concourse around the slipway.

Impressive is the picture, for now they see the vessel, the sublime result of so many combinations, charming in all her proportions, painted, gilded, ornamented, towering above the throng, with her Union and Ensign and Standard the unconquered and unconquerable flags of Old England, floating in the evening breeze.

As the tide flows silently to its height, so the artisans start to remove the supports, the bands play popular and national tunes and soon there is an intense and breathless interest as the blocks split out, the dog shores are cleared and the screw is applied.

The cry goes up - '*She creeps*' and the air is thick with waving hats and handkerchiefs, as, rapidly and majestically the vessel plunges into the water.

1789: George III visits the Royal Dockyard

Local Theatre at the end of the eighteenth century.

The Other Side of the Wall

As you might readily imagine the expansion of the Dock Yard has also led to the general swelling of the local population, as previously indicated. The figure has been further increased by the advent of our current conflict with the French, which has brought more activity than ever before to the Dock Yard and to the wider community that supports the working men and their families. When one takes account of the soldiers and sailors who also find themselves here for varying durations during the course of any war, then the cumulative number renders Plymouth Dock a principal town by any standards, not just in comparison with its now smaller Devon neighbours Plymouth and Exeter.

However, on account of this frequent influx of naval and army personnel and of strangers during war, it is inevitable that manners and customs are often unsettled and it should be noted that a spirit of unsociability prevails generally throughout the place. Two elements largely account for this: one, over-strained competition in almost every business or trade, and two, the great diversity of opinion that is to be found in religious matters.

The inhabitants are chiefly composed of workers from the Dock Yard and the Gun Wharf, tradesmen, mechanics, retailers, wholesalers, plus Officers and others belonging to the Army and Navy. There is scarcely a person here of any means who is not engaged in some kind of business or profession. There are but few gentlemen of leisure and literature and the arts meet with little encouragement. There is but one book club in the town and there is no other association or institution of a literary or scientific nature, and although several Circulating Libraries have been opened, these are mainly supported by the fairer sex.

Dock Theatre

The theatre, known as Dock Theatre, was opened in Cumberland Gardens in 1762. It has nothing to recommend it in its outward appearance but is neatly fitted up in the interior and is sufficiently spacious for the inhabitants, who are not very constant in their attendance. The theatre is currently conducted under the management of Mr Hughes, the proprietor, in spite of whose best efforts it tends to be a nightly scene of riot and debauchery – notwithstanding the presence of the Magistrates who use their privilege of admission not only for themselves, but for their friends.

The company are usually here from October to March every year and with the patronage of the Earl of Mount Edgcumbe, Lord George Lennox, the Officers of the Regiments in the barracks, and the Officers of the Navy and others, who make it their duty to countenance and support the manager and company in rotation, their seasons are generally above average. In times of peace, however, the theatre can barely support a company of performers.

Generally speaking the audiences here prefer the bawdier shows and patrons both smoke and drink as they watch, sitting or standing. They are also wont to engage their neighbours – and the actors – in repartee during the performance.

Outside of the theatre, tennis courts, billiard tables and other amusements of that sort are also supported by a respectable attendance. But the amusements of most of the inhabitants are few. Their main pleasures seems to arise from an inordinate love of dress – and in that almost all indulge with equal excess – and a devotion to playing cards, which can, and does, occupy whole evenings in succession.

The Longroom, West Stonehouse, before the construction of the Royal Marine Barracks.

The Assemblies

Our principal assembly room is at the Fountain Tavern in Fore Street. Assemblies begin on the first Monday after Michaelmas (at the beginning of October) and continue every second Monday for thirteen nights.

These popular entertainments can be booked by the season; subscribers are required to pay ten shillings and sixpence for each season, while the cost for non-subscribers is two-shillings and sixpence – gentlemen pay a further shilling each for tea.

At each assembly a Queen is drawn from among the married ladies and she chooses two stewards. Before tea ladies draw for partners and places, in the event of any dispute the Queen's verdict is final.

Dancing begins with a minuet at seven o'clock precisely and there are two country dances before tea. No dances are called after midnight.

The presence in Dock, during wartime, of a large number of Naval and Army officers, who are, in turn, often sons of noble gentlemen has done much to enhance the reputation of the town and the level of entertainments available to it, and to that list we must undoubtedly add the Long Room at Stonehouse. This is the place to which all genteel company from Dock and Plymouth resort during the summer for assemblies.

Every Thursday throughout the season there are concerts and assemblies here; the concerts begin at six and end at eight, at which time the dancing begins.

Again, most patrons subscribe for the season, non-subscribers pay three shillings and sixpence, for which they are entitled to have tea or coffee, although not if they arrive after nine o'clock. The dancing ends at eleven o'clock precisely and on public days gentlemen are requested not to wear swords in the room. Dogs are not permitted in the room on any days.

Dressing and dancing aside, Dock does not lend itself to the cultivation of the intellect – wealth is the universal idol and science has little encouragement. There are no manufactories in the town, nor till very recent times, has there been anything like commercial speculation, something that will always be difficult when all the land is leaseheld.

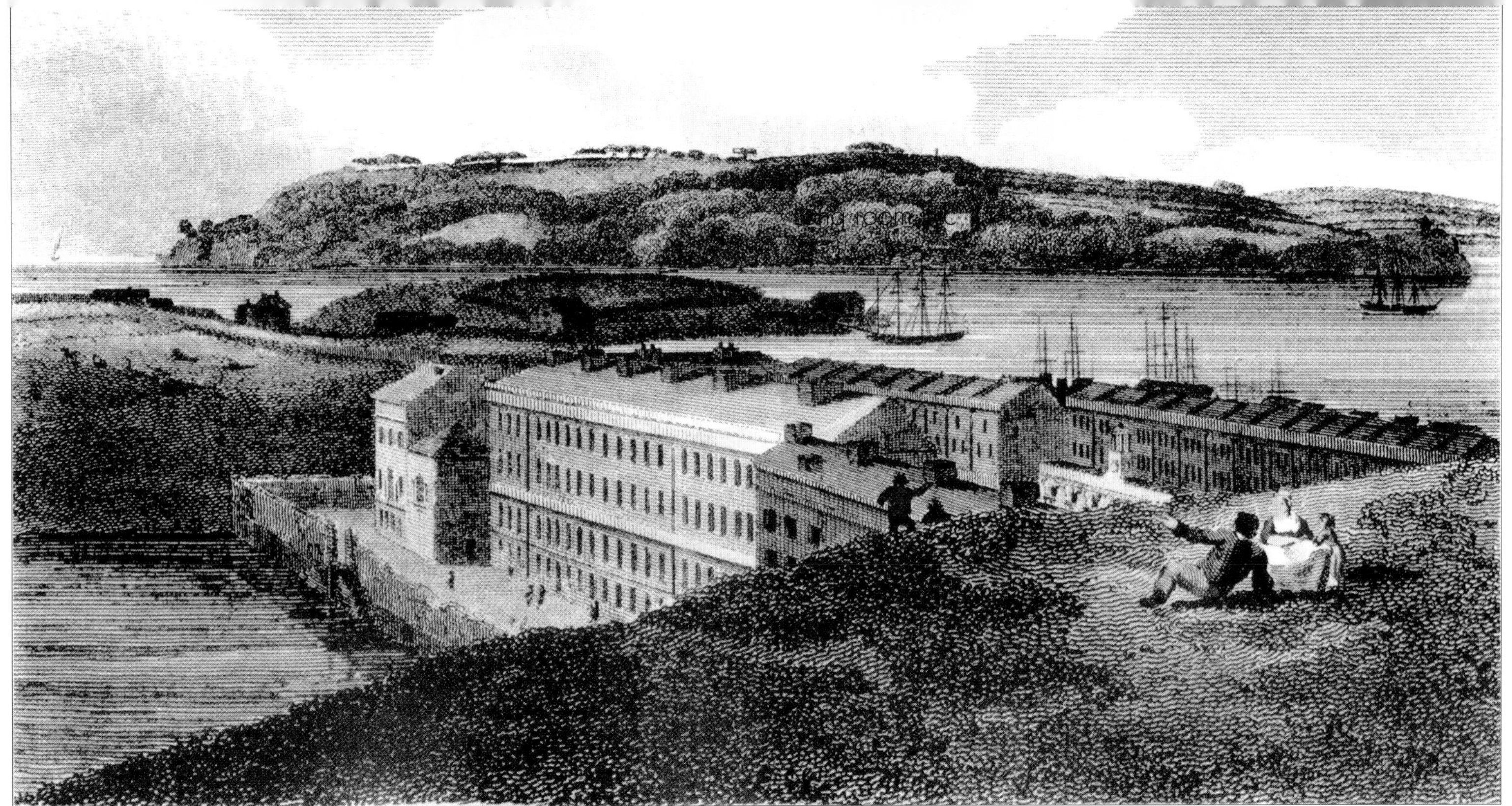

The Stonehouse peninsula with the recently erected (1783) barracks for the Plymouth Division of the Royal Marines.

Thus it is that we are so heavily reliant on the Dock Yard and ship building, not only for the work and wages but also for the fun and festivities.

In September 1786, twelve years after she had been laid down, the *Royal Sovereign* was launched with all the pomp and circumstance worthy of a first-rater carrying a hundred guns. One mass of seasoned British oak, her contour appealed to the imagination, and the noble figure of George III was beautifully carved. She took the water in view of the *Temeraire*, the French 74 that Admiral Boscawen had presented as an addition to the British Navy, and which, after splendid service in many a battle, now sat in the Hamoase as a floating battery.

In honour of the launch, the royal brothers, the sons of George III, attended a ball at the Longroom. When the three princes entered arm-in-arm, the eldest in the centre, they received the welcomes of the entire company; and returning the compliment with affability and ease, danced with the reigning beauties of the area.

On the following morning, they drove to Maker Heights to inspect the fortifications and returned to Dock to dine.

At a later hour they attended another ball at the Longroom, with its velvety lawn stretching down to the waterside – a situation that affords scope for fantastic displays of oil lamps and wax candles.

Here the brothers frisked light in frolic measure. The area possessed many charming women in the bloom of health, and envy and calumny were naturally at work.

But there was nothing more than a little flirtation. The princes enjoyed the ball exceedingly and their condescension made many ladies happy in selecting them for partners.

Prince William's extravagance, and his more serious sin of making love to the daughter of a Plymouth merchant, caused the Admiralty, at the request of the King, to cut short this agreeable sojourn.

Mutton Cove

A number of the foremost inhabitants of the town have become involved in shipping concerns under the auspices of the Dock Union Company and the company employs several vessels in the coasting trade. To this end they have converted a small quay and landing place at Mutton Cove (already used by the ferry to Mount Edgcumbe which had moved here from Devil's Point in 1750) into an excellent and spacious quay and little harbour, both for their vessels and for the general accommodation of boats landing there from the ships in the Hamoaze and in the Sound.

As you might expect there are a couple of inns here, but that is but a small fraction of the number in Dock as a whole, a number which is approaching two hundred - although many of them are taverns, primarily for the locals rather than for wayfarers and those looking for accommodation.

There has been some concern of late about the number of inns in the town and it is likely that the magistrates may soon make an attempt to limit them. There is already an obligation on the part of every inn keeper, to have a lamp over his door and for every tavern keeper to have two lamps - these are the only lamps in town.

Dock Inns

After the Fountain, in Fore Street, the next most respectable taverns in the town are the King's Arms and Prince George, both of which are to be found in Fore Street, nearly adjoining each other, and the Prince William Henry in Duke Street, opposite the Wind Mill.

There are many others, however, for the accommodation of travellers and others who may have occasion to visit.

Next to these are a large number of boarding and lodging houses which offer plenty of accommodation in times of peace, and even in time of war, such is the increase in the number of buildings in recent years that there is seldom much difficulty in obtaining comfortable lodgings at a moderate rate.

It would be unfair to pick out any particular locations but Morice Square and George Street at the two extremities of the town, and Fore Street itself, are preferred. Fore Street must be considered as an eligible situation for those who are fond of bustle and the noise of carriages; which will always attract the notice of travellers and others, both as the most spacious street in the town, and as the direct avenue to the Dock Yard.

Spies

It will be no great surprise to learn that foreign spies gravitate to the most populous areas and the most popular inns. As long as Plymouth and the Dockyard have been involved with the defence of the realm so they have been targets for would be invaders.

In 1764 the French hatched a plot to burn English dockyards with a newly invented kind of fire. Supplies of explosive were traced to various home ports, and two foreigners, who spoke the English tongue, were known to the be the organising conspirators, were watched closely from harbour to harbour. At one point they set off for France but returned to Plymouth in disguise and bribed to their assistance 'proper persons in the dockyard'.

The Port Admiral was told to keep a close eye on matters and to only confide in others where absolutely necessary. A Frenchman named Dumesnil, was detained by Admiral Pye on arrival while Peter Gony, his servant, who lived in the area for several months, was placed under arrest. Dumesnil managed to escape, deceiving a guard by placing an effigy in his bed.

In 1771 Mathuren Danet, under the name Monsieur Thebaud, frequented both Plymouth and Dock, lived in style and liberally treated local officers. His plan was to burn the dockyards and after firing that of Portsmouth he took the coach to Plymouth. Lodging at Beckford's Punch House in Butcher's Lane, he was apprehended at Mutton Cove where he was making 'suggestive enquiries'.

Five years later an American, James Aitken, who secured a job in the yard and was known to his colleagues as John the Painter attempted the same plan. He too was thwarted, by a vigilant watchman, and so went to Portsmouth where he managed to throw explosives into the Rope House and destroy the stores.

Mutton Cove c1830 by Captain GR Sartorius

Enemy Fleet in the Sound

In 1779 a bottle of explosives, a dark lantern and a long piece of fuse was found after an intruder had been surprised and shot at by the watchman outside the Hemp House.
The following year another spy, De La Motte, who had been attempting to supply details of our country's defences, the capabilities of our dockyards and the extent to which our ships were undermanned, was arrested. De La Motte had received help from an official in Plymouth and was sentenced to be hanged by the neck, but not till dead and then to be cut down and have his bowels taken out and burnt before him, his head to be then taken off his body and cut into four quarters.
That same year a Spanish spy, Jose Seyling was arrested after making too many questions when he was rowed around the harbour. When his lodgings were searched his trunk was found to contain maps of the coast, the dock, the magazine and other points. Like De La Motte, Seyling met his fate at the Tower of London.
Unquestionably the most dangerous of these men though was the accomplished linguist, Count de Parades. Liberally supplied with funds and thanks to the negligence of some and the corruption of others, Parades was able to get letters of introduction to obtain admission to the Dockyard. There he discovered someone who could supply him with the confidential orders for £100 a month. The information he discovered was then sent across the Channel by a trusty smuggler.
Meanwhile, having bribed his way around the Dockyard and the Citadel, Parades adopted the guise of a privateer and with the connivance of an unemployed mariner who was unhappy with the government and loaded with debts, Parades and his French backers kept a crew of seventy men happy with the capture of various American prizes.
With this as his ostensible reason for being in the area, the Count was able to befriend several officers, one of whom, after an excess of walnuts and wine, admitted that the port was undermanned; complained that the ammunition was at its lowest ebb and that the defence was practically dependent on the militia. Armed with this information Parades returned to France and urged that 4,000 men should embark at Brest and, feigning that their destination was America, sail direct for Plymouth, where he said there was not the slightest idea of the danger that threatened.
However, when the French Cabinet discussed the affair the ministers resolved to make a great affair of it, much to the Count's disappointment for he felt that surprise and small numbers was where success lay.
Notwithstanding the Count's dismay, an army of 30,000 was assembled sending shock waves back to England. Sixty-six French and Spanish ships set sail, and with help from pilots that Parades had enlisted, they anchored in Cawsand Bay, causing widespread alarm and terror in the villages and towns along the coast.
Fortunately the enemy had set out with insufficient provisions and Parades could not persuade the Admiral that batteries around the harbour were unfit for use and that, furthermore, he could arrange to supply the allies with food.
For four days the fleet lay at anchor, hundreds assembled on the heights of Rame and Staddon to assess how hostile the host actually were. On the fifth day a storm drove the allies out to sea and there they were met by Sir Charles Hardy and his fleet, but his fleet could hardly ride the waves and his men had little fight in them. The two sides drew up in battle order, but neither admiral had the confidence to go into action and, at sunset, the foreigners made for their own coast, with 'no other advantage save that of not having been defeated'.
It had been an uncomfortable moment for the people of Plymouth and Dock and in the subsequent theatrical comedy – 'Plymouth in Uproar' – there was an inn scene where fishermen, travellers, cowards and press-gangs were singing:
'We on the present hour relying, Think not of the future or past. But pall each moment as 'tis flying, The next, mayhap, may be our last.'

Natural Calamities

It wasn't just the enemy we had to worry about though, sometimes our Navy has sustained as much damage from the elements.
The calamities that befell Boscawen's fleet on leaving for the Channel were as devastating as a naval engagement.
In 1760, as thunder, lightning and hail was sweeping away scores of cottages locally, the newly launched *Conqueror* battleship was dashed against Drake's Island and the vessel was dashed to pieces.

At the same time HMS *Ramillies* was sailing from the port with other vessels when a westerly wind dispersed the squadron. In the thick and hazy weather, the *Ramillies* mistook Bolt Head for Rame Head and in the ensuing confusion the ship went down with 700 men. In 1774 the frigate *Torbay* caught fire and was burnt to the water's edge, while in a separate incident the *Kent* blew up in Plymouth Sound while a salute was being fired. Some sparks fell into an ammunition chest and a drummer who was sitting on the lid was blown into the air, and dropped, uninjured into the sea. Otherwise the catastrophe was too dreadful to be conceived, as more than fifty men were maimed and flayed by the crashing splinters, and many were scorched and blinded.

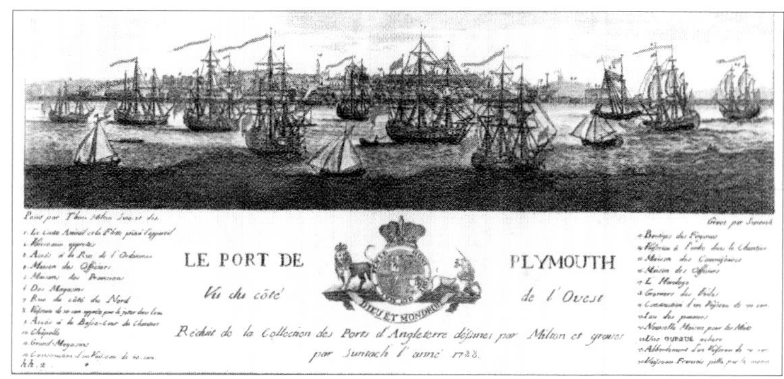

Above: *French view of Devonport.* Below: *Devonport Harbour, 1848 by Philip Rogers (1794-1853) oil on canvas (© Plymouth City Museum & Art Gallery)*

Getting About

For many years mounted - or foot - travellers bound for Plymouth or Dock or journeying outward to the metropolis came and went via Tavistock. Fording the shallow waters of the rivers they would enter fields through convenient gateways to avoid collision with horses carrying the extended crooks from which produce and merchandise were alike suspended.

At Longbridge a beaten track, which was subject to inundations and other impediments, traversed the tidal marshes. It communicated on the one side with the road leading from Leigham Gate to Knackersknowle Village, and with Plympton by means of a bridge across the river.

The stage coach was slow to reach this area and for a while the family of Sir John Rogers, Plymouth MP during the time of Queen Anne and the first King George, were the only people locally who used a carriage. This was a primitive affair, covered, and with roughly made wheels which excited lively interest whenever it entered the town. People ran to their doors as its approach was heralded; and, drawn by four long-tailed horses, it was looked upon as a weird example of man's ingenuity in an age of evolution.

As the eighteenth century approached its concluding decades so the necessities for transport have become more exacting and in the wake of the Turnpike Acts so the occasional coach started to appear, with radiant driver and cheery horn.

Mr Bignall, the proprietor of the Prince George Inn, the half-way house between Plymouth and Dock, attained the distinction, in 1760, of being the first to use a carriage for conveying the general public between the two communities.

Now, for those travelling out of town, a stage coach sets out every morning at six o'clock from the Fountain and calls at the Pope's Head and King's Arms in Plymouth before setting out for Exeter.

Meanwhile, Mr Goude's light balloon coach leaves from the neighbouring King's Arms in Fore Street at the same time each morning and proceeds to Exeter via the Prince George in Plymouth. If all goes smoothly, travellers arrive in Exeter before six in the evening. Typical fares are around ten shillings and sixpence for those travelling inside and seven shillings and sixpence if you are happy to sit outside.

For those looking to move belongings or large packages, the London waggon comes in on Thursdays and Saturdays and goes out on Wednesdays and Fridays. Warehouse and storage facilities are to be found at the Black Boy and Still in Plymouth. Meanwhile, there is warehousing available for the Launceston waggon at the Four Castles in Plymouth, and at the Prince George, in Fore Street, Dock, for items on the Barnstaple waggon. For yet larger goods, chartered vessels are continually going to and from Portsmouth and information regarding them may generally be gleaned from the public houses at the bottom of North Corner Street.

For those wishing just to travel into Plymouth (to the end of Old Town Street) diligences - quicker coaches - are generally ready from the stand in Fore Street from nine in the morning til nine in the evening (eight in winter time).

F. GOUDE,

KING's ARMS INN, FORE-STREET,

DOCK.

CHEAP TRAVELLING.

LIGHT BALLOON COACH, from DOCK to EXETER, every morning at Six o'clock. FARE.—

INSIDE, to EXETER, ...Half-a-Guinea,

OUTSIDE, ditto . . . . Seven-Shilling & Sixpence

The Royal MAIL COACH, every evening as usual, to EXETER, BATH, and LONDON.

POST CHAISE and ABLE HORSES, with careful drivers.

HEARSE and MOURNING COACHES to any part of England.

Moderate charges, and every attention paid.

Hackney chaises ply here the same as coaches in London – but from the filthiness of the sailors and their companions, who are the principal employers of these vehicles, they are often disgusting to more senses than one. The fares, which are regulated by Act of Parliament, are one shilling for a single person, one shilling and sixpence for two or three together. There is a fine for charging more than this fare, however should travellers wish to go beyond the stand at either end, or be put down or taken up elsewhere, additional fares may be implemented.

For travelling within Dock itself chairs can be hired and under the terms of a regulation passed a few years ago (17 February 1790) chairmen can charge, for carrying any person from any part of the town in the southern half – around George's, Clowance, Mount or Pembroke Street – to any part of the town to the north of Fore Street, the Dock Yard or Gun Wharf, ninepence, or vice versa coming the other way. All other, shorter, journeys across town are chargeable at sixpence and for every quarter of an hour that a chairman is kept in attendance he may charge an additional threepence.

Highways and Byways

The loneliness of the approaches to the Three Towns assists the designs of the evil disposed. In 1788, Philip Smith, a clerk in the Dock Yard, was set upon and murdered near Stoke Church. His cries reached persons near, who, on running in the direction heard men escaping through the bushes. The body was lifeless from fearful blows over the head and mouth, and a hat a bludgeon lay near at hand.

Not long afterwards John Richards, a labourer and an especially abandoned Dock character, who had already been suspected of waylaying and killing a sentry who refused to admit him into barracks after nightfall, drew attention to the serious probability of his complicity in Smith's murder by inferring that he knew who had committed the crime.

Not convinced by his story, one of the local constables, having noticed that Richards had been seen consorting with another ruffian as dissolute and disorderly as himself, one William Smith, made a search at Smith's home and found the stick. Richards confirmed that it was the stick, but that Smith was not the one he had seen carrying it. He also confided in others that he was glad that he was at home after bell ringing on the night of the crime. However, when questioned his landlady professed to know nothing of his movements, while Richard's wife reproached him for opening his 'blab mouth'.

Before long more evidence came to light and it transpired that Richards had planned the attack as revenge on an official who had discharged Richards from the Dock Yard. Furthermore, someone had seen the accused leaving via his back door on the night of the crime and someone else had seen him running across the Millbridge with wet blood on his hat.

Both Richards and Smith were convicted and the judge decreed that the usual course of giving their corpses to the surgeons should not be followed, but that they should be suspended between Heaven and Earth, as they were fit for neither. The two were hanged in Heavitree and their bodies subsequently conveyed to Stoke where they were hoisted on a transverse gibbet erected in the shallow opposite the Churchyard. Their remains, to the terror and disgust of many, loaded the air with putrefaction for months. It took fully seven years for the skeleton of Smith to drop as the other fell bit by bit into the mud. Thereafter the stump of the gibbet was used as a mooring buoy while an enterprising Dock carpenter has converted some of the soundest wood into snuff boxes.

1788: The gibbet on the edge of Deadlake, below Stoke Damerel Church

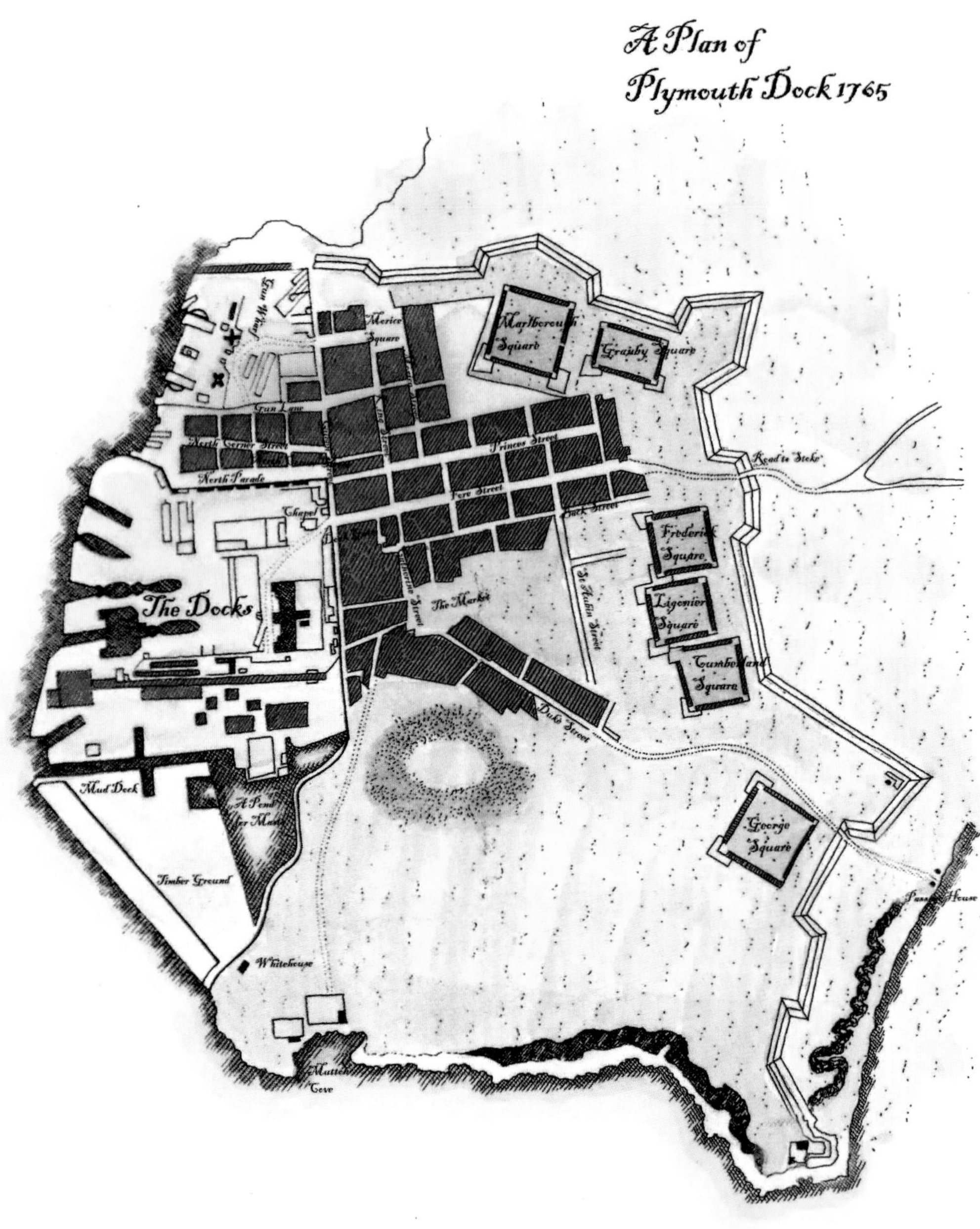

The Development of Dock

As can be seen by a comparison of these two plans the southern part of the town is very new indeed. The growth of the town since the escalation of development in the Dock Yard some thirty years since has been most remarkable. The construction of Mr Smeaton's bridge soon afterwards saw Duke Street thrown up with a similar speed to that of Fore Street which had appeared at the commencement of our story. Duke Street became the principal southern artery into the heart of Dock and once that had been almost fully lined so other streets sprang up in the southern half of Dock, such that now there are few sites that can be built upon that haven't already been developed.

As we can ascertain from our plan of 1765, but a small Part of St. Aubyn's-Street was built until almost 1770; there were a few irregular cottages in Chapel-Street, and the other Streets in that quarter, down to the market.

The date on the Chapel, and on Mr. Nelson's buildings at the south end of Chapel Street, are proof of its modern foundation. The road originally called Liberty Street and now known as Pembroke Street with the other Streets in that area are of still later date – around 1775.

Liberty Fields, the popular meeting place, was used as a Rope Walk. Not long afterwards George's-Street was begun to be built; and as the fashion for developing sites – the 'Speculations of Mechanics' – was at that point in time very prevalent, it wasn't long before Liberty Street and Clowance Street on that side, with Mount Street, and the Cross Streets which connect them, and Windmill Street, trod so fast upon the heels of each other, that they quickly occupied the full limits of the Town.

Morice, or the Town Square, was the favourite residence of the salaried classes.

The streets are regular and well built, and, with the obvious exceptions, nearly intersect each other at right angles. Their general width is from thirty to fifty feet, most of them having been built under the direction of the Commissioners appointed by Act of Parliament.

Three Lives

Only the field of Windmill Hill and the limits occupied by the Mill remain to be built; of which the tenancy of the former is at present held by an aged widow with whose Life that lease will terminate; upon the latter, we understand, there are two Lives existing, and it may probably continue many years in its present, undeveloped, condition. It is perhaps a good point here to explain that the whole of this town and parish is held by leases on Three Lives, or 99 years. In other words the houses in Dock have been wholly erected by the inhabitants under the terms of leases held from the Lord of the Manor. These leases are granted to a tenant who may then give the names of two of his children (or whoever) as the other two Lives in whom he would like the lease vested. Upon his death, assuming he is succeeded by his children, the lease passes to the first of the two, and thence, in the normal scheme of things, the third when the second 'Life' dies. Upon the death of the third named person the lease reverts to the Lord of the Manor, presently Sir John St Aubyn of Clowance.

A certain rent is reserved yearly to the Lord, according to the amount of land occupied; with a heriot or double rent payable on the death of any of the Three Lives. In recent years it has been thought expedient to grant leases on a 'Right of Perpetual Renewal' – and this modification seems to have been approved generally.

As for the Dock Yard and Ordnance Wharf, only a small part (about five acres out of seventy-one) is the property of the Government the rest is also the property of the Lord of the Manor and are leased to the Government at fifty shillings per acre, for twenty-one years, and constantly renewed every seven years – at a fine of £53 pounds or three years' value, under penalty of an entire forfeiture of the lease.

Incidentally the Lord of the Manor has free right to enter and leave the site at all times, and is entitled to forfeitures, in the case of premature deaths, in the same way within the Dock Yard as he is outside of it.

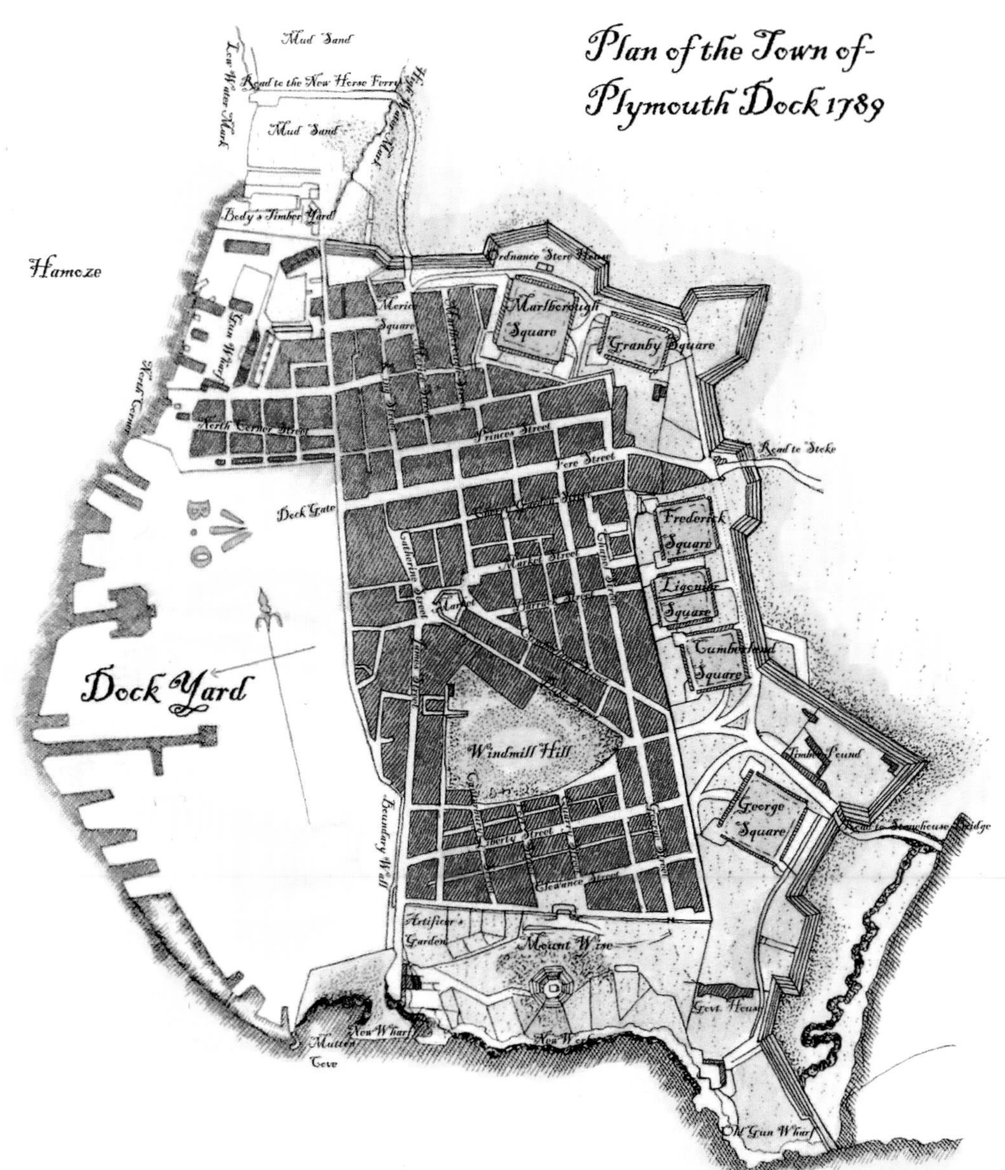

This page and facing: Plymouth Dock maps 1765 and 1789 redrawn by James Robinson 2010

Top; *Reynolds self-portrait c.1744.* (*© National Portrait Gallery, London*)
Above right: *First Lieutenant Paul Henry Ourry c.1744.*
Left: *George Edgcumbe (National Maritime Museum)*

Joshua Reynolds

One of the more celebrated figures at the Dockyard during this period of great expansion in the town was Captain Philip Vanbrugh who was appointed Commissioner on 8 January 1738. Brother of the architect and poet Sir John Vanbrugh, whose work had already had a major impact on the Yard, Philip Vanbrugh was painted in Dock, in 1743, by a young artist from Plympton – Joshua Reynolds.

Reynolds had been apprenticed to the portrait painter, Hudson, in London, but had quickly surpassed his master in the quality of his work. On his return to the County he was much employed painting portraits for the more prominent members of the community, among them George Gibbon, the Lieutenant Governor of Plymouth, various members of the Kendal family and a number of naval officers.

Master Reynolds' first stay was a brief one however, although he did return in 1746 when his father was taken ill. Joshua's father, Samuel, had been the schoolmaster at Plympton Grammar School and had done much to encourage his son's career. There was great sadness therefore when Samuel Reynolds' life was terminated on Christmas Day 1746.

Following the death of Samuel, the family was obliged to move out of the schoolmaster's house in St Maurice, Mrs Reynolds moved in with her married daughter while Joshua took a shop in Dock with his two unmarried sisters. The girls carried on a millinery business while Joshua painted portraits on the first floor.

Although Reynolds considered that his time in Dock saw him spend three years in company from whom little improvement could be got, he nevertheless painted many major works around this time.

The young artist attracted a bevy of lady patrons because, for the first time within their experience, justice was done to their loveliness, in a town where foreign imposters had hitherto only marred it by their ineffective treatment. Securing the Edgcumbes as his patrons, Reynolds painted each member of the family in turn, he also painted his first significant group study – of members of Lord Eliot's family – and a charming self-portrait with pencils and palette in one hand, shading the light from his eyes the other.

Reynolds also painted a number of naval officers, including Captain Edgcumbe's First Lieutenant, Paul Henry Ourry who would later become Commissioner of the Dockyard.

Reynolds' father had been friendly with Lord Edgcumbe and it was after consulting with him that Samuel had advised Joshua to return to Devon in 1743.

Six years later, through Lord Edgcumbe, young Reynolds met twenty-three-year-old Commander Keppel, two or three years his junior. Keppel had been entrusted with a diplomatic mission to the states of Barbary, on northern coast of Africa.

Sailing from Spithead on 25 April 1749 in the *Centurion*, problems with both topmasts obliged him to put into Dock for repairs and it was as a consequence of this unintended visit that Reynold's career took an unexpected turn.

Keppel was also a friend of Lord Edgcumbe and it was at the latter's residence that he became acquainted with the young artist and was so much pleased with him that he offered him a passage on board the *Centurion*. Reynolds readily accepted and went with the ship to Lisbon, Gibraltar and the Mediterranean, painting all the while.

Reynolds and Keppel struck up a lasting friendship and, after his return to London in 1752, Reynolds painted a full-length portrait of his erstwhile host as a kind of expression of his gratitude to Keppel, although Reynolds retained the painting for some time in his studio so that other sitters might see what might be achieved for them.

The painting, and the experience, gave Reynolds national recognition and assured his status as one of the area's most celebrated sons.

Eliot family painted by Reynolds c1743 (© Plymouth City Museum & Art Gallery)

Augustus Keppel, 1749 (National Maritime Museum)

The Parish Of Stoke Damerel

As previously mentioned, the whole of the town of Dock sits within the parish of Stoke Damerel, and with the rapid increase in population it will be easily appreciated that the parish church would need to be extended if it was going to be able to cater for its growing congregation.
At the beginning of the present century, the church was enlarged by the addition of an aisle on the northern side of the nave. As the numbers continued to swell, so the whole building, apart from the tower, was restyled (around 1750) to accommodate a southern aisle.
This new work altered the line of the main fabric of the building and many of the original fifteenth-century features were moved and incorporated in the new layout – most notably the large granite arch in the north wall. The tower formerly contained four bells which were known to date back at least as far as 1553, but in 1789 they were taken down and recast with additional metal into a peal of six.
The living is in the gift of Sir John St. Aubyn, the Lord of the Manor; and the present rector is the Rev. Thomas Williamson, who was appointed in 1791, upon the death of Edward Bridges Blackett, LL.D. who had been the incumbent here for nearly forty years. Stoke Damerel Church is remarkable for having a very good choir of singers.
Whatever changes effected at Stoke Damerel however, they were never going to be enough to cater for the great numbers moving into the area, thus it was that, in what would become Chapel Street, permission was granted, under the authority of an Act of Parliament, to erect a new edifice – St Aubyn Chapel. Conceived as a chapel of ease to Stoke Damerel it was completed around 1772 at a cost of £7,000.
The chapel has a gallery on the north side, and part of the south, with the west end, where there is a small organ. It has Divine Service regularly twice every Sunday, except Easter Day, when its minister pays homage of duty to and at the parish church. Every Wednesday evening also there is a sermon, and prayers on Friday evenings.
Its minister is excluded from christenings, burials, and all other occasional duties as these are entirely in the province of the parish church, and are performed by the minister or his curate. The exterior of St Aubyn Chapel is in the style of modern architecture, on which we shall not enlarge. It has a sun dial affixed on the western end, to show the time to the inhabitants; and on its small square tower, which contains but one bell, a neat and plain octagonal spire has been erected, surmounted by a vane to discover the direction of the wind. It is surrounded by a wall and balustrades; and has three entrances all at the west end, to the several aisles and to the galleries. The present curate is the Rev. Mr. Williams.
In addition to St Aubyn Chapel there is of course the Chapel in the Dock Yard, for the service of the officers and their families, and the artificers and families. Naval Officers and Ordinary also have pews assigned them, for their attendance on Divine Service. The present chaplain is the Rev. Mr. Hughes; who, besides his appointment, is entitled to fourpence per month for every man who is carried on the books of the Yard. Hence it is not easy to calculate the great Income of such a position.

William Payne c1790 Stoke Church At the west end is a plain and neat square tower which contains six bells. (West Country Studies Library)

Dissenting Chapels

Of the travelling evangelists, Whitfield and Wesley were the principal nonconformists. George Whitfield came to the area first but John Wesley made the greatest impression.
Wesley first visited Dock in 1746 addressing a crowd of adherents late one night and then again at five o'clock the next morning. On his return in June of the following year a hostile demonstration had been organised. All the Dock was in uproar - the house of his host, Mr Hide, was besieged by thousands of people and a constable was severely mauled and beaten in the struggle. Messengers were sent out to warn Mr Wesley that his life was in peril and to suggest he postpone his service. He replied by pushing his way into the town and penetrating the midst of the rioters, by whom he was immediately cheered in recognition of his courage.
As soon as he entered his lodgings, however, the crowd recovered its spirits and fought valiantly with the doors and windows until they were weary. Then they went home.
The next day Wesley, the great Revivalist, conferred with the members of the society and in the evening attempted to hold an open-air service.
While worshippers were rendering the opening hymn, an officer, a famous man, swaggered towards them with a retinue of soldiers, drummers and mob. As soon as the drums ceased, a gentleman barber made an attempt to speak, but his voice was drowned in the shouts of the multitude, growing fiercer and fiercer with the increase of numbers. Menacing as the crowd was, Wesley made his way to it with serene confidence and heartily grabbed the lieutenant by the hand. The sublime assurance thus displayed immediately won the officer, and he escorted the evangelist to Mr Hide's door, from which, as the mob grew better humoured, he spoke without further hindrance.
On the following day - Sunday - he preached in the Brickfields - the Common - to an earnest and well-behaved congregation.
Wesley returned to Dock four years later and found the locals more reconciled to his preaching. The night was far advanced when he rode into the town, but the moon gave them all the light they wanted.
Subsequent visits over the years saw a rain-soaked service in the square at Dock in 1768 and an indoor affair in 1787 that saw such a rise in Methodist support that the cleric had to be lifted over the seats to reach the pulpit.
There were many other visitations in between and if we were to make note of all the various groups of dissenters and religious societies, that do not correspond, in doctrine and practice with the established church we would readily fill these pages. It shall suffice to say, that besides the respective followers of Whitfield and Wesley, as professed followers of the doctrine of the Church of England, as Calvinist or as Lutherans; there are seceders from both, becoming one self-incorporated body; Calvinist, Baptist, and Moravians, who have distinct Meeting Houses, with many other lesser denominations.
Nor must we omit the New Unitarian Meeting House, opened in April 1791; in which, under the name of a reformed Liturgy, they reject the doctrine of the Trinity (Father, Son and Holy Ghost) and uphold instead the personal unity of God.
However these Unitarians are struggling to gain acceptance and that same year that their chapel here was opened three Unitarians were executed after a riot in Birmingham. Here in Dock, the Commissioner of the Yard, Captain Robert Fanshawe intimated that any Dockyardsmen who attended the new chapel would be dismissed as disloyal subjects.
Besides public places of worship, parties of the pious also assemble at each other's houses and would-be preachers practise the rudiments of their future calling. Many of them are uneducated mechanics and workers from the Dock Yard and overall they help contribute towards the somewhat distinct and incongruous spectacle that confronts outsiders. The most rigid sanctity and the most open and undisguised profaneness, as, on the one hand, we have the praises and prayers of devotional congregations, and on the other we have revels of debauchery and drunkenness. The temples of religion being surrounded by the temples of profligacy.
Of course this state of affairs is exaggerated during times of war, but it is commonplace when the country is in conflict and, in Dock, prostitutes walk the streets shameless and unabashed. Extortion also prevails, as if by mutual consent, most happy to participate in its advantages than to oppose its influence.

Moral Guardianship

Outside of the Church the moral guardianship of the town is largely in the hands of the County Magistrates in which, notwithstanding the number and respectability of the principal inhabitants, never less than two (currently Francis St Aubyn and R Morice) who constantly, twice a week, dedicate their time and attention to hear the complaints, and to restrain the irregularities, of the lower classes of people.
Whenever there is an exceptional influx of His Majesty's Ships, patrols are set up, by the Commissioners for Managing the Poor, to try and prevent any disorderly conduct of sailors while on shore.
The Poor House itself is an extensive building, occupying about an acre of ground and capable of accommodating three hundred persons - currently it is virtually at full capacity, there being just three fewer than that number in residence.
The only employment of those residents is picking oakum for the Dock Yard, a dusty, dirty job that cuts and blisters fingers. Inmates are given a weight of old rope that they have to unpick and clean by removing tar and any other matter to restore the original strands of hemp for re-use.
A Matron and a Governor are in charge and they, in turn, are appointed by, and subject to the control of, the Commissioners under the act for paving and lighting the town.
A good infirmary, a council room for the Magistrates and some other buildings for the separate accommodation of women and children have also been built within the precincts of the Poor House site.
The institution for the relief of distressed lying-in-women (women with child) was begun, and is entirely maintained, by subscriptions from women.

The Military Hospitals

Outside the town, near the pleasantly situated village that is Stoke - about half a mile from Dock - are the Military Hospitals.
Planned under the direction of the Duke of Richmond, they were actually erected under the superintendence of the Barrack Board during the recent war.
The reason for their being built, was a fatal illness that broke out on board a fleet of transport ships that had been held back in port by adverse winds in the early part of the war. The ships were full of troops and, as the disease spread, great numbers of men died, partly through a lack of ready accommodation when brought on shore.
The present buildings were then proposed and are thought to be well adapted for the purpose for which they are intended.
However, the establishment was originally planned to have been much larger and more complete, with offices and Officer's houses; but for some reason or other it was not carried into execution. To this day there is no military guard house and it was a long time before it was surrounded by a wall. It was intended to have ornamented the arcade with the King's Arms in the centre, and two others, one on each side, the places designed for them being carried up square.
The builder, Mr John Scoble, began and finished the project and it will always reflect on his integrity, honesty and ability, as long as the buildings remain, as it was not erected by contract, and no expense was spared to make it complete from beginning to end. The boundary is an excellent piece of rough lime wall, which will stand for ages - it is wider at the foundation and lessens gradually up to the coping.
The building is well supplied with soft water from the Dock Leat, which is conveyed by pipes to every floor; also a sufficient quantity of water for the water-closets near each ward; and water collected from the roofs is also conveyed to large tanks in the roof. The geometrical staircases are formed of large moor-stone steps, which give a peculiar lightness on entering the building, as well as uncommon strength and service.

Water Supply

While the essential spiritual needs of the town have never been without some basic provision, one of most basic human needs has, until recently, been the subject of much debate ... and that it is water.
Long before the population of this town outgrew that of Plymouth, it was apparent that we would need to invest in something akin to what Sir Francis Drake had provided that town with some two hundred years ago - a man-made waterway that would bring a supply of fresh water from the Moor.
Wells of enormous capacity were sunk by bakers and other large

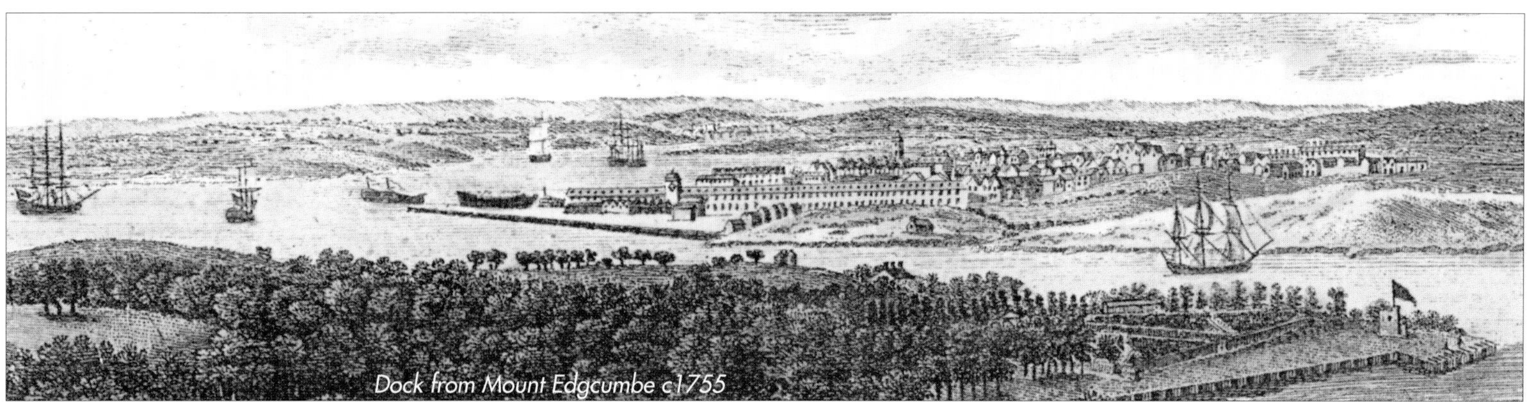
Dock from Mount Edgcumbe c1755

consumers. When supplies failed, as they did in dry or frosty weather, the water was fetched in carts from a distance of many miles, and sold at a shilling per hogshead.

In times of great need we have, on many occasions petitioned Plymouth for assistance and fresh water and more often than not we have been refused.

There have been times when the Dockers have been reduced to the greatest straits by drought; and, during the American War, the difficulty of supplying the military was so great that the Commanding Engineer applied to the Plymouth Corporation to permit the garrison to share in their plentitude on a fair basis of compensation.

An acrimonious controversy ensued, the humour of which is illustrated in a story that Boswell tells of Dr Johnson, who was then in the area visiting his friend, Sir Joshua Reynolds.

Assuming that, if man hates at all, he hates his neighbour, Johnson concluded that the new and rising Dock had already excited the envy and jealousy of the Plymothians. Accepting this to be the case, he mischievously set himself on the side of the old town and, professing to regard our people of Dock as upstarts and aliens, at the same time as laughing at himself for pretending to have a concern about something that he had no interest in, he exclaimed;

'No, no, I am against the Dockers: I am a Plymouth. Rogues! Let them die of thirst. They shall not have a drop of our water.'

Nevertheless, in 1779 the proposal would have been sanctioned had it not been for the obstinacy of Mr White, the Mayor, who refused to affix the Corporate seal to the contract on the ground that the yield of the leat was not adequate to deal with the wants of both boroughs.

Sir John St Aubyn, even offered to construct feeder streams out of his own pocket and then to pay Plymouth Corporation £200 a year for their supply, and yet still they would have none of it, protesting that the supply from the leat was only just enough to cover their own requirements.

Under these circumstances I am given to understand that some of the poorer people of Dock have, in the past, made some sort of living by collecting rain water and selling it to those who in turn needed fresh water to make a living themselves – like laundresses. It has also been suggested that others have in the past collected water from the Plymouth leat at locations not readily visible to prying eyes.

Now, however, we have the satisfaction to announce that water is brought home and conveyed in clay pipes, through every street. The leat is fed by three rivers high up on the Moor and brought to a reservoir for the sole use of Dock.

A scheme was first put forward seven years ago by Mr Thomas Bryer and Co., however it failed. Then, in 1792, Mr Bryer in conjunction with Messrs Jones and Grey and others submitted a plan to the inhabitants of Dock, as well as to the Government.

This proposal looked altogether more promising and the Corporation of Plymouth, doubtless jealous of the rapidly increasing importance of Dock, threw every obstacle in its way.

Furthermore they now suggested that their leat, which they had earlier declared to be incompetent to supply both Plymouth and the troops at Dock, was now large enough, or might be made so, to supply not only the troops but also the inhabitants there and the Naval Arsenals.

The people of Dock however, were sufficiently sensible to their own interests and rejected Plymouth's belated proposals and determined to support Bryer's plans. A bill was subsequently passed by the legislature and those plans have now been realised, but not without considerable opposition from Plymouth Corporation.

Nevertheless the inhabitants are now supplied with salubrious water on reasonable terms, while the Navy pay about £500 per year for their usage of it and the Ordnance Board around £200.

Dock Post Office

Thus it is that Dock is becoming increasingly self-sufficient and in recent years there have been one or two other notable developments in that direction; among them the setting up of a post office.

The introduction of the Torpoint Ferry has opened up many new mail routes; up until 1793 the post for Dock naturally came through Plymouth, but in that year a dedicated Dock office was set up under the guidance of our first Postmaster, Mr John Johnson, who still occupies that role today.

The official rate for sending a letter between Plymouth and Dock was initially tuppence – the normal rate for one post stage – but recently that was increased to threepence. Many correspondents deem this to be too much for a two-mile journey and as a consequence here, and in other instances where there are two Post Towns in close proximity, there has been an unofficial reduction by the local postmaster.

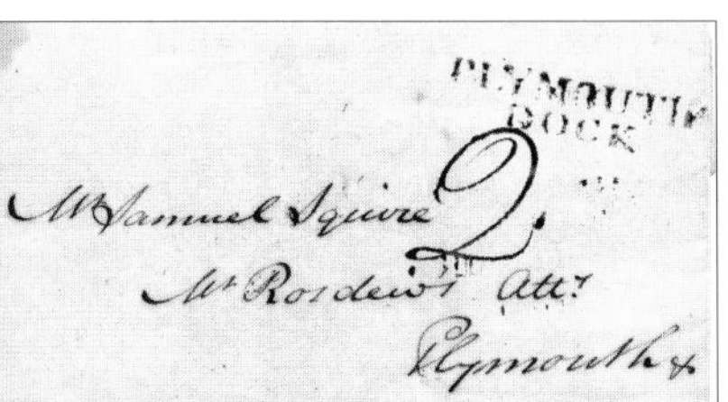

Above: *An early letter sent from Plymouth Dock – the 2 signifies tuppence.* Right: *8 April 1797. A missive received at Dock from HMS* Excellent *off Cadiz. Courtesy David Chamberlaine.*

Dock Bank

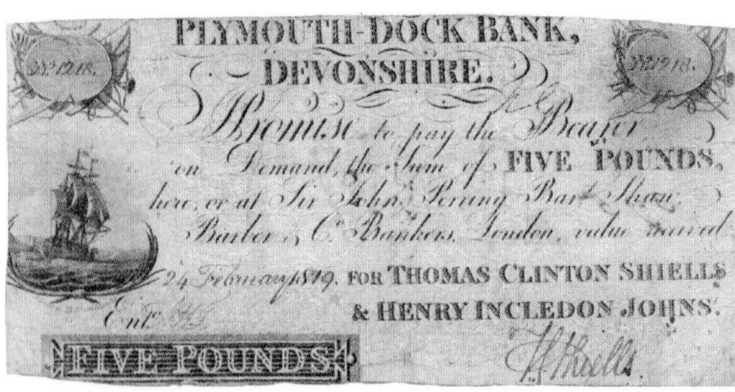

Early Dock banknote (courtesy John Heasman)

That same year our self-sufficiency was further aided by the establishment of a bank in Fore Street. Styled the 'Plymouth Dock Bank' it opened its doors for business on 18 December 1793, the proprietors being Messrs Nelson, St Aubyn & Chappell.

Mr Richard Nelson was formerly the proprietor of a naval outfitting business near the Dock Yard gate; Mr Francis St Aubyn is one of our magistrates and a member of the family who own the land upon which our town stands; and Mr William Chappell had recently sold his tannery business in Dobwalls and bought a new house in Chapel Street, Dock, where he had other business interests.

The bank, is one of only two hundred and fifty in the country and has given great facility to the trade and commerce of the town. Within a month or so of opening the proprietors were offering three per cent on notes deposited with them and soon they started to issue their own notes. Naval officers and merchants of the town quickly became patrons.

We may hope that the opening of the bank here will help curtail the endeavours of certain unscrupulous individuals who have, in many cases, started businesses without even a shilling.

Obtaining goods on credit from merchants and wholesale dealers in London and other places they have, in some instances, and after a few months' brisk trading, absconded with the money. Others, from an ignorance of the business they were engaged in, and extravagant living, soon obtained a residence in the Sheriff's ward of Exeter. Their places, however, are all too readily filled by others of the same description and goods supplied to them in the same way with equal eagerness. We can only assume that the speculations on the part of those who supplied the goods in the first place, must, on the whole, have been advantageous.

Extravagance

The lavish generosity and gullibility of seamen has long been the stuff of legend, and when a ship is paid off, the scenes surrounding the ship's company when they step ashore is a sight to behold. Trading sharks, wives and women waiting for money, shopkeepers and traders waiting for debts to be settled, encircle the men amid a babel of bawling, threatening, laughing and crying. Meanwhile the alehouses, bawdy houses and the theatre all look forward to benefitting from the ensuing spending spree.

For example when the crew of the *Hyena* were paid off, the Captain, Edward Thompson, merrily asked his men how long they would require to spend their money; and upon the majority saying that they would be satisfied with four days, he said he would give them six; *'And then I shall expect every man to be at his post.'*

On hearing this the chief dockyard official warned the captain that he would never see his men again, but Thompson was not worried.

On the following day 'The Fair Quaker of Deal' was staged at Plymouth Theatre, and, as Thompson's name was placed on the bills as author and patron, his crew resolved to witness the play.

At nightfall they hammered at the entrance and clamoured to be admitted without charge, on the ground that they were welcome to whatever belonged to their captain. There was a tremendous hubbub as the door was shut in their faces, and when the captain was told that his crew were storming the gallery, he replied; *'Let them in and I will pay for all hands.'* The men however had already surmounted every obstacle and on recognising their captain in the stage box, they cheered again and again, exclaiming: *'There's his honour, God bless him! He's got as good and tight a frigate as ever was manned in his Majesty's navy.'*

Then the jolly tars rendered in unison *'The Topsail Shivers in the Wind!'* a song *'full of heroism and tenderness'*, which the captain had composed and taught them. At the end of the six days not one of the crew was missing.

The thriftlessness and excesses are by no means confined to the sailors and soldiers however, as the workers in the Dock Yard themselves commonly earn double and frequently treble their wages when we are at war and they are similarly free with their money, as indeed are many of the other inhabitants who derive any benefit from this source of calamity to the world.

This free spending is concentrated chiefly upon personal decoration and luxurious living, such that social distinctions in dress and modes of living become almost extinct. The leading tradesmen emulate the excess of fashion that is observed at the various country seats. Pentille, Cothele, Mount Edgcumbe and Saltram are the centres of brilliant hospitalities, while the entertainments on board ships of the line can be splendid.

The Royal princes were regular visitors and generally little scrupulous in their selection of lodgings. The existence of the royal arms over an obscure house led to the discovery that every young prince of the Guelph family had honoured Dock with 'distinguishing attention'.

On one occasion the young Duke of Cumberland observed the royal arms in a 'very shabby street' near the Dock Yard. He asked who had lodged there and on being told that it was the late Duke of York, he replied; *'Then so will I.'*

'Your Highness will surely not lodge in so disagreeable a place as that?' asked his companion. *'And why not?'* rejoined the Prince; *'if it was pleasant enough for my uncle, it is good enough for me.'*

A disinterested observer would think that the whole aim of life was confined to the acquisition of wealth, licentious gratifications and ostentatious dress and that the only duties were regular attendance at church and the belief of certain undefinable notions and extravagant conceits which neither aid understanding, correct manners or improve the soul.

All the refinements of intellect, all the treasures of mental wealth, are despised. That such a general acquiescence in the frivolous and the sordid should exist under the apparent auspices of religion, is a situation that is perhaps peculiar to modern times. It is also primarily a condition of war and the very fluctuations occasioned by the alternate operation of peace and war has so far prevented the society of this place from acquiring any permanent feature. Under the influence of these opposite situations there is a remarkable contrast. Peace sees almost the annihilation of it: trade stagnates; speculation expires; numerous shops and houses are shut up. The streets are silent and inactivity and despondency pervades everywhere.

War instantly changes the scene, a new spirit is suddenly radiated in all directions and the greatest intensity of industry and emotion prevails.

The regular and frequent equipping of ships and the return of fleets, occasions the expenditure of immense sums of money and great numbers of speculators come here from all parts of the Kingdom to share the spoils. Shops of every description open in endless succession, not a house is vacant; hustle and bustle fills the streets and at length the whole place takes on the appearance of a fair.

1794 The Glorious First of June by Philippe-Jacques de Loutherbourg

The Wars with France

The growth of the military power of France was met in England by steady naval preparations. As the imperial armies marched triumphantly through Europe, huge stores were accumulated at Dock and the other arsenals, and grand battleships were added to the fleet. Thus, when the moderate republicans eventually took power in revolutionary France and challenged Britain to a death struggle, Dock became the scene of tremendous excitement as ships were commissioned and trading vessels were stripped of their crews.

In May 1794 it became known that the French had gathered twenty-six warships at Brest; and as they were on the point of setting out to secure the safety of a mighty crowd of merchantmen due from America, Lord Howe left Plymouth Dock with a corresponding strength. There prevailed a spirit of great enthusiasm as majestic three-deckers and frigates sailed in the full splendour of the summer sun.

Howe's subsequent success on the Glorious First of June gave England a victory that brought with it confirmation of our maritime supremacy.

Lord Howe himself brought the news of this great encounter back with him as his stately fleet, flying the banners of victory and mightily booming their return, arrived back in the Sound with six dismasted and riddled French battleships.

1794: The Glorious First of June, in the thick of the action.

The visitors anchored amid such tumults of joy as Plymouth and Dock had rarely witnessed – of salutes, of bell-ringing, of bands playing and of universal illumination. In each house a candle was burnt in every pane, and rows of lights were similarly ranged in perforated boards in every window of the various barracks – a spectacular effect which was regarded at the time as a triumph of ingenuity.

Disasters at Home

Defeat at sea didn't dampen the military ardour of the French however and her armed hosts continued their triumphant tramp throughout Europe.

In 1796 there were rumours of a proposed invasion of Ireland, and troops were continuously embarked from here to supplement the Irish garrisons. It was at this time that two heavy calamities befell the service within the limits of the harbour.

In January a gale of incredible fury had raged in the Sound. Monster breakers burst against the rocks and shot over the glacis of the Citadel, carrying away the sentry box, although it had been riveted to the ground with iron clamps.

At the height of the storm the *Dutton*, which was serving as a transport vessel, was dashed against the rocks under the Citadel. There she tossed with five hundred souls on board.

The guns of the Citadel boomed their sullen summons to rescue. Captain Edward Pellew, returning from a dinner engagement, heard the commotion and came down to the Hoe. Little headway was being made in the rescue attempt when Pellew called for volunteers through his speaking-trumpet.

1796 the Amphion explodes in the Hamoaze with the loss of 300 lives.

Only one, Lt Henry Edgell, stepped forward and the two men, fastened together, were drawn by a rope, through the raging sea to the stranded vessel. On board Pellew immediately assumed command and stood with his sword bared to deal with drunken insubordinates and more ropes were cast out. First-passage was secured for the women and children and eventually all were saved.

Pellew and Edgell remained at their post till the last, and the deck was under water as they were received on the rocks amid the cheers of the saved and spectators. The two men were subsequently feted as heroes and Pellew was presented with the Freedom of the Town.

By September French plans were apparently ripe for the threatened invasion and ships were despatched with incredible speed, and then, on 22 September 1796, there was another, even more dreadful disaster.

The frigate *Amphion* was being victualled in readiness for a special mission. Farewell dinner parties were given by the officers, and wives and sweethearts exchanged their boisterous pleasures with the sailors on deck.

In a moment the festivity was turned to terror, the masts lifted as though they were forced upwards, and the hull immediately sank. There followed an upheaval as of a mighty earthquake, the sky reddened, the air was thick with bleeding limbs and lifeless trunks, and heads blackened by gunpowder dropped in the water and floated on the surface.

The *Amphion* rose until her keel showed; then her masts flew into the air; and the waters boiled and hissed as the flames subsided. Captain Israel Pellew was thrown off his seat and partially stunned but, darting to his cabin window, cleared the ship with an amazing leap. Meanwhile Captain Swaffield, who had been sitting by his side, was crushed to death in the wreckage. The wife of one sailor was blown up with her child, and her arms were locked around the still living infant when her body was picked up. Three hundred persons perished.

1796; the Dutton is dashed against the rocks under the Citadel.

Mutiny

Despite their many setbacks at sea, the French were enjoying great military triumphs on land and with no intention of giving up their naval ambitions they continued to build ships and scores of transport vessels were waiting at various ports to pour a hundred thousand seasoned warriors onto our shores.

A friendly tempest happily thwarted that project, and the scare abated. But there were problems enough without leaving port as fear, famine and want were aggravated by widespread unhappiness in the navy. The short shrift that Robespierre had vouchsafed the French aristocracy occasioned revolutionary sentiments on the lower deck of every British battleship and here, at Dock, six Irish sailors who had been promoting such ideas were run up at the yard arm of their frigate.

Pay, the allocation of prize money from captured ships, and punishment for trivial offences, were the prime causes of agitation and once news that mutinous voices had made themselves heard at Spithead reached this far west, the red flag was run to the mainmast of every battleship amid a hurricane of cheers.

A promise to pay an extra shilling a day and to refrain from punishing the ringleaders had a calming effect, but once news arrived from the next Portsmouth coach that the Admiralty had violated their pledge to refrain from arrests and further that the leaders had been fired upon, the emblems of defiance were hoisted again.

Irritation developed into insanity at Dock, as a courier from Torquay announced that the squadron there had also revolted and sent the officers ashore. The epidemic spread like a prairie fire, and the officers were summarily evicted from their commands. Wooden gratings were improvised as rafts, and captains and lieutenants were towed to North Corner and Mutton Cove, and thrown on shore more dead than alive. Notorious disciplinarians were not allowed to escape so easily, for ropes were slung under their arms, and they were hoisted to the yardarms amid yells of delight, and dipped

1797: A contemporary cartoon lampoons the Mutineers.

until they begged for mercy. There was only one vessel in the harbour containing ammunition – the *Powerful* – and the dare-devils selected this as their headquarters. Popular sympathy ran with the men, and the town was given over to riot.
Obnoxious officers were paraded under bodyguards of sailors, and consigned for the night to the Black Hole in Fore Street. Known friends of the official classes, who barricaded their houses, were hotly besieged. Their doors were battered; and bedsteads, bedding, chairs and tables were thrown from the windows, piled upon waggons and paraded in triumph.
Loud were the jubilations as hilarious seamen mounted the trophies, and toasted the crowd in tankards of foaming ale.
However, once the strictness of the Ministers caused the movement to collapse at Spithead, the courage of the sailors at Dock evaporated.
Lord Keith accompanied by launches of armed sailors, who had made their peace, boarded the *Saturn*; and, addressing the crowd-denounced them for encouraging the enemies of England and demanded instant capitulation as the price of forgiveness. Fourteen men were condemned to death and many others to hundreds of lashes apiece; and for days the harbour was made hideous by the spectacle of dangling corpses and the ceaseless whish of the 'cat of nine-tails' around the fleet.

Cape St Vincent, Collingwood and Nelson

Despite this disaffection, the Navy soon performed great feats of valour. An attempt by the Spaniards to relieve Brest, so that the French fleet might make their escape, led Admiral Jervis to engage an overwhelming force of the allies of Cape St Vincent – the point that gave the name to the peerage with which he was rewarded. It was on this occasion that Nelson and Collingwood covered themselves with undying lustre by the fury with which they faced and fought the *San Josef* and the *Salvador del Mundo* – the noblest battleships in the Spanish fleet – and compelled the captains to haul down their colours as they menaced them upon their own decks. Whilst Jervis chased the flying Spaniards to Cadiz, Nelson brought the *San Josef* and *Salvador del Mundo* into Plymouth, where their arrival, with hundreds of prisoners, occasioned transports of joy. There had been a lingering suspense, but the anxiety that pervaded every class was broken by the ecstasies of victory.

The Admiral boards the enemy ship.

At first there were palpitating rumours, and then the convoys trumpeted the tidings of joy. Frenzied were the salutations as the royal messengers sped through the town in gaily-arranged coaches to acquaint the King and his Ministers, and the enthusiasm of the crowd could not be controlled when the prizes rolled in.
The town was alive with the record of Nelson's daring as the San Josef shadowed the waters of the Sound, and the officers in charge described the genius with which he broke the line of leading Spanish battleships and boarded one vessel after another until the crowning feat of the day was achieved!

1797: Nelson accepts the Spanish surrender on board the San Josef.

How the authorities at Dock laughed and rubbed their hands when the huge *San Josef* was towed in, with sails in rags and masts blown away, so strangely exemplified was the fortune of war in its fate!
When the Spanish Admiral visited Plymouth a few years earlier, his attention had been drawn to the works then approaching completion.
'Is not that the most capacious basin you have ever seen?' Gravini was confidently asked, and grievous was the disappointment of the superintendent when the Spaniard critically replied:
'The dock, although very large, would not hold the San Josef, our finest man-of-war.'
Yet, here, now, was Gravini's great monster berthed in the very space he had disparaged with such faint praise.

Prisoners and Prizes

It is customary for each power to bear the cost of maintaining the other's prisoners, but the French allowance was inadequate even to the provision of necessaries. To kill boredom or to add to their means, many of the captives resorted to gambling. Thus their destitution was aggravated, sickness ravaged their ranks and the more famished pledged the clothes in which they stood in order to sustain life. During the severe frosts captives were to be seen nude at Millbay Prison, and their only protection on board guardships was rotten straw. So weak with privation and suffering did these walking skeletons become that some of them fell out of their hammocks and broke their necks.
The French Government ventured to suggest that they treated Englishmen humanely as far as food and clothing was concerned and it was the duty of the British King to do the same. The advisors of George III vainly argued that there was no comparison in the numbers of prisoners, but the excuse was not accepted and the English ministers were told that they must accept the pleasures with the penalties of success. To this conclusion our ministers submitted and prisoners were supplied with warmer clothing and a more liberal allowance of food.
Early in 1799 we were cut off from the rest of the country by snow drifts and two frigates were driven ashore at Cattedown. In December similar tempests helped preserve the coast from foreign invasion. But there were yet more disasters in the Sound, including the dramatic loss of a man called Day, who claimed to have constructed a vessel in which he contended a man might live under water and subsequently restore himself to the surface. A twelve-hour experiment in the relatively shallow Cattewater proved a triumph, but despite walking confidently into his cabin, a subsequent attempt to repeat the feat in deeper water under the Hoe failed. Despite dockyard workers spending many days creeping and sweeping the sea bed, no trace of even the timbers could be found.
There was fighting in the Cattewater too, as the frigate *Clyde* sailed into port with the French vessel, *La Vestale* and firing broke out between the two, the French sailors, unhappy with the idea of surrender, eventually having to shriek for mercy.

Other prizes too came at a cost and soon after the 74-gun *Mars* brought home *L'Hercule*, a frigate of similar size, Captain Hood and other officers of the *Mars* died of wounds in the Royal Naval Hospital.

As the war raged on, victories in Holland prompted great local celebrations. Six thousand troops were massed in the Brickfields and orange colours were worn by the soldiers, as flowers and ribbons of similar hue were suspended from house to house.

The exultation quickly gave way to consternation when signals were flashed from the Lizard that the French fleet at Brest had slipped Lord Bridport and his barricade in a dense fog.

Not a moment was to be lost, for the enemy might be landing troops on the coast; and so every tavern in the Three Towns was ransacked by the officers, men on leave were recalled by drum and bugle, and courts and alleys were aroused to life and motion. There was no holding back, unless faculties had been deadened by drugs or drink, and responding with alacrity to the summons, the sailors worked through the night, getting in powder and shot, and guns as well.

The signal that the French were menacing the west was hoisted at Maker; and amid fluttering farewells from hundreds of craft, and cheers from thousands of throats, the fleet set forth to rendezvous off Cape Clear, if the enemy were not encountered nearer home.

In Whitsand Bay a French decoy was picked up, with bogus despatches in her cabin. In a day or two their contents were discounted, for the enemy were known to be steering south. There was now only one three-decker in Cawsand Bay, and the flagship was alone on the Hamoaze - a circumstance never remembered before.

In a few weeks Bridport returned for reinforcements, and dreadful casualties testified to the hurry. Sailors pacing the deck were killed by falling blocks, others were mutilated by the explosion of priming horns; some crashed from the maintop, and one man was transfixed on a bayonet of a patrol and his head pierced.

The Gun Wharf narrowly escaped destruction by the hasty handling of live six-inch shells, and the Three Towns were convulsed as by an earthquake as the fuses lit. The establishment was wrecked, and the survivors witnessed a horrid nightmare of flying limbs and maimed corpses - all so sudden and terrible that the number of the victims has never been ascertained.

Another fleet having been mobilized, eighteen sail of the line and four frigates moved from the Hamoaze in majestic combination.

In August crowds gathered on the Hoe to witness Indiamen - merchant vessels - being convoyed past the port. The horizon flashed with the white wings of world wide commerce as the traders stretched in splendour from Penlee Point to Bolt Head. Five hundred sail, floating emblems of Albion's proud Isles, emerged from a dense fog into the brilliance of a noonday sun. As the townsfolk contemplated the spectacle, picturesque, grand and interesting to every lover of his country's welfare, two French frigates were bold enough to harass the noble flotilla. They were silenced by a towering battleship, whose cannons roared when they steered the trespassers into the Hamoaze and into captivity.

There were many engagements like this that led to the crowding of harbour with prizes, few more enthusiastically welcomed as the arrival of the *Thetis* and the *San Brigida*. Sixty-three waggons were required to transport the treasure from the Dockyard for temporary deposit in the dungeons of the Citadel.

Great was the delight that so much treasure, once the property of the enemy, was soon to be in the pockets of our jolly tars.

French confidence was further eroded when *L'Engageante*, *La Pomone* and *La*

Action between the Cleopatra and the Nymphe

Babet were overwhelmed in the Channel and three splendid prizes with a thousand prisoners were brought back into the Hamoaze.

Then came the capture of the *Cleopatra* by Edward Pellew in the *Nymphe*. In a heavy battle the contending ships became enveloped in fire and smoke. The crew of the smaller, English vessel, stood on the defensive, until, taking advantage of the enemy's temporary hesitation, Pellew swept her decks, hauled down the French ship's colours and hoisted the English flag. Over a hundred men were killed in the encounter, and the list of wounded was much heavier.

c1800 a picture thought to be of Edward Pellew.

Press Gangs ... and Peace

As France readied itself for another invasion so every device was adopted that prudence could suggest for defending the coast. The wildest turmoil prevailed around the Three Towns and civilians were impressed in spite of privilege and protest. The press gangs acted like madmen, and stripped many vessels of the liquor as well as their crew. Prison-ships, slop-ships, privateers and traders were alike depleted of men; hundreds of impressed victims were brought from other ports under escorts of marines; the dockyard was alive and alight by night as well as by day, and every available coasting tub was fitted out for service.

The saucy French corvette, *La Bourdelais*, which had beaten the fastest of English cruisers, and had seized one hundred and sixty prizes in four years, was brought in by a frigate and classed for active service.

Nelson was given a tumultuous welcome when he arrived towards the end of 1800 to take up command of the *San Josef*, which had been refitted in the most complete style ever seen at Dock. His step-brother, and his friend Captain Hardy ever at his side, Nelson was greeted with almost reverent affection in the streets. There was hardly a day when he was not in evidence, and at a dinner held at the Fountain Inn, in Fore Street, Nelson was supported by Sir Edward Pellew and the fire-eating Jeremiah Coghlan.

1801: Sir James Saumarez's fleet prepares for battle.

Nelson subsequently cruised around the Devon coast, awaiting the signal for departure.

Meanwhile, due to the excessively heavy demand that conditions had created, food in the Three Towns was approaching famine prices and the sufferings of the poor were acute. Crowds paraded the streets, clamouring for relief, and ballad mongers fanned the flames by singing seditious songs. In March 1801 disturbances broke out in the Market where the populace were dispersed by the police. Receiving accessions, the mob marched about with crowbars and bludgeons, attacked the Shambles and retailed the meat to the bystanders at very small prices. They also stormed bakers' shops, carried away the loaves and threw about bags of flour and joints of beef and mutton.

The authorities attempted to ameliorate the situation but no measure proved effective until the Government authorised contractors in the area to sell army and navy supplies in the Three Towns. Compliance with this suggestion was followed by immediate relief, special constables were dismissed, military patrols were withdrawn, ringleaders restored to liberty and assistance was given to the poor.

Meanwhile, prizes continued to pour into Plymouth until the Cattewater presented the aspect of a naval wood of countless masts.

Making the outward journey, Sir James Saumarez left Plymouth to try to stop the Spanish and French fleets combining off Algeciras. With an inferior force of riddled ships and across two battles fought in July 1801, Saumarez thwarted the intended combination under forts of Cadiz.

The mail coach that brought news of this successful strategy entered the Three Towns flying the Royal Standard and the Union Jack; and blue flags were suspended from the hotel windows bearing the boast 'Saumarez and Victory'.

France was energetically prosecuting her plans for invasion, and England was responding to the challenge with extraordinary resource, when informal talks suggested peace might be attainable. Towards the end of 1801 the mail coach dashed into town, horses decorated with laurels. Joy pervaded every class when the news was released. Trading vessels of all nations displayed their colours in the harbours around the Three Towns, the *Extraordinary Gazette* was read to packed audiences at the theatres. Civilians hugged each other in the pit and females danced with soldiers and sailors in the

Sir James Saumarez's fleet in action off Algeciras, July 1801. One of a series of engravings from sketches by Captain Jaheel Brenton published in 1802 for the benefit of widows and orphans of the men who fought and fell on that Glorious Occasion.

galleries. Prisoners were thrown into raptures of delight and the sick left their berths to join in the merriment. 800 barrels of tar, oil and pitch were consumed in a monster bonfire on the Hoe.

Four thousand dockyard workers marched in procession carrying models of English sails of the line - symbols of those floating bulwarks which hurl their thunders at old England's enemies and surprise the world. Musicians in scarlet and gold, and banners, sublime and beautiful, constituted the grandest spectacle ever seen in the world. Artificers and shipwrights formed a circle at Morice Square, and sang 'God Save The King', 'Rule Britannia', and 'Fame Let thy Trumpet Sound'.

From the balcony of the Crown Hotel royal salutes were discharged, and local hostelries were resplendent with the portraits of heroes yet alive: one of Nelson, Saumarez and others, while another showed Britannia holding a weeping willow over the remains of Abercromby, Parker and the illustrious dead.

Not forgotten were the devotion of the reserve and volunteer regiments. The Royal Invalids took charge of the batteries of the Citadel, the Artillery held the fort at Eastern King, the Artificers that at Western

King, and the Cawsand Artillery commanded the bastions on Maker Heights. The remainder were massed within the lines at Dock – the Plymouth Blues, the Plymouth Volunteers, Langmead's Volunteers, Julian's Rangers, the Dock Volunteers, the Dock Association, Scobell's Artillery, and the Stonehouse Volunteers – and in every man's cap a cockade was fixed, with a sprig of laurel.

Always regarded as a family and constitutional corps, the Marines on this occasion were surrounded by the aristocracy of the West and a most brilliant ball was held at Pridham's Long Rooms.

As the men were paid off following the June 1802 Peace of Amiens, effervescing recklessness characterised the scenes; many seamen drank themselves to death, others were plundered by crimps as they lay helpless and unconscious. Fate was tempted with utter disregard as the men jumped into overcrowded boats and hustled, larked and danced in the streets. In some instances the occupants were suddenly immersed, and many exultant and hazardous spirits were drowned in this way.

An engraving after JMW Turner's happy view of Dock from Mount Edgcumbe

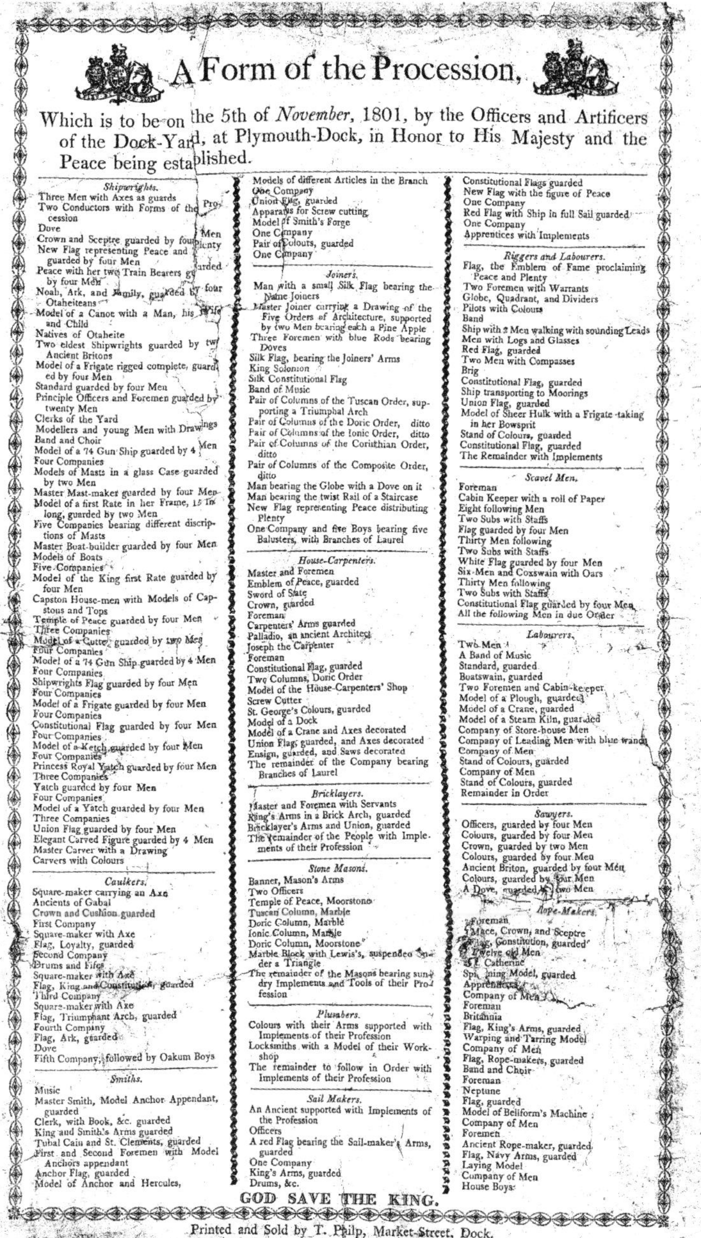

A Form of the Procession,

Which is to be on the 5th of *November*, 1801, by the Officers and Artificers of the Dock-Yard, at Plymouth-Dock, in Honor to His Majesty and the Peace being established.

Shipwrights.

Three Men with Axes as guards
Two Conductors with Forms of the Procession
Dove
Crown and Sceptre guarded by four Men
New Flag representing Peace and Plenty guarded by four Men
Peace with her two Train Bearers guarded by four Men
Noah, Ark, and Family, guarded by four Otaheiteans
Model of a Canoe with a Man, his Wife and Child
Natives of Otaheite
Two eldest Shipwrights guarded by two Ancient Britons
Model of a Frigate rigged complete, guarded by four Men
Standard guarded by four Men
Principle Officers and Foremen guarded by twenty Men
Clerks of the Yard
Modellers and young Men with Drawings
Band and Choir
Model of a 74 Gun Ship guarded by 4 Men
Four Companies
Models of Masts in a glass Case guarded by two Men
Master Mast-maker guarded by four Men
Model of a first Rate in her Frame, 15 In long, guarded by two Men
Five Companies bearing different discriptions of Masts
Master Boat-builder guarded by four Men
Models of Boats
Five Companies
Model of the King first Rate guarded by four Men
Capston House-men with Models of Capstous and Tops
Temple of Peace guarded by four Men
Three Companies
Model of a Cutter, guarded by two Men
Four Companies
Model of a 74 Gun Ship guarded by 4 Men
Four Companies
Shipwrights Flag guarded by four Men
Four Companies
Model of a Frigate guarded by four Men
Four Companies
Constitutional Flag guarded by four Men
Four Companies
Model of a Ketch guarded by four Men
Four Companies
Princess Royal Yatch guarded by four Men
Three Companies
Yatch guarded by four Men
Four Companies
Model of a Yatch guarded by four Men
Three Companies
Union Flag guarded by four Men
Elegant Carved Figure guarded by 4 Men
Master Carver with a Drawing
Carvers with Colours

Caulkers.

Square-maker carrying an Axe
Ancients of Gabal
Crown and Cushion guarded
First Company
Square-maker with Axe
Flag, Loyalty, guarded
Second Company
Drums and Fifes
Square-maker with Axe
Flag, King and Constitution, guarded
Third Company
Square-maker with Axe
Flag, Triumphant Arch, guarded
Fourth Company
Flag, Ark, guarded
Dove
Fifth Company, followed by Oakum Boys

Smiths.

Music
Master Smith, Model Anchor Appendant, guarded
Clerk, with Book, &c. guarded
King and Smith's Arms guarded
Tubal Cain and St. Clements, guarded
First and Second Foremen with Model Anchors appendant
Anchor Flag, guarded
Model of Anchor and Hercules,
Models of different Articles in the Branch
One Company
Union Flag, guarded
Apparatus for Screw cutting
Model of Smith's Forge
One Company
Pair of Colours, guarded
One Company

Joiners.

Man with a small Silk Flag bearing the Name Joiners
Master Joiner carrying a Drawing of the Five Orders of Architecture, supported by two Men bearing each a Pine Apple
Three Foremen with blue Rods bearing Doves
Silk Flag, bearing the Joiners' Arms
King Solomon
Silk Constitutional Flag
Band of Music
Pair of Columns of the Tuscan Order, supporting a Triumphal Arch
Pair of Columns of the Doric Order, ditto
Pair of Columns of the Ionic Order, ditto
Pair of Columns of the Corinthian Order, ditto
Pair of Columns of the Composite Order, ditto
Man bearing the Globe with a Dove on it
Man bearing the twist Rail of a Staircase
New Flag representing Peace distributing Plenty
One Company and five Boys bearing five Balusters, with Branches of Laurel

House-Carpenters.

Master and Foremen
Emblem of Peace, guarded
Sword of State
Crown, guarded
Foreman
Carpenters' Arms guarded
Palladio, an ancient Architect
Joseph the Carpenter
Foreman
Constitutional Flag, guarded
Two Columns, Doric Order
Model of the House-Carpenters' Shop
Screw Cutter
St. George's Colours, guarded
Model of a Dock
Model of a Crane and Axes decorated
Union Flag, guarded, and Axes decorated
Ensign, guarded, and Saws decorated
The remainder of the Company bearing Branches of Laurel

Bricklayers.

Master and Foremen with Servants
King's Arms in a Brick Arch, guarded
Bricklayer's Arms and Union, guarded
The remainder of the People with Implements of their Profession

Stone Masons.

Banner, Mason's Arms
Two Officers
Temple of Peace, Moorstone
Tuscan Column, Marble
Doric Column, Marble
Ionic Column, Marble
Doric Column, Moorstone
Marble Block with Lewis's, suspended under a Triangle
The remainder of the Masons bearing sundry Implements and Tools of their Profession

Plumbers.

Colours with their Arms supported with Implements of their Profession
Locksmiths with a Model of their Workshop
The remainder to follow in Order with Implements of their Profession

Sail Makers.

An Ancient supported with Implements of the Profession
Officers
A red Flag bearing the Sail-maker's Arms, guarded
One Company
King's Arms, guarded
Drums, &c.
Constitutional Flags guarded
New Flag with the figure of Peace
One Company
Red Flag with Ship in full Sail guarded
One Company
Apprentices with Implements

Riggers and Labourers.

Flag, the Emblem of Fame proclaiming Peace and Plenty
Two Foremen with Warrants
Globe, Quadrant, and Dividers
Pilots with Colours
Band
Ship with 2 Men walking with sounding Leads
Men with Logs and Glasses
Red Flag, guarded
Two Men with Compasses
Brig
Constitutional Flag, guarded
Ship transporting to Moorings
Union Flag, guarded
Model of Sheer Hulk with a Frigate taking in her Bowsprit
Stand of Colours, guarded
Constitutional Flag, guarded
The Remainder with Implements

Scavel Men.

Foreman
Cabin Keeper with a roll of Paper
Eight following Men
Two Subs with Staffs
Flag guarded by four Men
Thirty Men following
Two Subs with Staffs
White Flag guarded by four Men
Six Men and Coxswain with Oars
Thirty Men following
Two Subs with Staffs
Constitutional Flag guarded by four Men
All the following Men in due Order

Labourers.

Two Men
A Band of Music
Standard, guarded
Boatswain, guarded
Two Foremen and Cabin-keeper
Model of a Plough, guarded
Model of a Crane, guarded
Model of a Steam Kiln, guarded
Company of Store-house Men
Company of Leading Men with blue wands
Company of Men
Stand of Colours, guarded
Company of Men
Stand of Colours, guarded
Remainder in Order

Sawyers.

Officers, guarded by four Men
Colours, guarded by four Men
Crown, guarded by two Men
Colours, guarded by four Men
Ancient Briton, guarded by four Men
Colours, guarded by four Men
A Dove, guarded by two Men

Rope-Makers.

Foreman
Mace, Crown, and Sceptre
Flag, Constitution, guarded
Twelve old Men
St. Catherine
Spinning Model, guarded
Apprentices
Company of Men
Foreman
Britannia
Flag, King's Arms, guarded
Warping and Tarring Model
Company of Men
Flag, Rope-makers, guarded
Band and Choir
Foreman
Neptune
Flag, guarded
Model of Beliform's Machine
Company of Men
Foremen
Ancient Rope-maker, guarded
Flag, Navy Arms, guarded
Laying Model
Company of Men
House Boys

GOD SAVE THE KING.

Printed and Sold by T. Philp, Market-Street, Dock.

November 1801 a Dockyard procession to celebrate Peace.

Who the Devil's to Man the Ships?

Every effort was made to convince Napoleon that England intended to give the peace a fair trial: warships were hogged and their masts carefully laid aside. Night signals were discontinued, the militia were disbanded, and dockyard workers were restricted to normal hours. Petty officers were empowered to resume their rank in the event of another outbreak, sailors were restored by thousands to their freedom, and the press-gangs deprived of their warrants.

Lord St Vincent gave elaborate entertainments at his official residence in George Street and received the Freedom of Plymouth.

However, confidence in the peace was very thin and as soon as Napoleon had been made First Consul preparations were made for that invasion which was the absorbing passion of his life. Sailors rejoined the fleet and soldiers the army; naval trophies were surveyed at Dock for active service; discarded battleships were encased in one-inch oak - a new expedient - and artificers worked long after nightfall.

Then, one afternoon in May, 1803, a messenger galloped into Dock with instructions intended for the Commander-in-Chief alone: war was to be waged forthwith against the insolent upstart who declared that England could not fight without an ally.

Few fit men were safe from the heavy-handed Press Gangs

Within the hour Admiral Dacres had confined the soldiery to barracks, the various gates were bolted, and no one could leave either town without a written permit. As soon as the lamps were lit, the streets were paced by armed parties of Marines; the avenues to the Barbican, Mutton Cove and North Corner were surrounded; gin shops and vessels by the quays were invaded, every prime seaman was claimed and lusty landlubbers as well.

Each press gang member carried 'stretchers' pieces of wood that were ordinarily fixed at the bottoms of boats - things just as well in their proper place as flourishing about a man's head, especially if he hadn't his hat on.

Grim were the scruples of the press gang officers: *'take care you don't use any violence, my lads, but, if the fellows won't stop their nonsense, knock them down.'*

Inns were rushed, lights were suddenly doused. Fierce struggles followed. The use of stretchers was met by hurling pewter pots, and the raising of bumps found its retaliation in the cracking of skulls. As the mauled and maimed were thrown through the windows into the streets, shrieking women and children clung to the legs of the officer in charge. His reply to their appeals admitted of little controversy: *'Who the devil's to man the ships?'*

The bodies of the most reluctant were bared as soon as they were hauled on board ship and after the men had been tied to the gratings, they were lashed until the doctrine of submission had been sufficiently enforced. Then lacerated and bleeding they were flung below deck to keep company with half-suffocated wretches writhing as a result of similar flagellations.

The Three Towns were thus condemned to a state of siege and the agitation was intense as the press gangs continued their work.

Hundreds were torn from pleasures and occupations, and places of amusement were not privileged. The theatres were thrown into riotous confusion as the performances were in progress; and amid the shrieks of women and the curses of men, the galleries were cleared of the physically fit, and the way to the water's edge was a prolonged free fight, the press-gangs cleaving their course through the seething mass, with their bleeding victims bound by the wrists.

Terrorism was so general that watermen would not ply for hire between the Three Towns, Cremyll and Batten; traffic by these routes was suspended and apprentices went into hiding, although legally they could not be seized. But they were torn from their places of concealment, and the harshness of their fate was deplored in many a home.

Towns, villages and hamlets were regularly visited, and stout rustics and sturdy fishermen passed daily through Fore Street amid cheers of seasoned salts and pleasantries of the maimed.

Country bumpkins who journeyed to Plymouth to witness the local festivities were found good enough to serve the King. There were rough and tumble battles and much blood-letting, but pickets of soldiers protected the press-gangs from molestation and insult. Any apology for a uniform sufficed to clothe the recruits – a stained sailor's smock or an old soldier's tunic, the fit was of little account.

After a lull, parties were again judiciously placed on the turnpike roads and the escape of all fugitives checked.

Hostilities Renewed

Hostilities began in an unofficial way. *Le Frontier* mistook the disguised HMS *Doris* for an *East Indiaman*, and the latter remained passive until the French Captain assumed that she intended to surrender. At that point a body of marines leapt to her decks and the foreigners were mowed by a hail of musketry. *Le Frontier* lowered her flag and was brought back to Plymouth, where the details of this first encounter caused great amusement.

A couple of similar incidents followed but Napoleon had been postponing the inevitable until his East and West Indian fleets returned, but the advisers of George III decided that it was impolitic to wait upon his pleasure. Thus war was declared as the fleets returned, and as the Channel was swarming with the enemy's traders.

Over the next few weeks it rained prizes on the Plymouth cruisers. Brigs, corvettes, galliots, schooners and frigates congregated so rapidly that the agents could scarcely thread their way through the cluster and in three weeks, spoils to the value of two millions sterling was moored in the Cattewater – a mass of captures never previously witnessed in so short a time. The French merchantmen had left with these costly freights when there was every appearance of an enduring peace; and as few of them had effected risk insurances, their losses were peculiarly distressing.

These were now difficult times for any foreigners in the area. The Alien Laws were enforced with traditional rigour and proclamations were posted warning foreigners that they must disclose their presence under pain of imprisonment.

For all the excitement back at home though there was a sense of hush as everyone waited for the blow that was to determine England's fate. Nelson was steering after the French, as he assured a friend in Plymouth by letter, *'with every set sail'* confident that he would eventually overtake them.

The loss of the *Magnificent*, a noble frigate, which had been manned in the main by mariners from Stonehouse, of whom more than eighty perished on the rocks off Brest, accentuated the anxiety.

The thunders of Trafalgar burst the clouds and the tidings flashed like a morning radiance. The anguish that underlay the joy was evidenced by the scene at one of the local theatres, where, as the play was in progress, an artiste rushed on stage with the news of the victory. Hats, cloaks and doublets flew up, and Rule Britannia was sung before the play resumed.

Fervour again overflowed when a Corporal exclaimed in the third act: *'Victory and Old England for Ever'*.

Nelson pays the ultimate price for Victory.

'He will never fight for Old England again', one of the performers added in a pathetic aside; and, at this allusion to the death of the hero, there was not a dry eye in the house, the farce was abandoned, and the audience dispersed to mournful music.

The sorrow intensified as the prizes followed in the wake of the news, the battleships with their flags at half-masts.

The Sound presented a wonderfully diversified picture with belching of smoke; and responding orchestral effects of gun and drum reverberated with every important variation of the spectacle – privateers escorting their captures, Indiamen that the returning fleet had seized, and a few of the foreign line-of-battleships to testify to the completeness of the French defeat.

At the end of the encounter, the French and Spanish allies had lost twenty-two vessels, the English had lost none.

From the remotest towns of the west visitors made their way here so that they might hail the victors and inspect their trophies. The more curious visitors climbed on to the decks to inspect the bloodstained evidences of the carnage, and as they heard the moans of the wounded and inhaled the stenches that arose from the charnel-houses below, they turned shuddering and pained as from loathsome spectacles.

Not everyone was privy to such graphic first-hand experiences and across the country, so overflowing was the national pride that young members of aristocratic families rushed to join the navy; and with the arrival of each noble recruit, the battleships present brilliant examples of uniforms, and lavish hospitalities were dispensed on the eve of every fresh departure for the French Coast.

Swiss and other friendly foreigners were invited to join the service and they cheerfully co-operated. French prisoners were landed at Devil's Point in batches of hundreds, and drafted to the guardships in Hamoaze or removed inland. They were uncommonly impudent and overbearing, but the Plymouth Volunteers exercised iron discipline.

News Travels Faster

Up until this time instructions had been conveyed by colours burnt from battleship to battleship and station to station, but the system was now improved upon.

There were two sets of 'telegraphs' – one fixed within the Higher Lines at Dock, the other upon the heights of Saltram; and from lodges erected for the operators, messages were sent to the Admiralty and answers received in thirty minutes. Intimations were conveyed with such swiftness to London that replies were flashed back in ten or twelves minutes: a rapidity of conveying intelligence hitherto unknown in this part of the country, and one that represented a great saving in expresses – messages sent on horseback.

Night telegraphs were also evolved by the manipulation of various shades, simple and compound: A plane of convex or double convex lens formed hollow, and filled with transparent coloured liquids, was placed before the centre lamp, and a neck or tube admitted of the contraction or expansion of each lens. The process was capable of 63 changes, without varying the line of direction, and 252 signals in all were possible.

But the increase in speed of conveying information was not just confined to official avenues.

So insatiable was the demand from the public for news that two weekly journals were simultaneously started – the *Plymouth Chronicle* and the *Dock Telegraph*; and if the relations between these organs were at least as hostile as those of England and France, their records of the campaign, invested as they were with the varying emotions of the services, vividly illustrate the throb and palpitation of the port.

As the months rolled on and the despatch boats reached Dock with gloomy forecasts of the campaign in Gallicia, the suspense was afflicting. The first positive gleam of relief was afforded by the naval battle in the Basque Roads, and it is quaint to know that both local papers suspended publication until they could allay the anxiety, and no less instructive to observe the roundabout means by which the knowledge was acquired by the editors: *'The London mail which should have reached Dock at nine o'clock this morning did not appear till after three this afternoon. It brought neither papers nor letters, because the Bath coach, which usually delivers them at Exeter, was unable to travel by reason of the inundated state of the roads. The London mail, however, brought a gratifying and welcome announcement. The guard of the coach states that; "in coming to Exeter he met Sir H Burnard Neale proceeding express for town with despatches from Lord Gambier, containing the important news of the destruction of the French fleet in the Basque Roads. Those ships which were not destroyed lay on their beam ends".'*

More often than not, news from overseas came via the sea: 'The important information, which the arrival of the *Unicorn* enabled us

The Plymouth and Dock Telegraph;

OR, NAVAL AND COMMERCIAL REGISTER.

Printed and Published by L. CONGDON, No. 52, Fore Street, DOCK.

Vol 1.—*No* 1] *Saturday, March* 19, 1808. *Price Sixpence.*

TELEGRAPH-OFFICE,
DOCK, March 19, 1808.

IN laying before the public the first number of our paper, it may perhaps be expected that we should at the same time say something respecting the line of politics, or, in other words, the spirit of party which we mean to adopt. We beg leave, however, to assure our readers, that it is our intention steadily to adhere to the line of truth, equally unwarped by the influence of party, or the indiscriminate adulation of whoever may happen to be the minister of the day. We trust that, as Englishmen, we neither are nor ever shall be indifferent to the welfare and prosperity of our country, or the blessings of a Constitution under which we *yet* enjoy so many real comforts: but to suppose that OUR COUNTRY (or, more correctly speaking, the persons holding the reins of the executive government, *be they who they may*) could never err, would be to imply a species of perfection which could never yet be claimed by any earthly institution, however excellent in its nature

ment of a Newspaper requires a capital that ought not to be lightly embarked, we took time to collect the sentiments of our friends, and finding that they in every respect coincided with our own, an order was dispatched to town, EIGHT MONTHS SINCE, for the necessary founts of letter and other materials requisite for our undertaking: after the lapse of a considerable time, and in daily expectation of receiving our types, we were apprised by the founder to whom we sent, that, owing to a want of hands, and other causes, it was impossible to execute our order in less than four months; we then (EARLY IN NOVEMBER) sent to Messrs. Fry and Co. who promised that the order should be completed in six weeks; but, strange as it may appear, although sent by land, we did not receive the most essential part of our order till LAST MONDAY NIGHT! We must apologise for having thus taken up so much space, on a subject of such little import to our readers; "but circumstances have since arisen," which have called forth this explanation: an opponent has since started up, and entered into a competition with us for the meed of public

TO DRUGGISTS.

WANTED, a steady middle aged Man, in the DRUG LINE. One who can give advice occasionally will be preferred.
Apply to S. PAYNE, Plymouth.

ALL persons who have any claim on the estate of WILLIAM DAY, formerly of CAWSAND, deceased, are hereby desired to send the particulars thereof on or before the 1st of APRIL next, to Mr. BOZON, attorney at law, Dock, one of the persons who have been admitted administrators of the the said deceased's estate and effects.

H. B. SHILLIBEER,
AUCTIONEER and LAND SURVEYOR,
DOCK,

BEGS leave to return his sincere and unfeigned thanks to his numerous friends for the very liberal support he has hitherto experienced in the above branches, & assures them that the same assiduity and attention, which he flatters himself has always marked his conduct in executing their orders, shall continue to be paid to their future favors.

He begs also to announce to his professional friends, that he is appointed a Commissioner for taking special bail.

A. NOSWORTHY,
BOOKBINDER.

TAKES leave to inform his friends and the public, that he has commenced business for himself, at No. 70, PRINCES-STREET, PLYMOUTH DOCK, and solicits their patronage and support: BINDING in all its branches executed with neatness and dispatch, and on the most moderate terms. ACCOUNT BOOKS bound or ruled to any given pattern.

C. POTBURY, JUN.

BEGS leave to inform his friends and the public in general of PLYMOUTH, DOCK, and its vicinity, that, by the advice and recommendation of a number of most respectable persons, he has opened A SCHOOL in Scammel's-Row, PLYMOUTH, and also at Mr. REYNOLDS's, George's-Street, DOCK, for the purpose of teaching and grounding Pupils in the FRENCH LANGUAGE, with its proper Accent, in which he himself has been instructed (in France) by some of the most approved masters.

The strictest attention may be depended on, as it will be his study to give general satisfaction.

☞ The SPANISH Language also taught with the same purity and advantage.

JOHN PEARSE,
SADDLER AND HARNESS MAKER,
No. 94, FORE-STREET, DOCK,

RETURNS his sincere thanks to his friends and the public, for the numerous favours

HALEY,
UPHOLSTERER & CABINET-MAKER,
No 31, FORE-STREET, DOCK,

RETURNS his unfeigned thanks to his friends in general for the support he has experienced during the many years he has been in business, and particularly for the attention he was honoured with at his sale in Morice-square.

He takes this opportunity to assure his friends, that the report in circulation of his having quitted the business in consequence of his late sale, is entirely without foundation: He has engaged several workmen of the first abilities, to manufacture every article in the above branches, and trusts by his assiduity and attention, to merit a continuance of their support.

To the gentlemen of the Navy he feels a peculiar gratitude, from the conviction of his having received a greater share of their favors than any other tradesman of the same line in Dock, and it will be his particular study to execute their future orders with punctuality and dispatch.

Convenient and portable sofas and sofa beds, easy chairs; lounging ditto, to form occasional beds, bedding of every description.

CABINS COMPLETELY FURNISHED.

AN APPRENTICE WANTED.

FLAX FOR SALE;

By Virtue of a Commission of Appraisement and Sale, issued from the High Court of Admiralty, addressed to Edward Alder.

FOR SALE,

to lay before our readers last week (four days earlier than most of our contemporaries), has furnished the leading matter in the London papers of the current week – a striking priority which our situation enables us to command … The *Intelligence* gun-brig arrived here yesterday from Lisbon and reports a brilliant victory by the Patriots over the main body of the French army at Vittoria.'

And so the good – and the depressing – was reported. The worst of it in January 1809 when in the wake of Sir John Moore's death and the retreat from Spain (which had been annexed by Bonaparte) saw the remnants of his army transported back to the Sound.

Tears sprang unbidden to the eyes even of men as the poor fellows so eagerly sought the shelter of barracks and hospitals. The maimed were numbered by hundreds, arms and legs had been shot from many, portions of limbs had been amputated, and scores exposed wounds that were decomposing from neglect. As sufferers lays on stretchers awaiting removal, the effluvia caused the spectators to shrink, whilst their flesh crept, and the moans of the victims was piteous.

The women who had accompanied their husbands to Spain, and took part in the retreat though the narrow ice-bound passages, had endured unspeakable privations and hardships, and many perished despite the attentions of doctors who journeyed from every part to give them help. Over 2,000 sick and wounded soldiers were herded into the town in this extraordinary emergency, and, owing to the deplorable destitution of their families, a meeting was summoned by the Mayor. Subsequently, relief was forthwith given to 800 women; clothing was distributed by the ladies and Colonel Hawker's Volunteers sacrificed their uniforms so that the regulars might be clad. A general humiliation was proclaimed in Plymouth and Dock, and services held in churches and chapels, collections were made in aid of the distressed, £1,800 in all being raised.

No crock of gold at the end of this rainbow as peace brings its own problems.

The Peninsular War Ends

Sir Arthur Wellesley, soon to be Lord Wellington, personally superintended the embarkation at Plymouth of the army with which he was to retrieve the painful chapter of Corunna. In April 1809 soldiers flooded the town in one apparently unending stream of scarlet and artillery, ammunition and stores of provisions obstructed the approaches to the docks.

It was the check administered at Talavera that first restored confidence in the capacity of English generalship to outmanoeuvre and vanquish the French, and illuminations testified to the spirit of rejoicing that inspired every house and battleship.

More 'Glorious News' was reported in the *Dock Telegraph* in July 1810 when the *Eagle* cutter reported that Sir Charles Cotton, who had not long set out from the port (his residence was in Stoke), had taken five sail-of-the-line and 9,000 troops.

Two years later, in July 1812, after Wellington had endured weeks of frustration in Spain trying to engage the French, success at Salamanca gave those at home the assurance that Marmont's force was in full retreat. Wellington's combined force of 48,500 suffered 5,000 losses (2,000 of them Portuguese), while the French lost 13,000 of their 50,000 strong army.

Wellington, having forced the French foe out of Spain, eventually entered France in October 1813. His 120,000 strong allied force had effectively ended Napoleonic rule in Spain at Vittoria in June, with a crushing victory over King Joseph Bonaparte.

News of Napoleon Bonaparte's decisive defeat and retreat on Paris arrived via Falmouth. Bonfire responded to bonfire, and rockets carried the news to every village. Plymouth and Dock were overcome with joy.

At Dock every child was decorated with white ribbons and carried a wand tipper with laurel in one hand and a knife and fork in the other. Tables which groaned under the weight of Old English fare were laid through St Aubyn and Fore Streets. At the sound of trumpet, hats and caps flew off as by magic. Aged, crippled, maim and blind assembled in front of the Government House, and marched amid triumphal strains to the Dockyard Gates, where huge joints and plum puddings of four feet in diameter were sliced and the whole washed down with hogsheads of strong beer.

Plymouth Breakwater was depicted with the *Queen Charlotte* at anchor – the first ship moored within the bulwark when the earliest section was completed.

In Pembroke Street 'John Bull' drank the health of Wellington and Napoleon sat in melancholy posture and at the front of the theatre Bonaparte was dethroned and in chains, with a scroll proclaiming 'A long farewell to all my greatness' and over the balcony of the Crown Hotel, 'Time' pointed to the guillotine with the remark 'Victory! Victory! Vice is in Chains.'

Some sailors and marines and their sweethearts, imitating their betters, dined gloriously by the waterside at North Corner, to the extraordinary amusement of the public and nautical and other jokes and jibes of the most laughable description saluted the ears of the spectators.

Neither expense nor labour was spared to make the Dockyard procession one that Emperors, Kings, or Princes might gaze at with satisfactory emotions, and Dock was thronged by persons of all ranks, clad in engaging attire. Coaches and conveyances poured in from remote districts and hundreds of belated travellers finished their journey on foot because it was impossible to procure horses.

Over four thousand employees assembled in the King's ground outside the lines, and at nine o'clock the scavelmen and shipwrights entered Fore Street. Escorted by regimental bands the procession walked through Dock and Plymouth; and the festivities concluded with banquets at Goode's, Wheatley's and other hotels.

Napoleon returns from Exile

Napoleon repaid the clemency that had been shown him in sparing his life by landing in France and marching upon Paris at the head of a warrior host that wildly hailed his daring. Plymouth was again in arms, and the coast of Devon and Cornwall was swarming anew with French privateers. *Le Leocade* was seized off the port by the the *Sealark* and the captain cut his own throat when he learnt that his destination was the newly built prison on Dartmoor.

Napoleon's Hundred Days rule came to an abrupt end at Waterloo on 18 June 1815 courtesy of the Anglo-Prussian forces under Wellington. Napoleon fled and subsequently signed his second abdication.

Napoleon lent Eastlake his jacket to paint this portrait of the French Emperor in Plymouth Sound. (National Maritime Museum)

1815: Napoleon held captive on board the Bellerophon *in Plymouth Sound becomes one of the biggest visitor attractions the area has ever seen: Jules Girardet (1856-1938) oil on canvas (© Plymouth City Museum & Art Gallery)*

Ten days after the news reached Plymouth, thousands of prisoners were landed at Millbay and Stonehouse Pool in a truly deplorable condition. Only patches and shreds of clothing remained upon them, for the Prussions had appropriated everything portable; and as the captives were no less famished than filthy, the townsfolk gave them food to sustain them on the rough journey to Dartmoor. In conversation with bystanders the Frenchmen readily confessed the dash of the British, and avowed that nothing could withstand the sweep of their cavalry.

In a few weeks the Princetown settlement was more crowded than ever, and after that the local barracks and guardships. As many thousands were imported in a month as had been previously brought over in a year; food was at a premium; and the ovens of bakehouses were kept ablaze by night as well as day.

One French prisoner who was not allowed to land was Napoleon himself. As soon as his ship, the *Bellerophon*, anchored in the Sound, the captive was deprived of the usual deferences.

'The fascinating monster' was on view for many days, but it was impossible for even distinguished visitors to approach the prison ship, as the *Bellerophon* was now designated. Blank charges of musketry were fired to intimidate spectators from infringing the defined limits, and their greetings whenever Napoleon could be seen so exasperated the authorities that they rammed many shore boats for pulling within one hundred yards of the ship.

The Emperor's feeling was henceforth no more consulted than those of an ordinary prisoner of war, and his appeal that he might be treated as England's guest was contemptuously disregarded.

He refused to believe that communication with the land had been denied him, and the severity of the restrictions created quite a revulsion in his favour, indignant yachtsmen cheering 'the Corsican' and ladies wearing his floral emblem – the red carnation.

On the last day of July 1815, Lord Keith and Sir Henry Bunbury boarded the *Bellerophon* to advise the Emperor that he had been banished to St Helena.

The 'Little Tiger' protested that such a course would mean a sentence of death, but Lord Keith refused to discuss the matter. Local sympathy for the tyrant had exasperated Ministers and Plymouth was regarded as a hotbed of treason.

Napoleon become more retiring after this news, but as the weather was fine and the surface of the water calm, everything was in favour of the multitude which received daily accessions from every part of the country; and not only was the Breakwater used as a place of vantage, but thousands surveyed the *Bellerophon's* deck from the heights of Mount Edgcumbe.

During his stay Napoleon's linen was sent into Plymouth to be washed, and the fact that some of it was marked with an 'N' and an imperial crown, and the rest with an 'L' and the royal crown, let to the inference that the latter had been stolen from Louis. This moral reflection did not disturb the several residents of the town; for, with the connivance of the treacherous laundress, they tried on the shirts in order that they might boast they had worn them!

A plan to summon Napoleon to land to face a libel action that had been instituted by a naval officer prompted the authorities to hasten their plans to send the erstwhile Emperor to St Helena.

Hundreds of boats kept track of the *Bellerophon* as she rounded Penlee Point and a daring waterman was cut down by a gunboat and some of the passengers were drowned.

Out of the harbour, the *Bellerophon* was intercepted by the *Northumberland* and Sir George Cockburn received charge of the prisoner. Waiving all petty formalities, Cockburn emptied all weapons from Napoleon's suite, and requested that the Emperor surrender his pistols.

He then overhauled Napoleon's effects and left his valet fifteen hundred gold coins to meet his master's immediate wants.

When it came to the final parting between Emperor and his staff, some of them wept and others clung to his knees. Again and again Napoleon asked why he could not pass the rest of his life in rural England; and when an officer replied that he might have been surrendered to the Russians, he replied, with a shrug of the shoulders; *'God save me from them.'*

As his friends took their departure the Emperor waved them fond farewells until they disappeared in the *Eurotas* towards Plymouth. Their final and unfading reminiscence was the familiar picture of their hero in his green coat, with red facings and epaulettes, white waistcoat and breeches, silk stocking and chapeau bras with tricoloured cockade. With studied effect, Cockburn turned to Napoleon with the enquiry, *'At what hour, General, shall I receive you on board the* Northumberland?'

The Bellerophon is moored up off the Dock Yard.

Napoleon was profoundly agitated on being deprived of his title, and, stamping his foot and furiously taking snuff, he rapped out: *'The people who made me a General made me an Emperor, and you can no more deprive me of one designation than the other.'*
The last scene was the most ignominious of all, for Cockburn refused to allow his charge to distribute a hundred golden coins amongst the crew of the *Bellerophon*, on the ground that such a sum was too generous for a 'general' to disperse.
This haughtiness of manner confirmed the local opinion that unnecessary indignity had been heaped upon the fallen warrior.

Admiral Cockburn goes through the Emperor's personal effects.

Peace and Paying-Off

The departure of 'the Emperor' and the arrival of peace brought the promise of emancipation for tens of thousands of survivors of the fray, many of them pressed men.
In total more than 90,000 British sailors had been lost during the Napoleonic Wars, most of them however, had not died at the hands of the enemy, but through disease, shipwreck, or accident – less than 7,000 had been killed in action.
So when freedom came and with it - paying off - there was but scant regard for looking too far into the future. The streets of Dock were crowded with officers and sailors at liberty, and in possession of funds which they knew not how to disburse.
Carriages were in request at enormous prices, and young officers, who had hundreds of pounds to spend in a week, hired one for themselves, another for their gold-laced hats, and a third for their dirks or hangers. As for the sailors, they retained coaches to remain on the Fore Street stand, and danced hornpipes and reels on the roof to the harsh raspings of a violinist seated on the box.
At the end of these diversions they engaged in furious races, for ten or twenty guineas a-side, and urged the horses until they were ready to drop.
One singular scene in Fore Street on some such occasion may be recalled. Several sailors, just paid off, hired a hackney coach for a short cruise. The dilly was drawn up at the door of a public house for a 'moisture of the wet' before starting out, when the idea their brute companions ought to share in their entertainment. Accordingly the horses were supplied in their turn with beer; and, when their repugnance was gradually subsided, men and beasts were seen drinking from buckets.
When all was ready, the tars, instead of getting into the hold, mounted the backs of the harnessed creatures and the coachman, who felt his situation extremely awkward, accelerated the speed of his horses by whipping the shoulders of the sailors; who, communicating the impulse to those under them, thus made way before the wind.
'Jack' was a chartered libertine – an honest fellow with whom it was the height of indiscretion to to pick a quarrel, who snatched kisses in the taverns where he squandered his money, and embraced in the street with damsels to whom his addresses were not always

North Corner c.1812

agreeable. He walked abroad with pockets full of guineas if especially fortunate, or carried gold in his cap with a consuming passion to dissipate it.

At one paying-off a seaman came on deck with a pewter pot brimming over with guineas, and implored his captain's leave to go ashore; and on meeting with a refusal he tossed pot and contents into the sea with the remark: *'What's the good of money if you can't spend it?'*

Such scenes of debauchery delighted not only those who contributed to them, but also certain casual observers.

'North Corner is the place for Wilkie, for there is famous grouping - sailors and their lasses, drunk and sober; bearded Jews, salesmen and soldiers,' pronounced Plymouth painter Benjamin Haydon, about his Scottish friend and fellow artist David Wilkie.

The observation was made after Wilkie, then on a visit to the area, had astonished his host by evincing no taste for beautiful scenery, and emitting exclamations of real delight at the spectacle of a number of children romping on a dunghill. Inferring that David would prefer that bustling and dissipated landing place which is always so very crowded and busy in war time.

Captain Frederick Marryatt, who joined the Navy in 1806, has conveyed vivid impressions of paying off and sailing scenes that have rendered North Corner and Mutton Cove proverbial, via his wonderfully graphic novels: *The Naval Officer, Mr Midshipman Easy, Masterman Ready.*

Officers were as prone as seamen to dissolute proclivities. Admirals publicly admonished them to wear their uniforms and avoid public brawls and forbade them to enter disreputable public houses. But often these gentlemen were obliged to trust their crews for rescue, as with glittering swords recklessly flourished, they were hauled to prison by the watchmen.

Hundreds of pounds could be spent this way in just a few days, this at a time when the average wage in the Dock Yard itself was less than two pounds a week, although it was rising all the time, there being so many extra hours available, and further incentive being created by the offer of piece work.

Detail of the Revenge refitting from Nicholas Condy's painting of the inner harbour, c1830 - detail (© Plymouth City Museum & Art Gallery)

In the ten years leading up to Waterloo more new ships were launched in the yard than had ever been previously achievable during wartime.

Fearsome 120-gun wooden warriors were constructed, using up to 3,000 loads of oak, in something like half the time they had been just a few decades earlier.

When the mighty *St Vincent* was launched, shortly after Bonaparte's escape from Elba, 60,000 persons assembled at Dock to witness the event. Her proportions were contemplated with admiration approaching to awe, for she was a sublime specimen of naval architecture, destined to be the pride of the seas, and floated like some proud tower, menacing to England's foes and promising gallant achievements. Social celebrations took the form of balls on board the *Impregnable* and other battleships.

Pillage, Pilfering and Pillories

Generally, the artificers appeared to be contented and each individual was entitled to remain on the books until he was incapable of any further manual exertion. Nevertheless, every rank of person in the yard was accustomed to fraud and pilferings, and men of otherwise blameless character instituted important distinctions between the property of the nation and that of individuals, and excused without severe moral strain the general resort to embezzlement.

Heavy bribes were received by those who promoted plunder or shielded perpetrators, and crime became the rule and abuses multiplied. Attempts to eliminate these abuses were unavailing - there were so many officials who had always been ill-paid and who argued that they could not support themselves with decency, if the axe were put to the roots of corruption.

The pillage here alone was estimated at half a million a year.

There was such a struggle to obtain comfortable positions free from potential punishment that a bribe of £300 was paid for an office which carried a salary of just £40 a year; and when a Dock justice discovered that wholesale robbery was in progress, and hurried to inform the departmental head, he was told, with a colourful oath, to mind his own business, as '*such things have always been done, and will continue to be done, in spite of you or me.*'

Workers in the yard were allowed to carry to their homes, as firewood, a bundle of chips - but from chips the transition to timber was easy and the

Pilloried!

men cut up the best wood in their regular time. Within this supposed waste copper bolts were concealed and the metal was sold to the Hebrews who infested the lanes near the yard.

After a thorough investigation it was found that fragments estimated at sixpence were worth three times that amount, because first-class timber was destroyed to create the requisite supply.

Enough wood, in fact, was removed from the yard in one month to build a sloop of war. The chip allowance was stopped and a small financial consideration was substituted.

It didn't stop the fiddling though such was the scale of the theft of rope that firms employed staff to untwist the portions that contained the King's mark, and to eliminate the coloured strand which was introduced as a check upon fraud.

Another trick was to conceal articles in tall hats – a move that lead to the order that heads should be bared as workers passed out of the yard. Others rolled canvas around their wastes, and the pillage was only resented when the thief's appearance was too Falstaffian.

The dockyard stank of corruption and the higher the rank the greater the corruption.

Curiously enough it was to punish a blacksmith in the yard that the pillory was first introduced in Dock and as the wars progressed the resort to the pillory became frequent and offenders were flogged at the cat's tail amid the derision of their undetected colleagues.

In 1808 Daniel Crocker, a sailmaker, stood in the Fore Street pillory for two hours, exposed to the insults and the missiles of the mob, for stealing a role of canvas. John Geddy, the master of an Admiralty boy, was also condemned to the pillory for appropriating stores. And so it went on. In 1809 the Plymouth Dock Police Act was passed; under its provisions the justices had power over the waters of the Sound – and as the borough of Plymouth was thus included, its authorities were aflame with indignation and fear.

The fear and the punishments meted out on land however were a trifling compared with those handed out on board ship.

Given that the greater part of the crews were brought on board against their wills, dragged from their beds at night, or taken from traders to serve at inferior wages – there thus prevailed a sullen murmur of discontent and a silent brooding for revenge in almost every ship. Repression was the leading thought that animated officers, and from the firing of the daylight gun, when all hands were summoned to

wash the decks, until the signal to repair to hammocks, there was an atmosphere of hoarse blasphemy and muttered mutiny.

Sailors were lashed if a gleam of contempt were supposed to lurk in a glance towards an officer ...

'For he who freedom gives to all
Must bend at proud oppression's thrall;
And British Sailor upon the wave
Is but a name for British slave;
Oh! Let impressment meet the ear,
E'en tyranny must drop the tear;
Nor mercy to the black men roam,
When thousand whites are slaves at home.'

Flogging around the fleet was a barbarous institution, and young watermen, seized from their families at dead of night, who crept ashore at the first opportunity, were condemned to be shot or hanged, and occasionally reprieved to receive the 'milder' punishment of flogging.

On the day appointed for the torture, the yellow flag was hoisted from the mainmast; the boats' crews made their way in melancholy procession from every vessel; and the victim was towed from east to west to receive at each stage a certain number of lashes.

A surgeon saw that the loss of skin stopped short of death. Blood was drawn from the outset, but the hardy clenched their teeth until the fifth or sixth stroke, when their pent-up feelings found vent in shrieks that were enough to melt a heart of stone. The spectators groaned as the victim's back presented one horrible mass of lacerated flesh and blood, and sickened when a blanket steeped in vinegar and brine was spread over the wounds to 'prevent mortification'. From ship to ship the dreadful scene was repeated until the unconscious victim was reported as unfit for further punishment and taken to the Royal Naval Hospital at Stonehouse. Bodies of those who were hanged were also taken to the hospital, 'for the anatomical purposes of service surgeons'.

Not all of them regained consciousness and in 1801 Lieutenant George Rutherford was put on trial at Dock for flogging three men to death. Rutherford however leapt from his cabin, through the porthole of his ship and swam ashore.

A reward of £300 was offered, but the lieutenant was never heard of again.

After the Napoleonic Wars oppression was relaxed, and although the cat of nine tails was still used, persecution was not so marked a characteristic of some of the officers.

Contraband and Customs

Post Waterloo, however, the lack of occupation for sailors, soldiers and dockyardsmen, and the abject state to which merchants were reduced, led to the revival of smuggling on a skilful and ambitious scale.

There was a general search of Dock in 1808 and in one case the code of honour was amusingly violated. The premises of an old lady in Cherry Garden Street were marked, and she implored her neighbour, a cobbler, to accept storage until the inspection was over. Silks, tobacco and other stores were transferred to his shop and covered with skins of leather; the old lady's house was ransacked in vain, and the officers knew that they had been forestalled. The cobbler was asked in the morning to return the goods. In reply he laughed at the owner; and, when she threatened him, told the turbulent woman to do her worst. She at once told the excise authorities that they had searched the wrong house, and that the cobbler's would yield a harvest. In the afternoon the officers reappeared with smiles, to find the cobbler smiling more broadly, for he had removed the goods to his own haunt in the course of the night.

By sending out spies who wandered about country lanes in smock-frocks, and who kept their ears open in the drinking haunts of the suspects, the revenue officers did their best to obtain the necessary information of contemplated expeditions and expected returns.

In 1831 a crowd of some forty smugglers, armed with stout sticks, were pursued and overtaken by six preventive men. They had just received their cargo of fifty kegs of brandy from a sloop in Whitsand Bay, and were unloading the tubs at the foot of the cliffs, when the officers pounced upon them. A desperate fight ensued, and the preventive men fired ball-cartridge to restrain the marauders. Several of them fell wounded; but they were carried off by their companions, and the only man who fell into the hands of the officers was Sampson Trevan, who was taken, with a tub on his back, running towards Sheviock. In default of paying the fine of £100 he was sent to prison.

Those who could be identified were severely punished, but the majority escaped the toils of the law. And so the traffic continued well in to the 1840s; but doom was inevitable as law breakers were periodically sent for transportation and their smart craft sawn into separate portions for the edification of the sympathetic.

At the opening of the nineteenth century order was maintained by rounders and watchmen, armed with staves, lanterns, and rattles, and each force was controlled by its captain.

The Charleys (so called it is thought because Charles I improved the system of watchmen in London), were held in light esteem; but their occupation was hazardous, and they were the victims at times of murderous assaults.

In December 1810 a local officer observed four men coming up from the waterside with bags on their backs. Claiming they were carrying 'nothing but what belongs to us', the watchman offered to light their way back to their houses, whereupon one of the ruffians plunged a knife in the officer's stomach – the following morning he expired.

Earlier that same year, Mathurin Dagorn, a French pilot in the British service, in a jealous rage, shot his wife in Clowance Street and then

Excise officers at work near Cawsand Bay

put a similar end to his own existence. Thousands of spectators watched as his body was conveyed to Deadlake (Stonehouse Creek) and buried without any service.

For years after, the scene of the interment was reputed to be haunted and few would pass that way after nightfall lest they should see the spectre which floated in the air just over the unhallowed grave of the murdered and suicide and glowed with a phosphoric glare which made it plainly perceptible to the horrified beholder.

In 1817 a married Dock woman named Smith, who had gone to Ireland with a lover, and lived there for eighteen months, returned to her forgiving husband. Her lover, Jack Green, however followed her. She begged him to leave her alone with her husband but after a quarrel in the Lion and Anchor Inn, in Cherry Garden Street, Green stabbed the unfortunate woman to death. A case knife was found under a heap of shavings in the room and Green was subsequently executed.

Public whipping, the stocks, and the ducking-stool were in vogue for petty offences. Annie Wilcox, a widow living in St Aubyn Street, was indicted, in 1806 at the instance of Mr Shillabeer, an auctioneer, for being a 'common scold' and was sentenced to be dipped as a warning to numerous other noisy women in Dock who, *'daily raise their discordant voices to the disturbance of their peaceful and quiet neighbours'*. As she came up dank and dishevelled after her third immersion, the turbulent woman shrieked; *'And now I won't hold my tongue!'*

Law and Order

Burglary, highway robbery, arson, the maiming of cattle, mutilation of individuals, compounding of felonies, thefts of scrapers, knockers, lamps, bell-pulls, and leaden pipes were among the commoner outrages and recreations. Farms were entered at dusk, country lanes were infested and produce, sheep, cattle and horses were boldly carried off.

One Sunday night a body of armed servants were protecting an outhouse on a St Budeaux farm, where a notorious gang from Dock approached. The thieves attacked the watchers, but one them was shot dead and rest ran off. The jury returned a verdict of 'Justifiable Homicide.'

Other deaths followed duels. Impromptu dances were the fashion and love feuds often proceeded to extremes.

At an improvised entertainment in Pembroke Street, two midshipmen – Mr Armstrong and Mr Long – quarrelled and repaired to a field where, in the presence of friends, flushed from the night's frivolities, the hot-heads fought with pistols. Long was hit on the right side and the ball travelling to his left shoulder, he fell dead on the spot. All concerned rushed guiltily from the scene. The body was discovered in the field, his gilt-laced cap on his head and a cane by his side. Armstrong was clapped in irons and then publicly degraded and imprisoned.

Publicans took no responsibility. Licensed victuallers kept their houses open the greater part of the night and the scenes witnessed within them defied all description. Saturdays were the occasions of disgusting orgies, and tradesmen and workmen alike remained from their homes until an early hour.

Tavern keepers, who permitted women of loose character to revel in lewd dances did not hesitate to send cards to officers of foreign ships to attend balls in their honour, 'by the ladies of Dock'.

Card-playing, drinking, singing, and fighting were varied by daring robberies and outrageous practical joking even in the best conducted of these licensed establishments. Decked in gorgeous red shawls and beaver bonnets, women of a lower grade robbed Jack whilst he slept and were to be seen a few minutes later sitting upon the knees of redcoats.

Dock and the Hamoaze from King's Tamerton

Another view from King's Tamerton

So mischievous were these improper and immoral practices that Sunday was spent in recovering from or reviving Saturday night's drunkenness and families were plunged into poverty and distress for want of money thus spent in debauchery, to the evil example and destruction of the morals of the working classes.

Innkeepers transferred their licences without the knowledge of the magistrates and thus defied the laws for the regulation of victuallers; and a manifesto by the justices threatened to deprive offenders of further right to sell beer and spirits.

Furthermore, on 16 January 1812, a 'respectable' meeting of the inhabitants of the Plymouth Dock was called at the old Town Hall, with a view to the protection of 'the Persons and Property of Individuals from Violence and Plunder.'

Styling themselves the Plymouth-Dock Association, they resolved to unite together to prevent *'as far as possible, the occurrence of crimes in this neighbourhood, at least to operate as some check, and to bring the offenders to discovery and justice'* and further that having paid their ten-shilling annual subscription they shall offer and pay such rewards as seem appropriate in cases of *'burglary, highway robbery, setting fire to any house, grain, hay, &c., stealing, killing, or maiming cattle, stealing money, household goods, wearing apparel, provisions, hay, corn, implements of husbandry or trade, poultry, robbing and damaging fences, gardens, plantations, orchards, or vegetables in any enclosed ground, leaden pipes, palisadoes, scrapers, knockers, lamps, bell pulls,'* or any number of other offences, physical or otherwise, against members.

It was a growing concern: criminality and immorality were never more manifest than in the years following the peace of 1815, when thousands were thrown on their own resources.

One such response was in the manufacture of counterfeit coins. These were in general circulation in the Three Towns after Waterloo.

It was noted that after each fresh distribution a party of gypsies crossed from Stonehouse to Cawsand. Peace officers made their way over there and recognising one of the group raided a house where they found several men lacquering and polishing base coins. Milling and other implements were strewn about, counterfeit coins were piled in cupboards, and genuine guineas lay hoarded in the kitchen. The criminals were hanged at Bodmin.

Public celebration of such events went some way to lift the spirits as generally, and not for the first time, the people of Dock were suffering from 'peace depression' – the town was in need of cheering up.

Fore Street, c1828. Thomas Allom

Devonport *Henry Whitfeld*

The wars so inflated the prosperity of the Three Towns that certain far-sighted individuals dreaded the return of peace. When the merchants gambled in prize agencies and contraband goods, fortunes were rapidly made. But the wealth acquired was of little enduring value, for its recipients were demoralised by the ease with which they made it, and the methods of rivals did little to encourage success of legitimate trading. There were but few redeeming features associated with all this activity; successful men were generous with their hospitalities; a few useful institutions appeared suggesting some measure of pubic spirit; liberal support led to the building of the Theatre Royal and adjoining hotel in Plymouth; Sutton Pool and the Cattewater were improved; the Breakwater was begun; 'legal quays' were created and there were other symptoms of enterprise.

Thus it was not instantly that the depression was felt, although the worldly wise saw that it must come.

The overthrow of the Usurper, Napoleon, was welcomed as a cause for celebration, but, in a few months, money ceased to circulate with the old rapidity, and the port discovered that with peace it had lost the source of its maintenance as an auction centre for prizes and captured cargoes.

Escape from the gloom was sought in the development of the fishing industry and with the arrival of vessels from France filled with wines, spirits and tobacco. However, as the exportation of copper, tin, timber and fish was not authorised it was difficult for traders to fill these vessels back up in return and so the misery intensified.

Depression settled like night over Plymouth and Dock, and thousands were plunged into unutterable misery. Government cutbacks were such that two hundred men of war were laid off in a single month – only 12,000 sailors and 500 marines were retained. From every department there were wholesale discharges, and minor officials were reduced to nominal wages. Thus the stream that had nurtured the area suddenly dried up; every class was thrown back on its own resources; mutilated servicemen and unemployed artisans begged for the very necessities of life – 7,000 paupers received doles at the church doors.

A road around the Hoe was started to provide employment, meanwhile, droves of dockyard workers, soldiers and sailors emigrated to America.

Anti-government feeling was running high, and the King was rebuked as being the 'destroyer of his people', as the trading classes insisted that Plymouth and Dock should be as fully inhabited in times of peace as war.

The Prince Regent, in an attempt to ameliorate the situation, offered plots of land on Dartmoor, for experiments in cultivation, but this was not seen as bountiful gesture as the land produced neither heather, weeds, whins, brooms, nettles or thistles and was therefore extremely unlikely to satisfy starving workmen.

Devonport was indeed a dismal place and it was badly lit and lifeless. The existing park was a wilderness known as the Brickfields, and the present Brickfields went by the name of Parsonage Fields.

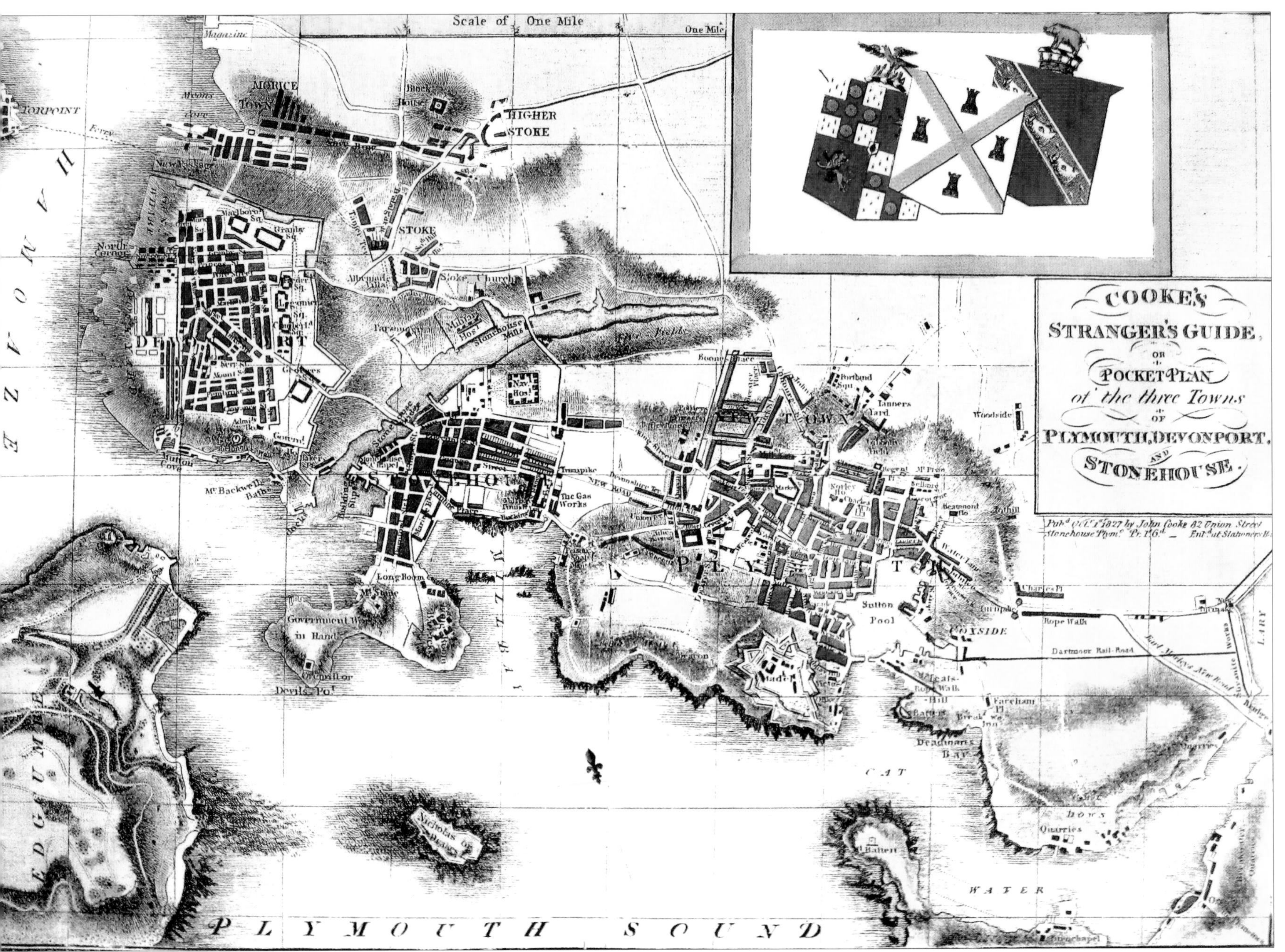

1827 Map of the Three Towns, shortly after the name change from Dock to Devonport

Entrance to the town was gained by a series of drawbridges, one, the most favoured, at the top of Stonehouse Hill, another on New Passage Hill and a third at the entrance to Fore Street – this particular route being the least popular because of the dread of footpads – horseless highwaymen.

Dilapidated huts were distributed over the area of the present Raglan Barracks, and in these the artillery and line regiments were accommodated. Blockhouses at Longroom and Stoke received the militia, and married couples were housed in St George's Barracks on Mount Wise. The site of Keyham Yard was agricultural land and Navy Row, the present Albert Road, was the only pretence of a street in Morice Town.

An official residence for the Port Admiral was built on the site of the old mansion at Mount Wise in 1809 and extensive ramparts were being thrown up around the town when the end of hostilities caused the officials to condemn the scheme as useless – however, it was completed a few years later with a view to giving work to the unemployed.

Plymouth Dock at this time had no political representation – not even at county level ... even though it had a population of around 40,000. Plymouth itself was not much better off; despite the fact the borough had more electors than most, there were but 163 men entitled to vote and most of them had little will of their own and could be bought off easily. As with most of the country, MPs were returned by *'aristocratic influence, ministerial manoeuvres and rotten corporations'* with individuals often buying seats for corrupt purposes – the enormous cost of political contests preventing independent individuals from even thinking about serving their country.

In Dock public business was conducted in a small Town Hall building in Duke Street which stood in immediate contact with the Workhouse. Ill-suited to its purpose, a number of leading inhabitants issued a manifesto declaring that they proposed to erect *'a building suitable to all useful and necessary purposes of public business, and their general accommodation, it is conceived to be perfectly compatible with the design and with a due regard to economy, to effect it upon such a scale, and in such a situation, as shall render it at the same time, ornamental and beneficial to the town.'*

Thus was the appeal made for subscriptions. A site was given by the Lord of the Manor and a new Town Hall was duly erected in Ker Street.

Filled with pride at this brand-new possession, a memorial was addressed to the King begging that a new name might be given to Plymouth Dock. Its tone breathed alike a spirit of importance and conscious indignity. Immense naval operations had been conducted in the town, and its arsenal had contributed to the glory and majesty of the empire. Dock had hailed the proud trophies so often and gallantly won, and had eagerly testified its attachment to the institutions of the country. But, protested the inhabitants in their petition, *'we deplore and keenly feel that although we exceed in population and extent every other town in Devonshire, we are only recognised as a mere offshoot of the borough of Plymouth and as an unimportant adjunct of a national establishment ...'*

Our town possesses chapels of ease in a addition to a parish church, a Town Hall *'unrivalled as to architecture and commodiousness'*; a public dispensary for the sick; two classical schools provided with masters *'who are ministers of the Established Church'* and various edifices dedicated to worship and charity.

Thus the petitioners hoped that *'your Majesty may not consider us unworthy of also participating in those political privileges which your Majesty has been pleased to confer upon other ports in your dominions.'*

Having dispatched their heart-felt plea a response was eagerly awaited

It was on Christmas Eve 1824 that the recently appointed Home Secretary, Robert Peel, sent the following from Whitehall:

"Gentlemen,

Having laid before the King your petition, praying, for the reasons therein stated, that the name of the town of Plymouth Dock might be changed, and that his Majesty would be pleased to confer on the said town the name of DEVONPORT, or such other name as to his Majesty should seem proper, I am commanded to acquaint you that his Majesty has been graciously pleased to comply with the prayer of the said petition, and to direct that, on and after the 1st day of January next, the town of Plymouth-Dock shall be called and known by the name of DEVONPORT, and a communication has been made to the several Public Departments accordingly.'

I am, Gentlemen

Your most obedient humble Servant,

Robert Peel

Top: *Robert Peel.* Middle and bottom: *The medal cast to commemorate the new name.*

Town Hall, Devonport Column, Mt. Zion Chapel and the Civil and Military Library) John Foulston FRIBA (1772-1842) (© Plymouth City Museum & Art Gallery)

On the day chosen for the changing of the name the proclamation was made with flourishes of trumpets, and the health and happiness of George IV were commended to the crowd amid further fanfares.

All over the town flags and arches uttered the momentous word; and the proclamation was recited from point to point by Mr Rodd the Town Clerk.

A pillar bore the name 'Devonport' in gilded letters in Cumberland Street and a public dinner was held at the 'Devonport' Royal Hotel. The town of 'Devonport' was toasted; the 'Devonport' march was played by the 'Devonport Amateur Band' and the 'ladies of Devonport' were complimented. 'Devonport' ale was distributed at the Tamar Brewery; a schooner was launched to which the new name was given; and the poor were liberally entertained.

A memorial column was designed by Foulston and the foundation stone was laid on the royal birthday. A medal, of which a cast in gold was presented to the King, represented Neptune in his carriage, drawn by sea-horses, surveying the town and harbour, and proclaiming to the world that he had selected Devonport as his head-quarters. A replica in silver was presented to the Duke of Clarence – the Sailor Prince, the one who, in reality, had secured the name change for the town in which he had spent so much of his youth.

Parliamentary Representation

The newly designated town was, however, still without Parliamentary representation and having raised concerns over this issue for the first time in 1827, the inhabitants took advantage of another visit from the Duke of Clarence, the following year, to press their case:

The Duke was not insensitive to local desire: *'I cannot undervalue the importance of Devonport, with its forty thousand loyal inhabitants, and am sure the gracious condescension of our beloved Sovereign will ever be gratefully remembered for having conferred a name upon a town in which exists so important a naval arsenal.'*

'I must always,' he added, *'remember the many happy hours I have spent in this place, and I thank you most sincerely for your kind wishes.'* The prince also conceded that the Dockyard, the Harbour and the Breakwater made the port the finest in the world.

Political enfranchisement did not follow straight away, however, and when the Reform agitation was at its height across the country, in 1831, a numerous and highly respectable meeting, constituting the opinion of the town, declared that whilst men of Devonport respected the claims of all, *'we cannot but feel aggrieved and degraded by our present situation, where, in a large town, and parish, containing 40,000 souls, six only can be found legally qualified by freeholds in the parish, to vote even for a county member, whatever their possessions might be or their payment of taxes.'*

The following year the tidal wave of Reform swept over the country and at last in 'The Town of Devonport and the Parish of Stoke Damerel and the Township of Stonehouse' the vote was given to: *'Every male person of full age, and not subject to any legal incapacity, who shall have occupied, for six months previously, any house of the said towns of the clear yearly value of ten pounds, or which shall have been for the same rated to the relief of the poor, or to the duty assessed upon inhabited houses, at a sum not less than ten pounds, shall have a right to vote for the election of members for such towns.'*

The number of householders enfranchised was 3,600 in Devonport and Stonehouse, and 2,500 in Plymouth. Thus 6,100 voters were created in the Three Towns, where, hitherto, two or three hundred had exercised the monopoly.

Thus it was that in 1832 tens of thousands of people across the country went to vote for the first time.

In Devonport, popular prejudice ran with Sir George Grey and Sir Edward Codrington, two moderate Liberals, but a third candidate – Mr Leach, a native of the town – entered the arena at the request of four hundred advanced Reformers, who thought him the least Conservative of the trio.

The town was daily paraded by rival bands, and each candidate retained a number of inns, which were variously distinguished by colours. Sir Edward Codrington further expressed his intention of giving a ball, and the ladies were all the more enthusiastic in displaying his favours. Grey, blue and pink ribbons were profusely exhibited on the nomination day; and the population flocked to the hustings erected beneath the portico of the Town Hall.

Sir George Grey pulled up in a barouche and four, and his friends displayed blue banners. Mr Leach was drawn by four greys, and his procession was headed by a band, while his supporters waved brilliant flags. Sir Edward Codrington arrived in a car that symbolised the stern and quarter-deck of the *Asia*, the ship in which he served at the Battle of Navarino; he was accompanied by several jolly tars in full sailing trim and his flag was *'nailed to the pole'*.

Silence at the hustings was demanded by the beadle: speeches were made and a show of hands taken. As it was in favour of Grey and Codrington, a poll was challenged by Mr Leach.

The candidates were early in the field the following morning, bands of music parading the streets, and committees and their friends rallying their forces. Booths were erected in front of George Square, on a site near Granby Barracks, outside Tamar Terrace, and on Stonehouse Quay. The polling was maintained with wonderful spirit, until, doubting the probability of his success, Mr Leach resigned. The following day at noon the result was declared: Grey 1,178; Codrington 891; Leach 575.

Mr Leach was consoled by a banquet, and, after asserting that Englishmen must look to the ballot for the preservation of their liberties, he denounced those who first solemnly pledged and then abandoned him as deserving of scorn, indignation and contempt of honest men. He then heartily toasted the 'unbought, unsold, incorruptible and glorious minority of 575, and unpolled Independent electors of the borough. A significant sentiment was proposed by Mr Ramsay: *'The people – may they know their rights, and, knowing, dare maintain them.'*

Borough Incorporation

The enfranchisement of Devonport was the prelude to the demand for municipal privileges. There was a far-sighted recommendation from the Boundary Commissioners that the Three Towns should be constituted one Corporation, and Devonport welcomed this proposal as pregnant with immediate and ulterior advantages. Then a section proposed that interests, habits, prejudices and passions were opposed to the union, although it was admitted that expense would be saved by having one Court, one Recorder, one Chief Magistrate, and one Police Establishment. It was suggested that amalgamation would embroil Plymouth and Devonport in perpetual contests over precedence and choice of officers. It was further argued that the combined Corporation would be the Corporation of Plymouth, that essential business would be conducted in the older borough, and all the important meetings held and municipal records preserved in its Townhall. There arrangements, it was suggested, would be unfair to Devonport, whose population was as large as that of Plymouth.

Amalgamation was supported by the Commissioners, it was alleged, because they dreaded the creation of a more influential authority than their own, in Devonport.

A joint committee of the parishioners and Commissioners sat for two months, and the majority eventually recommended the demand for a charter: Plymouth had debts - Devonport had none.

Plymouth had corporate property - Devonport had none. Plymouth was an ancient and commercial town, whose interests, habits and peculiarities were distinct from those of Devonport, where people depended for their prosperity on the establishments and the services. Whilst Devonport was thus anxious to secure independence, Plymouth was as little disposed to encourage union.

At the eleventh hour there was a mood of reaction, for the probable cost of incorporation troubled many Devonport people, and a finance meeting was summoned. The Admiral-Superintendent granted the Dockyard workforce two hours for dinner instead of one, so that they might attend in force; and, after a noisy interruption, it was decided to defer judgement until a financial estimate of the cost of a charter was known.

An assurance was received that it would not exceed £150, and by unanimous consent a petition for incorporation was approved.

In compliance with the appeal, a charter was duly granted by letters patent of Queen Victoria on 13 October 1837:

Sir John St Aubyn, by John Opie

'By virtue of the powers and authorities given to us by the 1835 Act for the regulation of the Municipal Corporations in England and Wales, we do hereby grant and declare that the inhabitants of the town of Devonport and the parish of Stoke Damerel shall be ever hereafter one body corporate and politic in deed, fact and manner, and that the said body corporate shall be called the Mayor, Alderman and Burgesses of the Borough of Devonport in the County of Devon.'

The number of electors for municipal purposes was less by nearly one hundred than those registered under the Parliamentary legislation, or the £10 franchise - a difference attributable to the three years' residential reservation, which was more operative in seaports than in inland communities.

There were to be twelve aldermen and thirty-six councillors elected across six wards.

Mr T Woollcombe was chosen as the first Town Clerk of the newly constituted borough and the first Mayor of Devonport, elected that same month in 1837, was Mr Edward St Aubyn. His father, the Lord of the Manor, Sir John St Aubyn, donated a mace for the Corporation, to celebrate the occasion and then, upon Sir John's death and Edward's unexpected accession to the estate in 1864 - when the Reverend WJ St Aubyn was ignored as the eldest son and the property conferred upon the youngest - Edward presented the Corporation with the massive gold chain worn by subsequent Mayors.

Devonport Life

Devonport's star had never burned so brightly, and across many spheres of cultural activity in the area, the Town shone.

One of the earliest major concerts had been staged in the Dock Theatre, at the beginning of the 1820s; the Dock Harmonic Society gave their first concert at the Philosophical Rooms in 1823. 'Mount Sinai', a new oratorio, was well presented at the Town Hall in 1831 with band and chorus selected from the professionals and amateurs of the Three Towns.

In 1834 the Devonport Choral Society acquitted themselves with distinction in 'The Witches' from *Macbeth*. Insufficient support and other difficulties were overcome in 1835 and the first Devonport Subscription Concert was held. Meanwhile, Mr and Mrs Crouch, the principal artists at concerts given by the Plymouth Harmonic Society, made Dock their place of residence.

Foulston's fourth, Egyptian-style, building at the top of Ker Street, the 1823 Devonport and Stonehouse Classical and Mathematical Subscription School, became, within a few years, the Devonport Library, complete with a *'highly valuable collection of books, both ancient and modern, and a constant supply of the London, provincial and local newspapers.'*

An earlier school, the Dock Public School for Boys, had been established, by subscription, in 1809, to *'counteract the baleful effects of ignorance and evil example in the rising generation'*.

With Sir John St Aubyn as the president, the school was run along Lancastrian lines, that is according to the tenets of Dr Bell and Mr Lancaster who had demonstrated that one master can educate a thousand boys in reading, writing and arithmetic as effectually, and with as little trouble, as twenty or thirty have ever been instructed by the usual modes of tuition, and *'it appears that a hundred boys may be educated at an expense not exceeding one pound each, including the master's salary.'*

Monsieur Huet taught French language, dancing and fencing at both Plymouth and Dock while Mr Philip Hill and Captain Bromley ran separate schools in the same building in Princes Street.

Mr Hill was a private teacher of mathematics and the 'higher' branches of education, while Captain Bromley was a public teacher of spelling, arithmetic and the 'lower' branches of education. Their two rooms were divided only by a cupboard with a wooden partition and through this partition Mr Hill's pupils bore sundry holes; then, fastening pins to thin sticks, drove them into the backs of Captain Bromley's pupils, causing them ever and anon to howl with pain.

The Captain retaliated by banging at the partition with his stick; and, entering Mr Hill's door, threatened him with personal chastisement. Bromley was charged before the magistrates with creating a riot, but the summons was dismissed.

With regular squabbles between schoolboys, soldiers, sailors and civilians it was not surprising that of the sports that most appealed to the temperament of the age, wrestling held the foremost place, and it was usually accompanied by bell-ringing matches for purses of guineas, cudgelling, jingling, jumping in bags and other competitions, including races for women and donkey hunts.

In the Three Town's neighbourhood there were many competitions between the champions of Devon and Cornwall, none more spectacular than the meeting between Abraham Cann, the Devon champion and James Polkinghorne, the pride of Cornwall.

The big match.

The long-anticipated encounter took place on 23 October 1826 at Tamar Green, Morice Town. On the evening before the contest the town was inundated, and the resources of the hotels and inns were taxed to the utmost. Truculent and redoubtable gladiators flocked to the scene – Kickers from Dartmoor, the recruiting ground of the Devonshire system; and bear-like huggers from the land of Tre Pol and Pen. Ten thousand persons bought tickets at a premium for the seats, and the hills around swarmed with spectators.

Excitement was at the highest possible pitch as the rivals entered the ring – Polkinghorne – the landlord of the Red Lion in St Columb Major who at 6'2" was considerably taller and heavier than his local adversary Cann – who was 5'8" and a bit and weighed 175 pounds – with a monstrous pair of shoes whose toes had been baked like flints.

Polkinghorne had been discounted as fat and unwieldy but the Devonians were dismayed to find that great as was his girth, his arms were tough and his shoulders immensely powerful. Cann displayed a more sinewy form, his figure was knit for strength and statuesquely proportioned.

The purse for the contest was £200 a side for the best of three back falls, over and above which hundreds of pounds worth of bets were placed on the event. The betting was in favour of Cann at the outset but it receded as the Cornishman impressed the multitude with his muscular superiority.

Abraham Cann, Devon wrestler.

With two experts from each county selected as sticklers. Polkinghorne won the first fall, and after several inconclusive rounds, Cann won the second. In the tenth round treating Cann's fearsome kicking with contempt, the Cornishman lifted his opponent over his head and dashed him to the ground.

However as Polkinghorne dropped on his knee the turn was disallowed. Polkinghorne then left the ring amid a mighty clamour and by reason of his default the stakes were awarded to Cann. The victor emerged from the terrific hugs of his opponent with a mass of bruises, which proved that kicking was only one degree more effective than bruises.

Uniformed Fighters

A more unsatisfactory issue could hardly have been conceived and the rival backers forthwith endeavoured to arrange another encounter. Polkinghorne however, refused to meet Cann unless he discarded his shoes.

Wrestling continued to thrill, however, and for some time matches were held on the Hoe, where they became such an obstruction to business that workmen could not be persuaded to attend their employment and the promenade was finally prohibited for such meetings. The arena then shifted to Chelson Meadow but the Cornishmen became increasingly reluctant to fight the Devonshire men in their increasingly lethal shoes.

There were further episodes of domestic fighting after the campaign against Turkey in 1827. Britain's interference, with France and Russia in the Greek War of Independence, saw the British Naval Squadron under Admiral Codrington virtually destroy the Turko-Egyptian fleet at the Battle of Navarino.

The paying-off scenes were scarcely less hilarious than those after Waterloo. To the accompaniment of fiddles and tambourines, the seamen whiled away the hours with dance and song, in the vicinity of Mutton Cove and North Corner; and as night darkened and the hours lengthened, the attempts of redcoats to intrude upon the privileges of the mariners involved taverns and town in the throes of a riot.

Heated with drink and inflamed with jealousies, the sailors matched their fists against the side arms of the soldiers; and when mere muscle did not prevail as against cold steel, they seized pokers, shovels and tongs and drove trespassers to the open. There in the midst of an uproarious crowd, the fights were resumed; but when the watchmen were summoned by rattle, soldiers and sailors made common cause and battered the constables with their own staves and maces.

During a revel held at Stoke, men and women were dancing in the Pear Tree Inn with the utmost good humour when a body of marines insisted upon choosing partners. After a struggle they were ejected, but, returning in increased numbers, they cleared the room at bayonet point. The majority escaped by jumping through windows, but one petty officer was killed and several others wounded.

On another occasion a crowd of men of both services were drinking together in Pembroke Street when a corporal struck a woman and a

sailor thumped him for his loutish behaviour and the fight became general. The soldiers fatally stabbed the seaman.
Another such scene was witnessed in James Street where scores of soldiers and sailors, stripped to the waist, fought in the roadway, and many were stretched insensible in the gutters. The men were encouraged and directed by their officers and, when the watchmen came on the scene, the combatants co-operated in overwhelming them. Companies of soldiery then appeared to suppress the riot, and two lieutenants and several sailors were carried face downwards to the Town Hall, where they answered to their names in the morning with black eyes, broken arms and bandaged heads. The officers were compounded for their offence and were released, but the men were sent to prison.

Animal Instincts

Such barbarism was not confined to human encounters as ratting, badger-baiting, bull-baiting and cock-fighting were much in favour throughout the West.
The object of bull baiting was to make the beef tender; and, although the sport was discouraged, the word went round whenever the performance was fixed. The last occasion on which a bull was baited in the area was in 1830 when a large number of people assembled in a field at Gilbert's Lane, Milehouse.
The admission charge was a shilling. The bull was tethered to the ground and dog after dog was let loose to worry it ready for the slaughter. By degrees the bull turned up the ground to find a refuge for its nose and mouth; and again and again one dog was tossed, another was gored, a third was caught by the farmer's wife, who ran about holding her apron open, so that she might intercept the pets and break their falls. 'Fresh dog – form a lane!' was the period cry as a new trainer came forward to gain experience for his animal and to prove its expertness.
By this time cock-fighting was forbidden, but this only served to increase interest and there was a good deal of training done in the area and regular encounters were held around the Three Towns.
Similarly and somewhat remarkably, the Brown Bear in Chapel Street, which had opened in 1774 as just 'The Bear', had a large bear pit in the cellar which had been used for bear fights.

Bull baiting always attracted a crowd.

Highways and Byways

The hardest working of all beasts in mankind's interest at this time though was the horse. As ever more business was conducted by road so it became all the more pressing to improve the highways and byways of the area.
The main roads between Plymouth and Devonport were contracted and filthy – one by-way of Stonehouse Lane and the other known as the road by Millbay, each sixteen feet wide, from hedge to hedge, and composed of materials very poorly laid. The hill into Dock, as it was, was a dreadful impediment which it was assumed that nothing short of an earthquake would diminish and the highway laws were so restrictive that it was taken for granted that the roads could never be widened.
After much persuasion an Act sanctioning the reconstruction of Millbridge and the levying of tolls was passed and as a result work was carried out to reduce the gradient of the hill on the Devonport side – hitherto it had been too steep to allow the ascent of animals. Stoke, Newpassage and Plymouth were brought into easier communication. Then, in 1828, Stonehouse Hill was lowered, and ascent and descent were considerably facilitated.

The route into Dock from Cornwall was from Cremyll across to Mutton Cove and, like the Saltash Ferry, this was invariably rowed by women – fit men were inevitably required for naval duties. Prior to the construction of the Breakwater these water passages were often subject to storms. The same was true of the Torpoint Ferry and in 1809, with a view to improving the service, the proprietors introduced a twopence charge for every horse &c, and one penny for every person, accompanying the same, 'whether going or returning'.

In 1836 a new road was cut from St Austell to Devonport, by way of Crafthole and St John's Lake to the north of Torpoint. Thence a steam-bridge was started, 'an ingenious contrivance' – a floating bridge – designed by Mr Rendle who, in 1827 had completed the area's first ever iron bridge for the Earl of Morley at Laira, thus bringing the South Hams into better contact with the Three Towns.

The first steam ferry, the *Jemima,* named in honour of the daughter of the co-proprietor of the service Reginald Pole Carew, was launched amid great excitement on 29 September 1829. However, the vessel didn't go into regular service until 1831 and even then it failed to live up to expectations. Poor *Jemima* was prone to being blown off course and being turned broadside when about to be offloaded and was soon relieved of her duties.

And so it was that the proprietors approached James Meadows Rendle who had already designed successful ferries at Dundee and Dartmouth. Rendel's solution was to create a chain-guided steam crossing, the first of which was introduced in 1834, and a second a year later.

With a lamp on each corner the new ferry crossed the river four times an hour taking eight minutes at high tide and seven at low tide.

Each vessel was capable of carrying three four-horse carriages, one two-horse carriage, seven saddle horses and sixty foot passengers.

Torpoint Ferry, W Briggs

High-Speed Links

Towards 1829 speedy travelling by water came into favour not just for simple crossings but also as auxiliary to coach travel.

Steamers plied between the Three Towns and Portsmouth, and coaches waited at the latter port to carry passengers to London. The vessels left Millbay at 12.30am and arrived at Portsmouth at 4pm, enabling passengers to enter the Metropolis at midnight. The entire journey was thus accomplished in *'the incredibly short time of twenty-three and a half hours.'* This was a mighty revolution in locomotion: *'What would our forefathers have said to this?'* was the question posed at the time, by those who rarely went to town without preparing their will and were six or seven days in performing the journey.

A memorable advance was made when a coach was started to run eleven miles an hour all the way to London.

There were some changes towards 1830, but the plan of travelling was always the same. The subscription New Light Coach conveying four inside and ten outside passengers, left at half-past three in the morning from Townshend's London Inn, Devonport; W Avent's Crown Inn, Stonehouse; and Hannaford's Commercial Inn, Plymouth; through Ridgeway, Ivybridge, Buckfastleigh, Ashburton, and Chudleigh, arriving at the Half Moon Hotel, Exeter, at four o'clock in the afternoon. It proceeded at six through Ilminster, Wincanton and Salisbury, and arrived at the Bull and Mouth, London, at half-past three-o'clock on the following afternoon.

The humour and inconvenience of the coach were alike illustrated in the rhyme of the period:

Having taken my place in the Plymouth stage,
To visit a friend I had promised an age,
I was rous'd in the morning before it was light,
With the prospect of rumbling and tumbling all night.
On mounting the coach 'twas my luck to be fix'd
Two very fat elderly ladies betwixt;
On the opposite seats were a brat and his nurse,
A sergeant, whose joy was to swagger and curse,
And between, a la bodkin, big, burly and staunch,
Mine host, that of Falstaff, might rival the paunch,
We had scarce clear'd the stones, when the road growing hilly,
To and fro', like a ship, roll'd the merciless dilly:
At this my good patrons, who sat on each side,
Were provok'd, one to cough, the other to chide;
The soldier to swear, and with none to say 'Fie,'
The landlord to snore, and the baby to cry:
If such be the charms of a stage, I'll take root;
Or if ever I travel I'll travel a-foot.'

As early as 1830 the germ of the Motor Car occurred to a Plymothian, Mr John Lee Stevens, who advocated that the application of steam to stage coaches so that transit between Plymouth and Devonport could be rapid and economical. Mr Steven's company did not float.

Expiring amid the romance of leafy lanes were those echoes of 'The Merry Ploughboy' that had for so many generations stirred the population with familiar resonance, and which never failed to attract a beaming crowd as the equipages rattled from the east end of Plymouth to the Dockyard gates.

The reality of the coach was passing into a picturesque dream, and the cheery horn and crisp whip were to be superseded by the snort and smoke of the iron horse. Soon the prevailing topic was the wonderful new machine for travelling without horses, which had a body of iron like a barrel, a furnace in the rear, and a perpendicular pipe ten feet high to carry off the smoke.

Stephenson's Rocket

At the first South Devon Railway meeting held in Plymouth, the engineer of the Great Western Company was chiefly concerned in dispelling the fears of the nervous. No accidents could occur – Mr Price pointed out – if passengers kept their seats until the train came to a standstill, and the rails would be so protected that stage coaches could not possibly drive over them.

These qualms settled, it was suggested that there was not sufficient traffic between Exeter and the Three Towns to justify the experiment; but Mr Rundle, MP for Tavistock, contended that the reduced cost of conveying passengers and stock would popularise travelling and lead to an increase of exchange.

Hitherto, farmers had been driving their cattle to London, impairing their strength and weight, whereas all produce would now be swiftly and economically carried. Emphasis was laid on the eminence of Plymouth as a port, and its possibilities of expansion, no less than on the facilities for carrying troops and stores. To this proviso George Stephenson attached the highest value, and there was a rush of railway projects aiming at the favour of the Three Towns.

Brunel was entrusted with the work, and warmly recommended Eldad, at the end of Five Fields, as the terminus, in order that an extension should be made into Cornwall, *'if this should be thought expedient'*.

Mr George Soltau warmly opposed the choice of 'No Place' for the purpose, because persons would find their way to Devonport instead of Plymouth, and he advocated Friary as a more appropriate station site. Mr Brunel laughed at the idea of conflicting interests.

'Although,' he said, *'you speak of your Three Towns, we only know one long, straggling, scattered community.'* He contended that no company would dream of approaching such a population at one extremity; but he so far yielded to pressure as to abandon his own idea and substitute land at the back of the Octagon.

This surrender aroused the fears of Devonport, whose citizens had subscribed on the understanding that a station would be placed near the North East Barrier Gate. Passionately protesting that there was neither public landing-place nor population at Millbay, they insisted on petitioning Parliament in favour of Devonport.

Their Town Clerk, Mr T Woollcombe, as chairman of the company, solemnly warned them that they would not improve their position by this course; and harsh though the hint sounded, it was justified.

Whilst the South Devon Railway was in the course of construction, in 1846, the Duke of Wellington left London on an official visit. The line had only reached Teignmouth, and he resumed the journey by coach. At Ivybridge there was no fresh relay of horses in readiness, and his Grace walked on to avoid mobbing. He was overtaken by the Tally-Ho coach, and Hex, the guard, asked him to honour the conveyance by taking a seat.

'No, I thank you,' was the prompt reply, *'I am waiting for my carriage.'*

Hex assured the Duke that he would be greatly delayed, but the old soldier rejoined: *'Never mind, they'll find horses to take me on. Besides,' he added, pointing to pedestrians with whom he was discussing the scenery, 'I have company'.*

The baffled driver hastened on and set the Three Towns alive with the report that the veteran was tramping his way to town.

1846: Duke of Wellington walks out of Ivybridge en route for Devonport

It was not until 1848 that the labour of years and anticipations of thousands were realised in the opening of the South Devon line to Laira. However, the Inspector General would not sanction a level crossing in Union Street and it wasn't until 1849 that a compromise was effected and the line was completed to Millbay.

Millbay itself was greatly developed, but an Admiralty veto put paid to proposals to run a line to Sutton Harbour.

Albermarle Villas c.1828, Thomas Allom

St Michael's Terrace c.1828, Thomas Allom.

Devonport Expands

Throughout this time there had been plenty of development in Devonport itself; the waste lands blossomed, the sites of market gardens were converted into villas, and the mother church counted the spires of several stately daughters. The unpretending graving docks were supplemented by others of larger capacity, and the Admiralty enclosure extended below the westernmost landing-place at Mutton Cove.

Then, as by a touch of the magician's wand, Keyham arose with its docks, wharves and factories.

It was in 1844 that the first spade was inserted, and Nasmyth's tilt hammer drove the piles that formed the coffer. The engine began its mighty task in 1845, to the wonder of spectators, and a a dam of 1,600 feet, in which 800 loads of timber were used, was soon completed, the area of 74 acres being intersected with railways and the excavated soil thus early removed. Over 1,200 men, 100 horses and 70 boats were used in the construction of Keyham Steam Yard and the eventual cost of the project was said to be over £2,000,000.

1865 Keyham Steam Yard, W Hake

38 acres of land and 43 acres of foreshore were purchased from the trustees of the will of Sir I St Aubyn and the first lord of the Admiralty, the Rt. Hon Earl of Auckland laid the official foundation block, containing all the current coins of the realm.

The vast factory area, encompassing about six acres under one glass roof, was designed by Charles Barry, the London architect who had designed the new Houses of Parliament in 1836.

1853: HMS Queen *marks the official opening of the new Steam Yard.*

The basin was opened to admit water for the first time in 1850 but it was to be another three years before the official opening, an event that was marked by the admission into the basin of HMS *Queen*. Devonport had produced its first steam fighting ship over twenty years earlier, the 813-ton paddle-steam-powered *Rhadamanthus*, however, like the 1845 steam-paddle frigate *Avenger*, both had been sailed elsewhere (Woolwich and Deptford respectively) to have engines fitted.

Keyham Stream Yard opens for business, W Hake.

North gate into Devonport from the Torpoint Ferry and Keyham, c1860. (Bob Cook)

Less than twelve months after the new Steam Yard had opened, Britain found itself in the grip of an almost hysterical clamour for war.
There had been nearly forty years of comparative peace and it was that a test of the nation's manhood was long overdue. So it was that, primarily on the pretext of asserting public law against a transgressor, Aberdeen, his Chancellor, and Gladstone, took the country into a war, over 3,000 miles away, in support of Turkey, who had actually turned down terms that we had agreed with their aggressors, Russia. Furthermore, we were also to be fighting alongside the French, who, only a year earlier had been generating rumours of a British invasion.
The degree to which the whole event was treated as a public spectacle was obvious from an account published in *The Times* according to which some *'thirty Russian ladies went out of Sebastopol to see the battle of Alma as though they were going to a picnic. They were quite assured of the success of the Russian troops and great was their alarm and dismay when they found themselves obliged to leave the telegraph house on the hill and flee for their lives in their carriages.'* British officers too were accompanied by wives and their maids and some wealthy individuals cancelled their holidays to follow the Army and see all the fun.
It was against this backdrop that work began, that same year, 1854, on improving the barrack facilities in Devonport. First it was necessary to pull down the old single-storey blocks - George, Cumberland, Frederick and Ligonier - that had been erected almost 100 years earlier in 1757. In all, eleven acres were cleared for the construction of the new accommodation with well over a third of the space left to be laid out as a parade ground. The number of soldiery thus increased dramatically and in 1856 the Garrison Chapel was built for the Military in Devonport although civilians were allowed in, by the south door, to fill the seats left unoccupied by the troops at the morning parade service.
On Sunday evenings the chapel was free and open. These services were very popular as a surpliced choir, mainly composed of soldiers and soldiers' sons, led the singing.
St Stephen's, meanwhile, was the fourth of four daughter churches that were designed for Devonport by J Piers St Aubyn and was completed in 1852. The other three were St James' and St Paul's (1851) and St Mary's (1852): the sites for the four churches were given by the Lord of the Manor, the head of the St Aubyn family.

Garrison Church

Raglan Barracks, W Hake.

St Stephen's Church

Cholera, Small Pox and Insanitation

It was just prior to this frenzy of church construction that the Three Towns were hit by a second attack of cholera.

The first outbreak had been in 1831 and it had stalked through the area like a scythe-armed spectre.

Keen pressure on the part of the doctors led to the creation of a Local Board of Health, Plymouth and Devonport were mapped into districts and empty buildings were hired as hospitals. Attempts to move poor patients were met with crazed protests and agonised creatures were rescued from the nurses and restored to their homes to expire of fright and exhaustion. This objection to removal was due to a suspicion – which the disclaimers failed to eradicate – that the doctors desired subjects for dissection, and the prudential refusal to admit to the mortuary the friends of those who expired lent colour to the notion and caused repeated riots.

Every other person who was attacked by the disease succumbed and for a while the doctors despaired of arresting the plague. Improved methods of treatment resulted in the reduction of the mortality to one-third, and eventually ignorant and prejudiced people were impressed with the devotion of the medical men, aided by private citizens, some of whom were attacked in the course of the work.

The neighbourhood of 'The Marsh' (Union Street) and Sutton Pool were festering scenes of squalor, and, alarmed by the reports of horrors witnessed in these districts, the wealthier classes left the town to reside in the moorland villages – only to find that every hamlet became contaminated and that they were just as safe in their own homes. Months passed before the disease spent itself, and the bereaved carried corpses to the cemetery in unfinished coffins.

Poor families were wholly swept away and, in not a few instances, only one member – and that a child – lived to tell the tale. After the terror had ceased, a medal was struck in honour of much self-denial, and the medical men were presented with snuff-boxes bearing inscriptions that testified to their *'humane and unceasing attention to the poor during the awful visitation of malignant cholera at Plymouth AD 1832.'*

During the second appearance of the plague, in 1850, ten per cent of the population were attacked. Nine hundred victims succumbed,

The Dockyard Doctor's surgery.

but, as in the former outbreak, it was impossible to ascertain the full extent of the calamity.

Improvement in the condition of housing at Devonport had been attempted some years prior to the second visitation, but the manorial system – the housing being leasehold not freehold – accustomed the inhabitants to look to the Lord of the Manor instead of trusting to their own efforts. The sites for the Town Hall, Public Library, Mechanic's Institute and various places of worship were invariably granted in answer to memorials requesting free gifts on public grounds; but the streets remained unwidened, obstructions continued to exist and slums were untouched.

Plymouth had advanced to commercial success so rapidly in relation to Devonport, in the first half of the century that the Court Leet jury at Devonport recommended the manor authorities to resume perpetual renewal and the buying off of existing leases. However in fear that this departure would involve *'legal doubts and personal risks'* owing to the *'very peculiar circumstances in which the property is place'* the trustees declined to sanction so radical a change. They did offer though, to encourage new houses *'of a superior class'* by conceding terms of from sixty to ninety years; and they also undertook, where leases had been granted on three lives subsequent to 1842, that the lessee may *'hereinafter renew within one year after the dropping off of each life, on payment of a fine, to be calculated with reference to the ages of existing lives, according to tables which will be prepared and kept at the Manor Office and be open at all time to the inspection of the lessee.'*

It was while these relatively modest symptoms of improvement were being effected that the second cholera visitation occurred, and found the squalid area of Quarry Lane in a beastly state from end to end, the houses being worse than the most common privies. There were loathsome cesspits and temporary contrivances; improvised drains overflowed through dilapidated premises and the pestilential odours were intolerable.

Every room was crammed with wretched, beastly and degraded creatures swarming with vermin and wallowing in filth; tenants washed and dried their clothes in the rooms in which they ate, drank, slept and cooked; and the fetid and sickening smell arising from these abodes of wretchedness baffled all description and was enough to produce the very worst of consequences.

Quarry Court was a similar abode of misery, calculated to sicken the heart and create abhorrence, disgust and pity. It swarmed with children, who bordered on a state of nudity and the women and men were not much better clothed. Anaemic infants and adults laid on foul straw mattresses stretched on mud floors and in the courts pools of stagnant water collected.

Morice Town meanwhile, was the haunt of every vice and misery of which human nature is capable, every third house was an inn; and the children swarmed in lanes in 'absolutely heathen ignorance'.

In his report, Mr Rawlinson, the Local Government Board Inspector, declared that Devonport and Plymouth ranked with Warsaw – the most insanitary town on the Continent.

These criticisms were resented by the Plymouth Improvement Commissioners who were rewarded for their neglect and formal statements of public grievance by an Act that improved them out of existence. However, nothing was done in Devonport until 1858 when Dr Row found fault with the manor authorities for allowing the abandoned workhouse in Duke Street to be colonised by 227 persons. A demand was raised for model dwellings, baths and washhouses, and a deputation was appointed to meet the ground-rent land-owner to promote these ends. However, difficulties were raised as to the suitability of sites and neither project was pursued.

Nevertheless, certain old streets, lanes and alleys in Devonport vanished over the next quarter of a century and ghosts of the past would have searched in vain for their former haunts.

When Fore Street was first remodelled, the houses facing the site of the Public Hall were recessed beyond the existing street line and the old-fashioned Rising Sun stood at the corner of Andrew's Lane, the narrow thoroughfare that led to Cherry Garden Street. The site of the existing South Western Hotel and Temperance Hall was a piece of No Man's Land and here travelling showmen, menageries, cheap jacks and others pitched their tents and caravans. A butcher's shop occupied the site of the Post Office and the way to Chapel Street was through Coxworthy's Court, a group of ancient tenements where many a deal took place in smuggled goods.

The Crown Hotel vanished and the Workhouse in Duke Street was demolished. Keame (Keyham) House still remained with its weather-beaten masonries – a delightful old mansion with quaint rooms, rambling passages and antiquated stairways. Its windows were furnished with stone sills and mullions, leaded lights and diamond frames and its hall was paved with marble.

The Three Towns were periodically decimated by smallpox and the heaviness of the affliction was due to the persistence with which, in spite of the medical manifestos, parents insisted upon inoculating their children, for smallpox, without using cowpox.

The disease made frightful ravages, every other person walking the streets appeared to be disfigured, and the few ladies who escaped with their beauty unimpaired were more than ever admired.

At the beginning of this century a number of our eminent local doctors – Vaughan May, Robert Sargent, Daniel Little, Richard Dunning, Digory Morris Spry, John Smith, John Lower, John Penkivil and John Bone – issued a statement lamenting the spread of the contagion by deliberate inoculation of the smallpox and detailed how they found inoculating their own families with *cow-pox* exclusively, to be the most decisive and satisfactory means of conveying to the public their reliance on this preventive for protection against the smallpox.

In 1872 the area was revisited by smallpox and hundreds of victims were mowed down. Panic was so widespread that the newspapers were prevailed upon not to publish the daily death toll.

When the epidemic had spent itself, I published a pamphlet, 'Overcrowded Plymouth' detailing the degree to which Plymouth had become, in certain areas, a dismal, overcrowded and insanitary place and parts of Devonport were no better.

Devonport Park and the Fore Street drawbridge c1860. (Bob Cook)

Before leases on lives were conceded here, every street contained insignificant and incongruous elevations, with windows of small diamond panes. After the concession the town awoke from its lethargy, and the main streets exhibited marked improvements:

Keyham Factory was finished; Raglan Barracks were completed; and the fleets more often in evidence. The flush of prosperity caused reconstruction to be steadily carried out. Weakley's Hotel passed away with its romantic roadside memories. A few doors west, the Fountain Inn was cleared, business premises rose upon the ruins, and 'The Modern Pompeii' as Devonport had been designated, emerged from desolation into daylight.

Mount Edgcumbe Terrace offered invitations to residential classes, Osborne and Wingfield Villas followed, and then Collingwood, Nelson and Argaum. Thus the suburb of Stoke became charming to view, and Mannamead advanced to greet her sister with graceful movement.

The old Brickfields, or Ordnance Fields, were conceded by the military authorities and converted by ready subscription into a Public Park in the late 1850s. The Swiss Lodge at the entrance, designed by Norman, followed the fashion set by Prince Albert, when he redesigned grounds and gardens of the royal residence, Osborne House, on the Isle of Wight. The upland that made Devonport Park was cleared at a cost of £1,000 and dedicated to the recreation of the inhabitants. The principal fountain in the park was erected to the memory of Sir Charles Napier, by seamen and marines.

Upon the sites of notorious rendezvous, churches and chapels were reared; St Mary's in James Street, St Stephen's in Clowance Street and St Paul's in Morice Square, were all built on land formerly covered by disreputable dens. Hope Chapel, in Fore Street, extinguished another 'loathsome by-way' and the Unitarian Chapel in Duke Street, blotted out a most unsavoury haunt.

The old search for the Post Office in Ker Street revealed the state of affairs in that district, socially and structurally. Virtuous ladies, eager for a line from their absent spouses, were compelled to take a circuit of half a mile in order to avoid the insults of Billing's Row, and the annoyance of Pembroke Street. Parents and children wondered what road to select and the worst nuisances to avoid.

After the tottering dwelling and narrow passage that supplied the entrance to Chapel Street were demolished, a new Post Office was raised and open access was provided to Fore Street. The barrier gates were condemned as a hindrance, dangerous and a nuisance and were removed 'without regrets'.

1849: Devonport's new Post Office

In 1855 there were only three freehold patches of land in the borough of Devonport – one of thirty-two acres, the property of the Couch family, and situated in Ford; Earl's Acre; and a portion of the Swilly estate, consisting of fifty-one acres.

The piece of freehold land outside manorial rights, belonging to the Couches, then became available, and attracted the eye of a local syndicate – the Devon and Cornwall Freehold Land Society. Mr GH Rundle was the moving spirit in its formation, and Mr Alfred Norman designed dwellings with open spaces that were unfortunately much curtailed.

Ford sprang into existence to meet the demand for workman's houses to which an unappreciative ear had hitherto been turned. At the manor dinner in 1872, the steward announced having made *'careful enquiry of the number of houses that he himself had authorised to be built since 1862, on the ground belonging to Sir Edward St Aubyn, and the total was 192 in the ten years.'* That was an evidence of prosperity which he thought was not at all discouraging.

The condition of 'The Cribs' next arrested the attention of the authorities. These warrens threatened to tumble around the ears of their occupants – persons so repellent that no citizen could enter without certainty of insult.

Bragg's Alley, an infamous spot, once tenanted by Admirals whom Nelson was accustomed to visit, was now abandoned to the corpulency and cracks, and the visitor wandered from court to alley, from alley to square, and from square to passage, until he despaired of escape from these infernal regions.

Bragg's Alley and its island squalors were extinguished under an Artizans' Dwelling Scheme, which found in Dr May an ardent enthusiast. The original intention was for the Corporation to complete the work they inaugurated, but the manor authorities recovered the freehold by erecting the houses, and the town raised to a common level the pits that abounded. As a result thoroughfares were widened, but the alterations intensified the overcrowding by driving the populations into districts no less dense.

The Railway comes to Devonport

Devonport never ceased to lament the sacrifice of its interests by the South Devon Railway Company, and its irritation resulted in the introduction of the narrow gauge system. A line, wholly independent of the South Western Company, was projected by the Devon and Cornwall Company, with an important station near Albermarle Villas.

The House of Commons passed the Bill, but, when the Lords were reached, the Great Western and South Devon interests were combined for opposition, and the measure was thrown out.

Indignation in Devonport found vent in a proposal to call upon the Town Clerk to resign his office. Councillor Aunger was the author of the resolution, basing his action on the fact that Mr Woollcombe had throughout been the chairman of the South Devon Railway Company, and that its board of directors had always been the enemy of Devonport. Reacting to the strength of feeling in the town following the rejection of the bill, the promoters determined to renew the application.

After a bitter battle of gauges and protracted arguments over sites, North Road Station was erected and the Devon and Cornwall Railway were empowered to carry a loop line to Devonport, and from the terminal station near the Rectory Grounds a branch to Stonehouse Pool was effected. Running powers over a portion of the Cornish Railway admitted of an entrance to Keyham, as well as over the South Devon Line into Sutton Pool.

Thus Devonport attained, in May 1876, much for which it had clamoured. All parts of the borough were decorated with flags and mottoes on the arrival of the first train, and the municipal procession and troopings of the guard were witnessed by delighted crowds. Eight hundred persons sat down to a banquet in the Goods' Shed, and several of the innkeepers closed their premises in the evening because their supplies of liquor were exhausted. The commemorative ode proclaimed:

The town will no longer be left in the shade
As the rail will be used both for pleasure and trade!
All hail to our guests: those who strove in the past,
To obtain us fair play, have secured it at last!

Devonport Market

The impact of the railway on local commerce was apparent long before this, however, and within three years of the railway penetrating as far west as Millbay, the foundation stone was laid (on 13 July 1852) for a new, purpose-built market complex in Devonport. The Italianate clock tower with commodious halls and accommodation either side were constructed to the designs of J Piers St Aubyn at a cost of £2,000.

Devonport Market seemingly as proposed by St Aubyn with an impressive gate and statue that never materialised. Plymouth Auction Rooms.

Even as the new market was being built work was underway to improve communications yet further. After much planning and an expenditure of more than £100,000, the Cornwall Railway Company secured an Act of Parliament authorising it to construct a railway through the county. Royal Assent was received on 3 August 1846 and although Isambard Brunel came down to look at the scale of the problem – of bridging the Tamar that same year, it was a long time before sufficient funding was available.

Brunel's father, Marc, himself an eminent engineer, had ruled out the possibility of a solution, but his son felt equal to the task and although lack of capital caused several years of inactivity (1849–52). By the summer of 1857 the western tube and truss section were ready to be floated into position and Brunel chose 1 September for the great event.

Across the Three Towns the occasion was treated as a cause for a general holiday with low computations estimating crowds in the region of 30,000–40,000. Brunel himself conducted the operation and no one was disappointed. Eighteen months later, when the second tube had been placed and the bridge was opened for the first time Brunel, who was very ill and soon to leave this mortal coil, viewed his masterpiece from a couch on an open carriage.

Prince Albert, having made the six-hour journey down from Windsor, performed the official opening ceremony some weeks before that, and the bridge was named 'the Royal Albert' in his honour.

2 May 1859: Prince Albert opens Brunel's Bridge.

Charitable Institutions

The same honour was bestowed upon the Prince Consort, albeit posthumously, four years later when the Royal Albert Hospital was opened on 1 December 1863.
The provision of a hospital for Devonport was due to Mr Thomas Woollcombe, Mr Alfred Norman – by whom the plans were prepared – and Miss Florence Nightingale, who arranged the chief wards.
The memorial stone was laid by Lord Mount Edgcumbe, on 17 June 1862, some six months after Prince Albert had died. Lord Mount Edgcumbe placed the promoters of the scheme, and every other local charity, under recurring obligations, by allowing his park to be used for fetes and garden parties to swell subscription funds.
Some five hundred people joined the procession from Devonport Town Hall to the grounds of the site. An address was delivered by the Rev John Huyshe, Grand Chaplin of England, and Corinthian, Doric and Ionic lights were displayed by the brethren.
The Government granted £3,500 towards the Lock Wards, then instituted for the treatment of unfortunate women – women with sexually transmitted diseases. However, the Act of Parliament which legitimised compulsory examination of women resulted in occasional abuses, and its repeal was advocated on the grounds that the liberty of the individual was violated and the statute law rendered it ethically indefensible. The Act was largely brought in, in the first place, because there was a major problem with the ranks both in the Army and Navy, but the men did not want to subject themselves to compulsory inspection, neither did the surgeons want to have to inspect all the men.

July 1862: the Earl of Mount Edgcumbe lays the foundation stone of the new hospital.

Devonport was an active centre of the propaganda and prosecutions were taken out against the constabulary for molesting virtuous females. As more and more women were detained on suspicion of being prostitutes so the level of protest grew. Thomas Woollcombe was the staunchest defender of the Act and did his utmost to preserve it, eventually public opinion prevailed and the Act was abandoned by Mr Gladstone's Government. After its Repeal women voluntarily tendered themselves for treatment when their case was desperate.

Even more distressing was the plight of the fatherless. So numerous were the bereaved of sailors and soldiers, and so urgent their claims, that Mrs Tripe, the wife of Dr Tripe, an old Devonport resident, made it her mission to do something about it.
Her efforts were not too warmly received, but after some years she enlisted sufficient support to witness the inauguration, in 1834, of the Devon and Cornwall Female Asylum in Lockyer Street. Concluding that a similar institution ought to be erected in Devonport, the Royal British Female Orphan Asylum was eventually set up with the expressed sympathy and financial support of Queen Victoria.
A house was rented as a temporary asylum until 1845, when the foundation stone of the new building was laid with Masonic ritual, in the presence of thirty thousand people. The building was completed at a cost of £5,000 and it was occupied by twenty orphans on the anniversary of Waterloo, in 1846.
As time went on the numbers largely increased, and the cholera epidemic of 1849, the fatal outbreak of disease on the *Eclair*, the destruction of the *Amazon* by fire, the wreck of the *Avenger*, and the foundering of the *Birkenhead*, found the doors open to many destitute children. The Crimean War and the Indian Mutiny next taxed available resources, and Mr Metham (Mrs Tripe's grandson, who continued her work), issued eloquent appeals to the nation, and the orphaned were furnished with timely shelter.
In 1872 national depression resulted in famine prices, and the home grew so overcrowded that extension was imperative. The Admiralty set aside £4,000 a year for the support of 200 girls, and this

particular asylum received fifty. The committee then made provision for a hundred more children at a cost of £6,000, and the Duke of Edinburgh laid the memorial stone of the new wings in 1874.
The loss of the *Eurydice, Atlanta, Serpent* and *Victoria*, with their chapters of harrowing grief for so many Devonport families, found the Asylum prompt in offers of relief, and the Afghan, Zulu and Egyptian Wars evoked the same merciful consideration and corresponding public benevolence.
Meanwhile, for establishing the Sailors' Rest thousands of gallant fellows owed an irredeemable debt to Miss Agnes Weston, who not only provided for their care on shore, but championed the interests of their wives and children. This noble woman, by offering a home to the seamen, was instrumental, more than any one person of her generation, in changing the habits of the service by preserving thousands from the perils of 'paying-off' and sending them to their wives and families flush of funds.

Left: *Naval cadet painted in Stoke c1850.*
Above: *Royal Sailors' Rest, Fore Street.*

Arriving in Devonport from Bath in 1873, to visit sailors she had been corresponding with, Miss Weston was asked – by a group of men from HMS *Dryad* – the following year to set up a temperance house close to the Dockyard entrance in Fore Street.
Two years later and working with Miss Sophia Wintz, with whose family Miss Weston had first lodged when in Devonport, she had raised sufficient capital to acquire a large house in Fore Street. Here they offered 'Coffee, Comfort and Company, for One Penny.'
Adjoining the property was a large hall, with a separate entrance to the street, and it was there Miss Weston held religious services. Before long another property had been added at the back of the premises and this was to be converted into dormitory accommodation for seventy men.
In emergencies caused by the loss of ships and men, Miss Weston was quick to take action: when Devonport was inconsolable for the loss of brave sons, and the Patriotic Commissioners jealously hoarded their accumulated stores, she sprang to the help of the bereaved with immediate relief. Chilling indifference and niggardly allowances were so clearly exposed by Miss Weston and Mr Kearly, MP for the borough, that the basis of administration was changed by Parliament.

Fire

Not all disasters happened at sea, or on the battlefield: fires were the occasion, as a rule, of serious panics, for buildings were so closely herded together, and the means of suppressing outbreaks so limited, that the worst was invariably feared. Whenever the alarm was raised, guns were fired from the ramparts, the drums beat to arms, lines of soldiery and sailors surrounded the district, the parish engine rattled to the scene, generally to be discarded by reason of rust or want of sufficient force, and an unending stream of workers passed in procession from wells, waterside or conduits, singing in hoarse chorus:
Fire, fire, fire down below
Bring a bucket of water
Fire down below!!
A dreadful outbreak laid waste to Pembroke Street in 1810. Pans, pitchers and vessels of every kind were requisitioned to keep the engine going, but all such efforts were unavailing, and it was only by destroying the roofs of several houses that the progress of the conflagration was checked. Five men fell with a dwelling that collapsed, but, strange to relate, then emerged unscathed from the smoking ruins.

The parish fire engine made its first appearance at a fire in Catherine Street, in 1828. When the outbreak first occurred not a soul was seen in the street, and the watchman did not present himself with his rattle until the flames had extended to the adjoining premises. The whole district was threatened for some time, and the troops experienced the utmost difficulty in preventing the crowd from plundering the deserted shops.

On another occasion, early one morning in January 1840, smoke was seen issuing from the Royal Hotel, in Fore Street. The start of the conflagration was in a bedroom occupied by Colonel Horndon of Callington. The floor gave way before he could be reached, taking the aged occupant with it. Guests and servants lost their way in the corridors, and it was only the shouts of the rescuers that enabled them to escape, blackened and burnt, to the open air. Bursting through the roof the flames shed illumination over the town, and, with the collapse of the walls, the parish engine was buried in the debris.

Later that same year, in September, the Dockyard was devastated by a fire that was little less than a national calamity, the destruction resulting in the loss of two line-of-battle ships and a frigate.

It was four o'clock on a Friday morning that policemen on duty near the three northern docks were suddenly alarmed by the appearance of smoke from the bows of the *Talavera*. This, with the *Minden*, another 74-gun craft, was being fitted out for demonstration purposes; and, in close proximity, was the frigate *Imogene*, which had been prepared for commission.

Cries and shouts induced the sentinels to fire their muskets in the air, and, in a few minutes, a large force of military and police was summoned. By this time the interior of the *Talavera* was on fire and the flames lit up the surrounding workshops, docks, and jetties, and a number of battleships in addition to those just mentioned.

The ringing of the yard bell, and the firing of guns, summoned the engines from various stations in the Three Towns, but their combined

September 1840, fire devastates part of the Dockyard.

efforts failed to stay the course of the conflagration. The hissing of timbers of the *Talavera* strained and parted with explosive gusts, and all expectation of saving her was abandoned. Attempts were thereupon made to preserve the Adelaide gallery, which, with its wide-spreading sheds, rose in imposing tiers to the left and right, the intermediate openings being filled with deals and loose timber. In this 'walk' as it was called, were stored the mementos of many a hard-fought battle, and scores of figure-heads of ships that had borne the brunt of some of the most famous naval actions in British History. At one end hung the flag under which Nelson fought and died at Trafalgar; and, at the other, the banner which streamed from the poop of the *Queen Charlotte* during the bombardment of Algiers. Here too lay the capstan of the *St George*, only just recovered at Spithead after it had lain buried for fifty years, and a Sphinx which had recently been rescued from the sands of Egypt and was supposed to be three thousand years old. All these relics of former times, after having passed the ordeal of fiery tempest action and rushing tempest, were now doomed to destruction,

The flames from the *Talavera* darted from under the coping of the shed in terrific volumes, ran along the paper-covered top, and engulfed the entire range of the gallery with its combustible contents. Roaring like a furnace the fire shot into the air; and thick masses of smoke rolled over the yard, now brightened to a dull red colour, as some portion of the building crashed.

The Talavera *and the* Imogene *burn to the water's edge.*

From the roof of the Adelaide gallery the flames spread to the covering of the south dock in which lay the *Imogene*. The frigate itself was ablaze, and the fire attained such dimension that the safety of the entire yard was seriously questioned.

In the near vicinity of the *Talavera* lay the *Minden*, and again and again the flames played across her bows. Water from a dozen engines was continuously poured upon her main-deck timbers and the planks of the forecastle; and, by superhuman efforts, the *Minden* was saved from the fate of her neighbour.

Meanwhile the flames raged with the utmost violence on board the *Talavera* and the *Imogene*, and along the sheds and the Adelaide gallery. As the dock occupied by the *Imogene* was surrounded by timber, and the stacks communicated with the sail-loft and storehouses, desperate efforts were made to destroy the connections.

In an hour and a half of the alarm the conflagration reached its climax. Amid hoarse cries, stubborn shouts, and wild cheers, the work of battling this volcano went forward. Shortly after six o'clock the *Talavera* and *Imogene* were burnt to the waters edge, the pyramids of fire settled down for want of fresh fuel, and bare and discoloured walls alone remained of the sheds and stores. The disaster was variously attributed to dockyard discontent, official stinginess, and the plot of a foreign power whose spies were *'seen gloating'* over the devastation.

The view that was finally obtained was that the presence of combustible material was sufficient to explain the calamity, and that the use of coal tar to prevent the *Talavera's* timbers from contracting dry rot accounted for her sudden envelopment.

Desperate as the situation was, it could have been much worse and happily, the *Minden*, which had been launched in 1831 was subsequently converted for use as a hospital ship and was relaunched eighteen months after the fire.

It had been in May 1834 that the Admiralty had started employing a Dockyard Police Force, although the service had actually been instituted the previous year in the wake of Sir Robert Peel's creation of the modern Police Force in 1829. Formed by remodelling the existing collection of Watchmen and Warders in the Yard, they had previously been without uniform, but now they were equipped with stove pipe hats and silver buttoned blue frock-coats, cut away at the front from the waist downwards.

Fore Street.

They carried an ornately decorated truncheon with the Sovereign's Coat of Arms and their own number and a rattle to raise any alarm. Happily Devonport remained free from alarms until February 1855, when Mr Hudd's spirit stores in Fore Street, ignited.

It was impossible to work the parish fire engine, due to a lack of water, and as the flames reached across to the other side of the street, so roofs and walls soon crashed there as well. A piercing wind blew in furious gusts, and the frost coated the hats of the firemen and icicles formed on the scorched timbers.

Eight years later Fore Street was again the scene of a serious outbreak. Mr Emmett, the proprietor of some oil stores in Princes Street, was going down to his cellar, to obtain a supply from a large drum, when the vapour came into contact with the lighted candle he was carrying.

The premises were ablaze on the instant, and the flames, now bright when the turpentine was being consumed, changed to deep orange or vivid blue as the sugar or tallows were reached.

The powdered remains of Mr Emmett were dug out from the cellars; and the Commercial Rooms which were built by Mr Thomas Husband, 'for reading and conversation', disappeared for ever.

The Dockyard Gears up for War Again

The susceptibility of wooden warships to fire, improved armaments and the weather, all helped hasten the demise of the graceful triple-deckers, but it was by no means an overnight change. These discoveries were not all made at once, and although steam was slowly asserting itself as the real method of propulsion and iron as the only defence against the devastating shell, the launch of the *Phoebe*, a frigate of fifty guns, shortly after the declaration of hostilities in the Crimea, showed that faith in wooden walls had yet to be abandoned. *Phoebe* was, in her way, a noble addition to the British Navy and, as the *Nile* quitted her moorings the same day, the occasion excited unbounded gratification. The *Nile* steamed down the harbour against wind and tide, at no very dashing rate, as it was considered imprudent to strain her engines to get under weigh but, after rounding Devil's Point, the speed was increased, and naval men were satisfied that steam would soon be the indispensable motive power.

An hour later, the *Phoebe* was despatched from the stocks, and glided into the Hamoaze amid loud and sustained huzzas.

Intense was the interest excited by the launch of the *St Jean*

1854: launch of the Phoebe.

D'Acre, the largest vessel yet constructed for the reception of a screw propeller, the invention that was rapidly revolutionising naval architecture. By connoisseurs she was voted a masterpiece of strength, and a superb combination of skill and beauty.

Soon the country had need of every ship and seaman it could command. Drive was the order of the day, past errors had to be rectified, and wondrous things were achieved in incredibly short periods. The completion of the *Exmouth* was urged and, amid the drinking of wine and the crashing of the indispensable bottle, she advanced to meet the rushing waters.

A few weeks later, on an ideal summer's day, the *Conqueror*, a line-of-battle ship of larger dimensions, although of the same class as the *St Jean D'Acre*, was consecrated to her purpose.

1876: Devonport from Mount Edgcumbe, Newman - detail (© Plymouth City Museum & Art Gallery)

Stirring were the scenes as the troops embarked for the Crimea, and the excitement overflowed as the Hussars pranced into Plymouth. The streets were thronged as the gallant fellows made their picturesque ride into Devonport; and after being billeted in the various inns, they assembled in Fore Street in the morning to gratify the locals. Men and horses alike were in splendid condition, and mighty cheers were raised when they moved towards the Dockyard gates, holding aloft the flashing sabres with which they proposed to shave the Russians.
As they embarked upon the transports, volley upon volley of cheering rose from the clustered decks of the steamships, and the cries were re-echoed from the manned yards of the picturesque three-deckers. Similar demonstrations marked the departure of the First Royals, and, as the regiment marched from the Citadel, and a sinuous line of a thousand men was seen coursing its way through the serried civilian mass.
And so the fervour of the Three Towns was rekindled by these patriotic displays, followed by moments of serious anxiety. Suspense was broken by overwhelming rejoicings when the success on the Alma and the storming of the heights of Inkerman came over the telegraph. The vessels in the harbour were resplendent with flags, salutes were fired from battery to battleship and from battleship to battery, and the church bells testified to abounding pride and universal relief.
The landings of hundreds of Russian prisoners from successive transports left no doubt as to the reality of the successes in the bleak Crimea; and the Millbay and other barracks once more overflowed with prisoners.
Thousands journeyed by road and rail in May, 1856, to witness the commemoration of the peace. Church bells pealed, ships fired salutes, troops were reviewed in the Brickfields, and the artillery thundered forth their rejoicing salvos. After dark the fleet burst into a blaze of light, on an arranged signal rockets formed variegated devices, and illuminations culminated in an emblematic device 'Peace'.
With the cessation of the war followed rigorous retrenchment and depression. The Dockyard regulations became more rigid, workmen were overhauled on leaving the workshops, and officers were detained if they could not give the watchword after nightfall.
Employees were often subjected to a second search and, if a wisp of oakum were found, they were summarily dismissed, so that the few survivors of the ancient prerogatives were suppressed with merciless hands. The close of war was marked, however, by an increasing tendency to more humane punishment. Although examples of petty tyranny were to be met with, the disposition was less brutal.
Thus a carpenter's mate who resented the goading tactics of a boatswain by cleaving his skull with an axe was tried in Hamoaze and sentenced to be hanged. When the prisoner heard the decree he fell to the deck, but the persecution was so clearly established that he was reprieved and the boatswain was degraded to the ranks. It wasn't long after that that the cat was abolished too.

Russian Prisoners at the Octagon.

Vanguard Rock

In 1858 attempts were made to displace the mass at the entrance to the Hamoaze, which was known as Vanguard Rock, because a ship of that name struck upon it. One of the huge cylinders that had been sent out to blow up the sunken fleet at Sebastopol, and had not been required, was filled with a ton of gunpowder and sunk so that the end rested in a cavity of the rock. Efforts to fire the explosive by galvanism and safety fuses were continued until successful, the cylinder eventually bursting within thirteen minutes after the ignition

1858: Vanguard Rock

of the fuse, and throwing up a cone of spray one hundred feet in diameter at the base and forty in height. So tremendous was the effect upon the surrounding water that sand and seaweed were piled in masses: the shore vibrated as with an earthquake, thousands of fish jumped into the air, and a heavy ground swell followed as after a storm. Many tons of stone were detached, and the rest was so split and cracked that the application of grappling irons and haulage easily effected its removal.

1878: breaking up the Racoon.

Iron and Steam

Over forty years had now elapsed since a squadron of fleet cast anchor in Cawsand Bay. In the early days of the century, Nelson's three-deckers were clawing off the shore. In 1872 Admiral Hornby's flagship was flying the signal 'Prepare to Ram' and ironclads were propelled through the water in pursuit of a 'powderless programme'. The old salts conjectured what the admirals of the Napoleonic era would have thought if they could have watched the winches, compressors and other machinery by which the *Sultan's* 400 pounders were moved with as much ease as the carronades of the old frigates, with their 18 and 32 pounders. The spectacle of a fleet of ironclads was no less a revelation to the Three Towns, and the shoreline was crowded with spectators when it steamed to sea.

Ships are all of iron now,
Floating tubs with rams for bow;
Nelson's tars would stare to view
What the Navy has come to!
Seamen walk in private suits,
Smart felt hats and patent boots;
And they're all teetotallers: Gracious! Whew!
What is the Navy coming to?

With the introduction of steam a large class of warship immediately became unsuited for modern warfare, and wooden ships that had never been to sea were sold, broken up, or sent to swell the procession in the Hamoaze, which became known as 'Rotten Row'.
The disposition of these vessels occasioned the Government a vast amount of difficulty; for whilst they were inevitably abandoned, it was necessary to prevent them from falling into the hands of a hostile country. Eventually they were broken up in the private yards, under the supervision of Government inspectors, the copper bolts being returned by arrangement.

Palmerston's Forts

At this period much activity was displayed in strengthening the defences of the Three Towns and a fort was placed at the western end of the Breakwater. Others were raised at Tregantle, equally commanding the Channel and Hamoaze; and Scraesdon, to prevent the approach of an enemy landing at Fowey. Staddon Heights, Picklecombe, Laira and other points were also rendered equally inaccessible. Ancient embrasures were removed from the Citadel, Armstrong guns were erected on concrete foundations, and a grand chain of communication around Plymouth, Stonehouse and Devonport was thus effected. As it transpired, the feared French invasion that stimulated this activity here and at Portsmouth never materialised. However, the construction of twenty-two major fortifications around the area gave a much needed boost to the local economy, during the 1860s.

Around the same time the North Bastion was removed (1864) having been superseded by the new fortifications and also in order to facilitate improvement in the contact between the two dockyards and to make way for other development in the area.

The North Bastion shortly before its removal in 1864.

The Zulu War

The Zulu War revived impressions in 1879, when the marines and other troops were despatched from the area. The troops made their way to the Dockyard through a tremendous crush and amid a ringing fire of cheering which at times overpowered the strains of the massed bands. The embarkation of soldiery was soon effected, and the *Jumna* steamship moved into the Sound amid the noisy shouts of thousands of dockyard workers who crowded the jetty, and tens of thousands of visitors who swarmed the slopes of Mount Wise and the rocks at Devil's Point.

And so the brave fellows embarked to the strains of a song specially written for the occasion:

So cheer up, my lads, let us join hands
Like Royal Marines in our brotherhood bands,
God Save the Queen, our watchword shall be,
Wives and sweethearts at home and Zululand free!

1879: the heroes of Rorke's Drift.

Local interest in the struggle was displayed not so much when the news of the reverse of Isandula came to hand, to excite a wave of humiliation and sorrow, as when the inhabitants heard, with immense relief and pride, of the glorious stand which was subsequently made at Rorke's Drift, at the instance of a St Budeaux boy, Major John Chard.
Elated by their victory, the Zulus were over-running the country, and it would have been no discredit if Chard and his comrade, Bromhead, had fallen back, as there were so many thousands of savage warriors in eager pursuit.
Resolving to stop an onrush which would have placed the colony at the mercy of the dusky warriors, Chard strengthened the small station at Rorke's Drift, of which he had been left in charge and, from behind a barricade of biscuit tins and mealy bags, he and his devoted little band fought many hours, brave fellows, continually falling around, the adjoining farmhouse ablaze, with wounded comrades within.
Exercising unwavering intrepidity, Chard wore down the Zulus, the horde withdrew discomfited, and credit of Great Britain was preserved.
In all on that night of 22-23 January 1879 some eighty men of the 24th Regiment of the British Army, held some 4,000 Zulu warriors at bay. It was the night after Isandula and the men were there to guard the commissariat stores and the hospital of Lord Chelmsford's force. Rorke's Drift was a station on the Buffalo River, in Zululand, South Africa.
Chard and Bromhead were both awarded the Victoria Cross and Chard well feted back in the Three Towns, with the Plymouth sword being presented to him in front of 3,000 leading inhabitants.
However, before Major Chard made his hero's return, Cetewayo, the Zulu King was brought to the port as a prisoner of war, and he left for London with as much attire about his prodigious form as when he was driven at bay after the battle at Coomassie.
When he returned to take his departure the noble native wore a faultless frock-coat and silk hat, and his gloved hand carried a silver-mounted walking stick presented by 'my brother, the Prince of Wales'.
Twelve months later the British troops emerged successfully from Tel-el-Kebir, and the Plymouth detachment of Royal Marines and members of the Royal Naval Brigade serving in the port were entertained at the Devonport Public Hall.

1865: The Royal Albert Hospital and the drawbridge at the top of Passage Hill.

Royal Visits

The Prince of Wales himself was no stranger to the area. In 1865, two years after his wedding which had been greatly celebrated in the Three Towns, the young couple paid a visit to the Royal Agricultural Society Show which was held at Pennycomequick, on the showground behind Devonport Prison.
Attended by the Countess de Grey, the Earl of Mount Edgcumbe, and a guard of honour, the Prince and Princess drove from the Royal William Yard, where they landed from their yacht, through the streets that were filled with multitudes and spanned by triumphal arches.
After lunching at the show yard, the royal pair and their suite went to Saltash Passage, and visited the warships of several nations that were then at anchor in the port.
A ball of unusual splendour was held at the Victualling Yard, at which the Austrian and French officers were specially welcomed and the Prince ascended a gilded throne to survey the scene.
On the following day the royal party visited Mount Edgcumbe, and the in the evening the Prince entertained a party on board the *Osborne*. The vessel was a blaze of illuminations, and the movements of guests were watched by thousands from the shore.

1865: the showground surrounds Devonport Prison.

Queen Victoria herself had made her first visit, as the 'future Queen of England' in 1833 and had been lucky to escape injury when the Royal Yacht, *Emerald*, had been carried under a hulk, causing the mainmast to spring in two places. Sail and gaff fell upon the deck and narrowly missed the Princess and her mother.

Here for several days, the Princess attended the Dockyard Chapel for a Sunday Service after which the party crossed to Mount Edgcumbe.

Ten years later, and now as Queen, Victoria and Prince Albert included the port in their marine excursion. Studious silence was preserved by the authorities as to their arrangements, but whispers of preparations escaped from the Dockyard.

When the royal yacht approached the port, the heights were swarmed by devoted subjects and a flotilla of pleasure boats sailed out to accord the fair young monarch welcoming cheers.

The *Hindostan*, a ship of ninety guns, then recently launched, was minutely inspected in the Dockyard, and the Prince was struck with astonishment at the panorama at Bunker's Hill.

The Queen was received on landing by the authorities of Devonport; and, reinforced by the officers of the garrison and the Lords of the Admiralty, the cavalcade moved towards Stonehouse. There the Mayor of Plymouth extended a welcome, and Her Majesty was escorted through Union Street to the Citadel. The party returned through Hoe Gate to No Place and thence to Fore Street.

Devonport tendered its thanksgiving to the Queen;

'Since the period at which we were last honoured by the presence of Royalty, most eventful changes have occurred in the domestic annals of the Borough. Its importance as one of your Majesty's naval arsenals has been acknowledged by the favour of his late Majesty King George IV, who bestowed upon it that name which now distinguishes it. The political changes which occurred in the reign of your Majesty's august predecessor have entitled us to address the legislature through representatives of our own election; but we owe to your Majesty's especial grace that final boon which by extending to us the benefit of municipal institutions, now enables us to express our loyalty and gratitude in a corporate capacity.'

As a reward for these compliments, the Queen sanctioned the substitution of the name of Devonport for Plymouth Dock 'in every bill, warrant, or quittance' and official letters were for the first time authorised to be addressed to 'Devonport' instead of 'Plymouth'.

The Queen paid her next visit to Plymouth in April 1846 and, on this occasion she received the municipal authorities on the quarter-deck of her yacht – the more fully to convince them that she wanted no public

1865: The Prince and Princess of Wales sail through a squadron of ironclads in Plymouth.

demonstrations. The chief object of the visit was to inspect Cothele. On sailing down the Hamoaze, the Royal Standard was dipped three times by way of homage to the battleships there lying in repose, and a crowd of officials and citizens on the deck of the frigate *Thetis,* which had just been launched, gave three hearty cheers. These salutes were re-echoed from the fleet of boats that extended from Cremyll Beach to Mutton Cove. On returning to the anchorage, there were some presentations, which were meant to have been formal. The commandant of the marines, however, much to the surprise of his brother officers, entered into a quiet chat with Her Majesty, asked as to her health, hoped the voyage had been agreeable, and enquired if she were a good sailor. The Queen did not resent these familiarities, but replied in her usual affable manner that the trip had been very pleasant, although she had suffered from sickness, and could scarcely claim to be hardy upon the water.

That night, as her yacht lay in the Sound, the lusty tars danced hornpipes, and rendered glee songs, in the presence of the Queen, and there was no attempt to abridge freedom or damp pleasures.

Six years elapsed 'ere the Queen revisited the Three Towns, and a request was on this occasion conveyed that no popular displays should be made. Nevertheless, each evening clusters of craft surrounded the yacht off Barnpool, and the varying hues constituted a lovely scene in the moonlight.

The Queen and Prince Albert landing at Devonport Dockyard.

1846 'Lusty tars' dance before Her Majesty and Prince Albert on board Royal Yacht.

The Queen's last visit to Plymouth was due to the accident of weather. She left Cowes in August 1856, to make for Jersey, but the squadron was compelled by gales to stand down Channel to westward. Her Majesty's arrival in the Sound, although unexpected by the public, was anticipated by the officials, and the *Victoria and Albert* entered Hamoaze amid a bright panorama of dressed ships and manned yards. In the storm the royal yacht had rolled heavily, and the Queen suffered severely from sea sickness. Upon her recovery, she visited Mount Edgcumbe and Endsleigh and drove through Devonport to visit the new steam factory. The troops were exercised on Mount Wise, but the artillery raised such clouds of dust that the review was abruptly curtailed.

As the weather remained gusty, the Queen returned to Windsor by rail, and, although Millbay Station was crowded with municipal officials, no attempt was made to interfere with her freedom of action, a consideration that Her Majesty evidently appreciated.

Transatlantic Cable

The year after her Majesty's last visit, a major experiment was undertaken to attempt the laying of telegraph cable from one side of the Atlantic to the other. In 1857, however, the attempt failed as the loss of 300 miles of cable rendered the quantity available insufficient for the task. Thus it was that in May the following year, Mr Cyrus Field, the American financier behind the project, funded a renewed attempt, which saw the two ships that had previously been involved – the *Agamemnon* and the *Niagara* – in the new Keyham yard, loading some 3,000 miles of cable to span the 1,950-mile gap.

Great was the rejoicing that August when the first transatlantic message was received in County Kerry from Trinity Bay, Newfoundland, and equally great the grief, two weeks later, when the cable broke – somewhere beneath the ocean, with no-one knowing if it could be repaired or not.

Mr Field, who had set up the New York, Newfoundland and London Telegraph Company in 1854, and who had exclusive rights to lay the cables, promised that if repair attempts failed he would simply have another cable laid. And that is precisely what came to pass, but only after another seven years had elapsed.

Even then it took another year before the link had been made effective, and our unfortunate Mr Field, who had made a fortune as a paper manufacturer, was to die a poor man, in 1892.

1858: transatlantic cable layers – Agamemnon *and* Niagara *in Keyham steam yard.*

Devonport Prison

Devonport Prison

At Pennycomequick, the extremity of the borough of Devonport, was erected, in 1850-51, from the designs of Mr Piers St Aubyn: the Devonport Borough Prison. It was completed just months after Plymouth Prison had been constructed without the precincts of the town, at the top of Greenbank Hill.

The style of architecture adopted is that of the fourteenth century. The officers' houses are placed together in the south front and designed in the domestic character of that period. The prison is provided with a chapel, necessary offices, and warming apparatus.

Deemed to be one of the most efficient prisons in England in its day, the weekly food bill per prisoner was one shilling and eight pence in 1870. Inmates received for the most part nothing other than bread and potatoes or Indian meal pudding in their first week, with soup, suet pudding and cheese (on Sundays only), for those serving longer terms. While the diet was fractionally below the minimum of a sustaining diet, even during inactivity, it is found that one short but tedious week of comparative fasting is quite long enough to affect the plumpness of the most robust prisoners, but as it is never prolonged beyond that period, it can rarely do harm.

In 1877 another Prison Act brought nationalisation of the service and of the 113 prisons that were subsequently taken over, Devonport was one of 38 that was closed. It was sold in 1881.

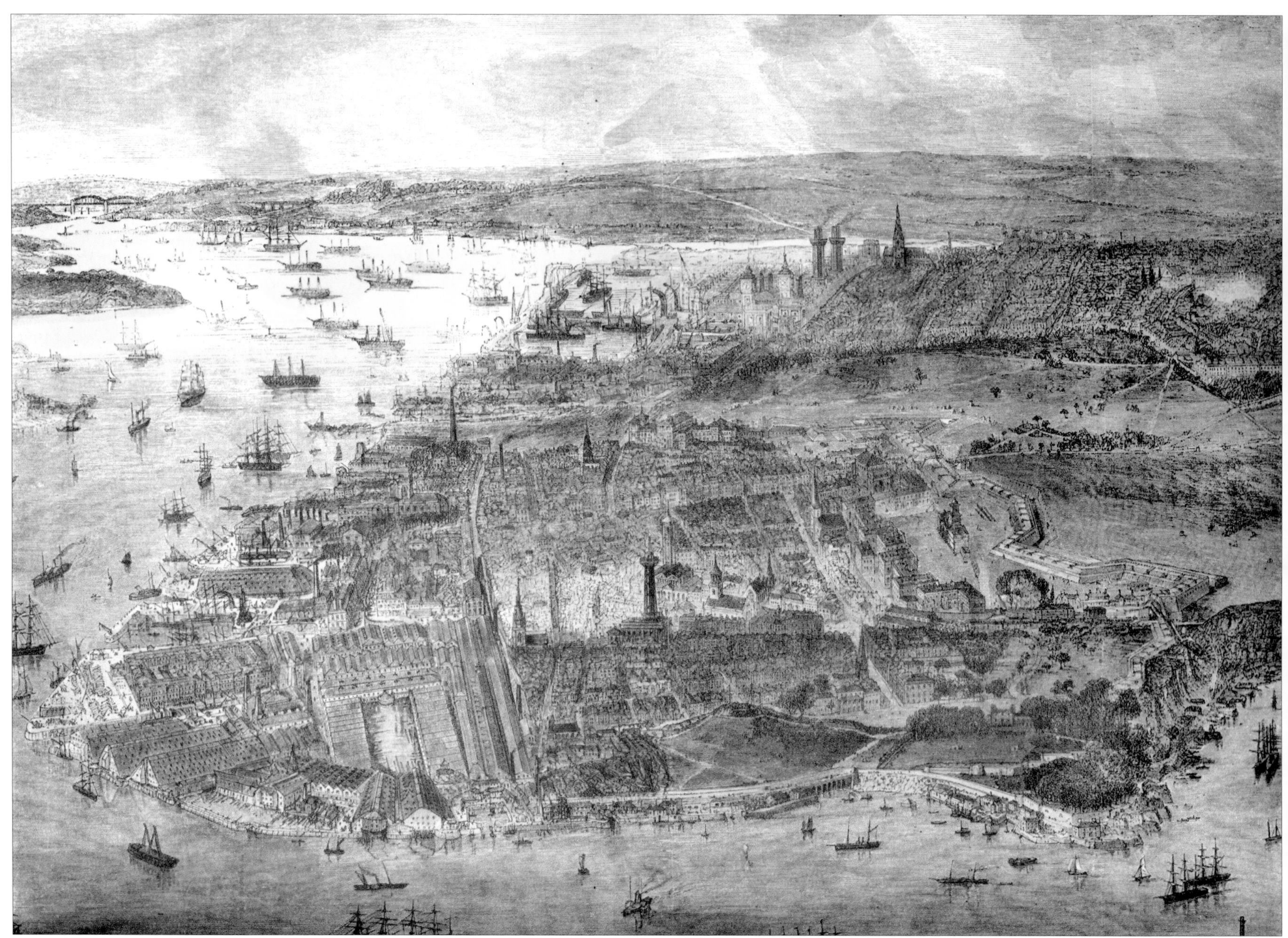

14 September 1872: Detail from a large format engraving that appeared as a 'Special Supplement' on that day to The Illustrated London News.

Devonport: A bird's-eye view in 1872

A most spectacular view of the Three Towns was issued as a Special Supplement with *The Illustrated London News* on 14 September 1872, for many people around the country - and beyond - it was the first opportunity they would have had to gain an appreciation of what this area was like and how the towns related to each other; here we show the Devonport section of that illustration and append the accompanying relevant passages of text.

The estuary of the Tamar, which divides Cornwall from Devon on the western side, expands into a grand piece of water called the Hamoaze, four miles long and nowhere less than half a mile wide, with a depth of fifteen to twenty fathoms, and anchorage for a hundred large ships.

The town of Plymouth, which has 62,000 inhabitants, is chiefly built on the west shore of Sutton Pool, with its seaward front upon a range of cliffs named the Hoe, from the Citadel to Mill Bay.

The town of Devonport, nearly a mile west of Plymouth, stands on the shore of the Hamoaze, where the naval docks are situated; it has a population of 51,000. Stonehouse, with about 14,000 inhabitants, but with great manufacturing establishments of the Admiralty, is a suburb between Plymouth and Devonport, on a rocky promontory, separated from Plymouth by Mill Bay, and from Devonport, by Stonehouse Pool.

The land side of Devonport has a strong line of fortifications, for which a broad belt of ground is kept open; and the inlet between this and Stonehouse runs up so far as to detach the town of the dockyards completely from its eastern neighbours; but there is easy passage to and fro by the bridges.

Devonport, which was first called Plymouth Dock, came into existence in the reign of William III, when a naval arsenal and dock were established at this place. Several other docks were constructed in the early part of George III's reign, and the Keyham steam-ship factory has been created in the last twenty-five years. Devonport obtained its incorporations as an independent town in 1824.

Boswell's Johnson, commenting on the tendency of mankind to disparage each other's merit, once remarked that *'the good people of Plymouth thought themselves very superior to the good people of Plymouth Dock'*. Neither of these equally respectable towns, we believe, is now inclined to turn up its social or municipal nose at the other.

Plymouth is the elder sister, the one more independent of Government patronage, and has more to do with the county aristocracy and gentry. It has fine public buildings; the Theatre, Assembly Room, and Royal Hotel forming one handsome pile of Ionic architecture; the Athenaeum, in the Doric style; and several stately churches, streets, crescents, and terraces of good private houses are to be found in Plymouth.

The architectural ornaments of Devonport are the Townhall and the Post Office, which are Doric; the Library, which is Egyptian; and Mount Zion Chapel, which is 'a curious combination of Gothic, Saracenic, and Hindoo'.

The dockyards, however, remain the chief objects of interest in this town; the Military and Naval Hospitals, and the official mansions on Mount Wise, where the Admiral and General commanding this station reside, are characteristic of its dependence on the two gallant services. A visit to the works of the ship building and repairing yards, the anchor smithery, the chain-cable store-house, the rope houses, the mast-house, the gun-wharf, and the steamer-factory, will excite the stranger's wonder.

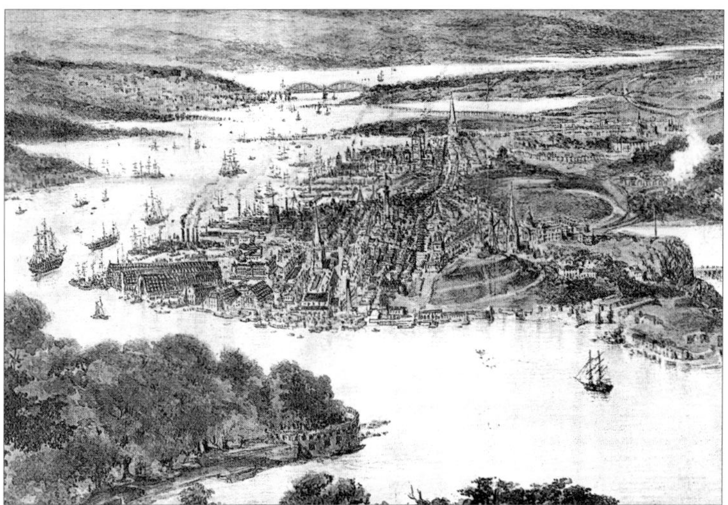

1873: Another, slightly less detailed, 'bird's eye view.

Pressing Issues

A fortune of war or flaw of fate caused the first number of the *Plymouth and Dock Telegraph*, or *Naval and Commercial Register*, to appear one week later than its contemporary, the *Plymouth Chronicle*, and the irritation of the former at being out-manoeuvred was ill-concealed.

The proprietors had resolved on the publication of the Telegraph twelve months previously and orders for type and other material were then despatched. *'Strange to say, we did not receive the most essential part of our plant until last Monday night and, in the meantime, an opponent has started up and entered into competition with us for the meed of public favour.'*

The two papers were the same size and price, the Dock paper being printed by L Congdon of 52 Fore Street, Dock. From the very beginning the relations between the papers were suggestive of the spirit of rivalry that scorned fraternal relations.

Occasionally there were problems with supplies of stamped newspaper sheets to print on – all papers were subject to heavy stamp duty and when the Legislature passed an Act allowing proprietors to charge an additional halfpenny on each paper, both the *Chronicle* and the *Telegraph* raised their prices to sixpence ha'penny, which, after tax, left only a penny ha'penny to defray the expense of newsmen, journeyman's wages, wear of material, and other incidental and unavoidable charges.

Thriving on the hunger for news during wartime, the crushing of Napoleon and the depression that followed the Peace proved fatal to the *Chronicle* and the two papers thereafter merged.

DOCK

[Price Seven-Pence.

Newspaper broadsheets had to have the tax stamp.

1819 saw the launch of the *Plymouth Gazette*, but it exhausted its resources and invective in fifteen months and was then withdrawn from the scope of public criticism.

The enfranchisement of Devonport and the extension of the suffrage in Plymouth led to the multiplication of ephemerals and between 1832 and 1836 some thirty different journals were started in and around the Three Towns.

THE

Telegraph and Chronicle.

PLYMOUTH.

SATURDAY, FEBRUARY 19.

Interment of his late excellent Majesty.

On Wednesday evening last the venerable remains of our good old King were deposited in a cell of mortality prepared by himself, wherein, sooner or later, he will be surrounded by the corpses of his numerous progeny, some of whom, to the second generation, by the providential inversion of the order of nature, are there before him, each in turn attesting the frailty of the life that now is, and sinking under the inexorable conditions of human existence!

1820 news breaks of the death of King George III

Many ephemerals were of the catch-penny order, but some – the *Devonport Independent*, *Plymouth Herald* and *Plymouth Journal* – were reared on more enduring foundations. Ever seeking to outdo their rivals, on the occasion of one particularly important Parliamentary division, which was challenged at three o'clock on a Friday morning, the *Dock Telegraph* went to press with the numbers within twenty-four hours and, as the distance from London was 216 miles, this was an instance of despatch never equalled by any provincial paper.

No sooner was the *Dock Telegraph* printed than the *Devonport Independent* obtained an early copy, and most unhandsomely reproduced the report without the least acknowledgement.

In 1851, when the 'taxes upon knowledge' were reduced, the *Telegraph* doubled the number of its pages.

In 1860 local journalism took a new and permanent departure when the first *Western Morning News* – a small four-paged paper – was published and six months later the *Western Daily Mercury* was started – on independent and undeviating Liberal principles.
The existence of two daily papers soon told disastrously upon the weeklies. In 1862 the *Plymouth Mail* was absorbed by the *Western Morning News* and, after a gallant struggle, the *Dock Telegraph* issued its last number in June 1863.
Expectation was strong when the *Western Daily Standard* was started in 1869, as the promoters had enlisted the support of influential partisans throughout the West of England, but in less than a year its proprietors confessed the utter futility of contending against their contemporaries.
The *Western Globe* represented another effort of the Conservatives to claim a political organ. It was started in 1873, and the county court proceedings that followed its demise indicated that its mission was rather mercenary than political.
In more recent years (in 1891) the *Devonport Independent* passed into my editorship and, relaunched as the *Western Independent*, recovered immediate reputation.
In the first article of the revised organ we set out our stall;
'The Western Independent *shall be the medium for ventilating and redressing grievances. It shall deprecate shams whatever their paternity may be. It shall excite attention whenever the drum of hollowness is being sounded. It shall protect the weak and encourage the strong to be generous. The intolerable evil of the household system it will not hesitate to impeach, and the axiom that property has its duties as well as its privileges we shall impress on Lords of the Manor with such object lessons as may occur at our doors.'*
A few years later the *Western Daily Mercury* passed into the hands of the Western Newspaper Company and, for the first time in its existence, was developed with ample working capital and the proprietors suddenly launched the *Western Evening Herald*, with Mr RAJ Walling at the helm.
In 1899, Councillor TH Gill, a Conservative, evincing the power of the press, confessed in public that the campaign against overcrowding, which mainly inspired the propaganda of the *Western Independent,* had led to the uprooting of the worst of the old manorial traditions of Devonport.

The Modern Pompeii

In 1882 the Lord of the Manor reported at the court-leet dinner that the amount of building during the year had been very limited, and was chiefly confined to completing works already begun. By not hurrying on unduly they avoided the danger of over-building. It was a bad thing when the desire to build was greater than the demand for houses, and houses became tenanted by a class of persons lower than those for whom they were intended.
Nevertheless, the Devonport Mercantile Association, especially through Mr William Lamb and Mr William Ford, as successive secretaries, continued to press upon the different authorities the need of increased accommodation for the working classes, and Mr Josiah Clark gave evidence on behalf of the town at the Royal Commission on Leasehold Enfranchisement, showing how closely associated were the depression for which Devonport suffered, and the dilapidations and overcrowding complained of. Mr Kearly, MP, reiterated the complaints in the House of Commons.
In 1895, I addressed an open letter to the Lady of the Manor: it was titled 'The Boy From The Back of Morice Square'. As a result of the pathetic revelations made by this typical street urchin, the Dockyard Dwellings Company was inaugurated, and land was conceded at sixpence per foot – subsequently raised to one shilling per foot – to admit of building operations without the interposition of middle-man or rack renter.

1895: the back of Morice Square.

Two years later I produced another pamphlet – 'The Curse of Devonport' – and in one day alone it sold 12,000 copies. In the preface I wrote:

Proceeding systematically through the borough slums, I could not fail to be impressed with those recurring views of ruined and collapsed houses which a casual visitor from a volcanic country might be excused for regarding as the evidences of a nineteenth century earthquake. Whilst Plymouth, indeed, has still its overcrowding evils, and is trying to cure them, the Manorial System of Devonport results in structural decay and public indifference.

The sanitary aspect, in truth, is almost inferior to the commercial consequences of that Leasehold Curse which has so long hung over the borough like a depressing cloud. Without malice, and extenuating nothing, the facts have been set forth, in the hope that revelation may be followed by reform so comprehensive and complete that Devonport may not only vie with Plymouth in the application of social remedies in the interest of the poor, but may prevail upon the Manor Authorities to loosen that uncommercial grasp on available sites which has for years been the cause of impoverishment to nearly every class of its community by giving to land in the borough a purely arbitrary value.

1895: more squalor at the back of Morice Square

One of the most interesting of the experiences was encountered at the back of Monument Street, where the cells of the old Devonport lock-up were being used as living – and dying – apartments. The ascent of 'Jacob's Ladder' as the place was historically known, I described thus:

As we mount this Jacob's Ladder by one flight of stone steps, and wind our way downwards by another flight of a similar kind – for the malefactors were introduced by one route and the officials by the other – we begin to speculate that the Lord may not be in this place – this Jacob's Ladder at the back of Monument Street – for the purpose of bringing home to the consciences of men in authority some sense of their responsibility.

What must be the state of affairs in Devonport, when cells, that passed muster in the days before prison reform became a phrase, are still used for the habitations of young children?

1895: James Street, soon to be the site of the 1899 Municipal Buildings.

Does not the existence of this ancient lock-up, does not the survival of the unfittest in this locality, point the moral of these disclosures, and demand that the note of human honour shall be loudly sounded in the borough!

'Just think of the sewage-sodden shillet, with those excrescences in the form of dwellings, shored up and buttressed to prevent their falling into the lane, tenants and all – for the sickening mass lurches forward every now and then, and supplies new cracks for escapement – and then put it to yourself whether we have not here idealised the Curse of Devonport.

As a result of these disclosures public opinion was aroused in the borough, and I was elected by the ratepayers of one of the most overcrowded wards – Clowance – to stimulate the movement. Feeling ran painfully high and, incidentally, led to administrative changes in the Council, Mr AB Pilling being elected Town Clerk.

The Mayor, Mr Thomas Waddon Martyn, a young man of exceptional gifts, threw himself into the work with passionate zeal, and the movement promised immediate realisation when his untimely death occurred. An overwhelming demonstration of sorrow ill atoned for a loss which much retarded progress.

I was elected Chairman of the Housing Committee and the wild rendezvous for cats and rats in Clowance Lane, James Street, and other districts, were cleared and reconstructed. The Housing Committee then undertook what their opponents ridiculed as a holiday trip to ascertain the methods pursued by other municipalities and, on return, counselled the immediate utilization of a site acquired for street improvement purposes in James Street, as also the area known as the Back of Morice Square or Ordnance Row.

There were accustomed delays interposed by the Local Goverment Board but, in October, 1899, in the Mayoralty of Mr W Hornbrook, I laid the foundation stone for the new buildings.

The effects of the agitation, however, had already been to induce the manor to throw their land upon a more open market: the inclusion of the freehold system of St Budeaux within the borough kindled for the first time in the history of Devonport the instinct of competition; and hundreds of houses were raised in advance of the achievement of the municipal programme itself.

1895: the rear of the dilapidated James Street dwellings.

Water, Fire and Snow

Another Devonport body I came to chair was the Water Committee. Elm pipes were used as the means of distribution for many years, but there was no provision for storage until 1830, when a site for a reservoir to contain four days' supply was utilised at Stoke. Before it was completed the leat was blocked by a heavy snowstorm, and the inhabitants were dependent on wells. When these began to give out and distress was universal, the Plymouth Corporation, who had maintained a free current by employing detachments of labourers, offered their neighbours the entire use of their night supply.

Just as the connections were being established at Brooklands the thermometer fell, and the snow storm was so heavy that the work could not be completed. Water was thereupon carried from Plymouth to Dock in hogsheads, for which 1s3d was charged. A town's committee visited the rise of the stream at Blackabrook and on returning they dispatched gangs to the scene of the obstruction and the leat was cleared.

Devonport was aroused to the peril of its public health in 1868 by the contiguity of Dartmoor Prisons to the Company's leat. The stream passed across uncultivated land lying between Princetown and the settlement, and the village soil was carried over the cut in a wooden trough, and that of the prisons underneath by means of a dyke. These troughs were so saturated that more sewage passed into the leat than over it or under it.

For the purpose of irrigation and manuring, the adjacent land was also traversed by open drains, and thus the surface overflow was carried direct to the stream. A dyke running parallel conveyed the drainage to the various troughs, and the contents had found their way to the supply. The condition of the banks generally was so disgusting that Dr Munro was called in by the Council to report in detail, and Dr Wilson testified that monstrous rats waxed fat and sported in the leat by the dozen.

Loud were the calls for instant redress, but the Company argued that the Government ought to remedy the difficulty. Application was made in 1876 for an Act conferring power to carry out filtering beds and other works. Resistance to increased charges was unavailing, and the rate, which then stood at 16s, with 8s for water closet, on houses within the lines, and at 20s a year, with 10s, for water closet, on houses without the lines, was raised in harmony with rentals, the highest being £3.10s a year for houses not exceeding the annual value of £80.

In 1895 a court case concerning the Company's charges led to a clamour for the Devonport's Municipal body to purchase the water works. The principal was endorsed by the Council in 1898, but the sudden death of the Mayor Martyn, who had animated the dry bones of Devonport with his reforming zeal, dislocated the various schemes with which he had been associated. Some months later, as Chairman of the Water Committee, I reintroduced the subject, but despite winning several major votes on the matter over the next few months, there was sufficient disharmony to prompt my resignation and the committee was dissolved.

Local water supplies were severely tested one night in June 1894 when there was another serious fire in the Dockyard. Attributed to the leaving of an unextinguished pipe in the coat pocket of a workman, the scene of the fire was a large store opposite the Quadrangle in which the authorities reside. The alarm was set at ten o'clock on a Saturday night, and an unmanageable crowd gathered in a few minutes and the precincts were impassable. The store was full of combustibles, and the flames shot to a great height. Excitement was unbounded as the workmen dreaded a catastrophe that would deprive them of employment. The fire was suppressed in two hours, however the building was gutted.

Devonport Corporation cleansing department team c.1900.

There had been another major fire three years earlier, during the blizzard of March 1891. In one night the streets of the Three Towns were covered with snow to the depth of several inches, trees were uprooted within the town, houses were unroofed, and attempts at vehicular traffic were abandoned.

The fire that broke out that night was at Wingfield Villa, and the flames could be seen from all parts of the Three Towns. Thick flakes of snow dropped upon huge tongues of fire, the falling water froze into fantastic icicles on the angles of the building, and the hair of Mr J Burns, the captain of the Devonport brigade, and that of his colleagues, was rigid from the same cause.

Crowds endeavoured to reach the scene via Millbridge, but the force of the hurricane rendered it impossible to pass, and the waters of Stonehouse Pool could be heard dashing against the walls.

At daybreak, the area was isolated from the rest of the country. Trains ceased to run, several were snowed in, a few came into collision with serious results to life and limb, and the telegraph wires were everywhere blown down. Huge drifts blocked the doors to hundreds of dwellings, windows were enveloped in frozen snow and the Plymouth and Devonport leats were so buried under masses of ice, that the water supplies ceased to flow.

1891: the snowbound water steps – Milehouse.

A notable side effect of the blizzard was that it precipitated plans for the building of a reservoir on the moor. The massive undertaking was eventually completed seven years later and a medal was struck bearing the legend: '*Burrator Reservoir, constructed to avert the danger and hardship to which the town was formerly liable.*'

The year following, 1899, the Three Towns were visited by a drought of unusual duration, and the inhabitants of Devonport were partly supplied from the reserves which their neighbours had been able to make – the supply taken by the company amounting on some days to a million gallons.

1891: the Great Blizzard hits Devonport Park.

Devonport Dockyard Expands Again

Coincident with the development of Devonport, and the adaption of its dock to the most ponderous types of battleships, was the appointment of Sir William White as Chief Constructor of the Navy. His genius had evolved more splendid examples of the ironclad than all other shipbuilders of the modern world, so that if Devonport failed to produce an admiral of enduring memory, its training school for young apprentices yielded one man whom England required in her increasing struggle to maintain indisputable maritime supremacy.

Devonport, which had hitherto been restricted to the construction of second-or third-class cruisers, was now admitted to the privilege of turning out leviathan ironclads; and modern slipways were constructed to admit of their being successfully launched.

The *Ocean* was the first of the class to be laid down, a vessel of 12,950 tons displacement, with engines of 13,500 horse-power. She was christened in July 1898, by the Princess Louise, in the presence of a brilliant throng of spectators, and launched amid a chorus of sirens and foghorns.

Preparations were forthwith made for building in the same space an even more gigantic battleship, the *Implacable*, an improved *Majestic*, of 14,900 tons displacement.

1899: launch of the Implaccable.

She was launched in March 1899, after being seven months on the slip, by Lady Ernestine Edgcumbe, gliding majestically to the waves, and so easily that scarcely a ripple disturbed the surface of the Hamoaze.

Thus Devonport was restored, in an incredibly short space of time, to one of the first of the national shipbuilding establishments and £10,000 was paid every Friday in Dockyard wages.

No sooner was the *Implacable* despatched than the *Bulwark* was laid down – the stateliest and most imposing ship of the trio. She was launched in September, 1899, when the port was once more throbbing with war sensations, departures of troops and preparations for meeting the challenge to the Boers for supremacy in the Transvaal. The suspense was less prolonged, though no less acute than of yore, for the telegraph was now at work; but the enthusiasm was as high as ever as regiment after regiment marched to the railway stations, and fired their royal salutes from the carriage windows whilst the engines raised their first puffs towards Southampton, the chief port of embarkation.

Once more Plymouth rejoiced over the thrilling charge up the almost inaccessible hill at Glencoe, which was led by its heroic and familiar neighbour, General Symons, of Hatt, near Saltash, and gloried in the achievements of the Devon Regiment at Elandslaagte.

1902: start of work on No.5 basin of the Dockyard extension.

Further imposing naval additions and gigantic dock extensions at Keyham were simultaneously in progress. One hundred acres were enclosed within a huge dam by the contractor, Sir John Jackson, and forests of timber were imported for the purpose of carrying out a scheme admittedly destined to render Devonport the first naval rendezvous in the world.

A huge tidal basin with a water area of over thirty-five acres, or four times the size of the largest basin in existence at Keyham, is the leading feature of this development, whilst a tidal caisson will admit of direct communication with Hamoaze.

Three graving docks, to be connected with the basin, and an entrance dock, all in parallel lines, are to communicate at one end with the tidal basin, and at the other with an open basin, so that battleships of the largest class may hereafter be docked at Devonport.

When the millions of sterling contemplated for the purpose have been expended, one long line of Government depots, docks, and ships will extend from Devil's Point to Bull Point.

1903: the Dockyard extension takes shape.

Growth of the Three Towns

The character of the County Council's Bill in 1888 was so revolutionary that it almost took away the municipal breath. Devonshire was to be constituted a parliament for purposes of local government, and instinctively jealous of Exeter as the capital, the Three Towns urged the responsible minister, Mr Ritchie, so to divide the county that the Southern and Western representatives should assemble at Plymouth, and urged that such an authority would be powerful enough to kill many of the evils to which *'cliques, cabals, and caucuses have too long been giving rise'*.

As Mr Ritchie nervously yielded before sundry persistent opponents the disposition in Plymouth was to contract the scope of reform by becoming a county of its own; and, in Stonehouse, Dr Christopher Bulteel earnestly commended the amalgamation of the Three Towns. Whilst Plymouth sought to preserve its integrity, Devonport grew apprehensive of absorption, and its representatives made desperate efforts to reduce the standard of population of the exempted boroughs so that it might also be constituted a County Council.

Mr Ritchie was not sympathetic to such proposals and nor did he think there was mileage in grouping Plymouth, Stonehouse and Devonport, 'which are geographically one large town, and contain 140,000 inhabitants', as a county.

Finally it was argued that Plymouth should be made a county of itself, the measure was emasculated to meet that and similar cases, the downgrade continued to grow in favour, and Devonport was equally successful in continuing its own identity, although it was below the minimum limit of population. Soon afterwards an act was passed that abolished the scratching system of electing guardians, and the ballot was substituted in its stead. To complete the scheme of uniformity the Devonport Board of Commissioners were replaced by a more compact and regularly elected body of Poor-law representatives.

Plymouth grew apace and in 1894 it applied for powers to amalgamate the parishes of East Stonehouse, Compton, Eggbuckland and Laira, and with the exception of Stonehouse, was successful.

Controversial plans to convert the Cattewater into a harbour capable of accommodating ocean liners were eventually approved by a public vote but were then vetoed by the Lords of the Admiralty, who blocked the scheme on the grounds that ocean liners in numbers would too largely draw upon the two deep water channels that admit of entrance to the Sound.

Nevertheless, the town continued to grow, but there was a temporary pause in the Plymouth pace in the wake of the sudden loosening of land in Devonport in response to the insistent demands for workmen's homes.

In 1897, the advent of Mr AB Pilling as Town Clerk, a scheme of borough extension, which had for a long time existed in a nebulous condition, became materialised at Devonport. There were many reasons for the desired annexations. The population of the old borough had overflowed into the outlying districts, and converted them into thickly populated areas, which, though urban in character, remained under rural government. So little had the District Council coped with the needs of these districts that the inhabitants applied for powers to transform St Budeaux into an urban community. Another reason for the expansion was the necessity of safeguarding the health of Devonport by controlling these suburbs. Insanitary conditions prevailed that might easily become a general menace, and it was advisable to control the mudbanks, covered with water at high tide, known as Weston Mill Creek, which formed part of the northern boundary.

Another important reason for amalgamation arose from the fact that land in the old borough was almost entirely within the disposition of the Lord of the Manor. The absence of free trade in building had made Devonport one of the most overcrowded towns in the country, and, by the enlargement of the borough, it was anticipated that a gradual dispersion of the inhabitants would take place, and the congestion would be steadily relieved.

As Devonport was bounded on the south and west by the water of the Hamoaze, and on the east by Plymouth and Stonehouse, the only possible direction of development was northwards. Despite vigorous opposition from St Budeaux Parish Council and other local bodies the order was confirmed in the House of Lords.

The old borough consisted of 1,925 acres, with a population of 60,000; the extended borough comprised 3,173 acres, with a population of 63,000. The added areas were granted a representation on the Council of twelve members, and the number was thus raised from 48 to 60.

The extension of the Devonport boundaries was followed by the investiture of Sir William White (the Chief Constructor of the Navy), Alderman JW Ryder and Alderman Joseph May, with the freedom of the borough. Mr William Waycott was Mayor when the extension order was passed and confirmed. The bounds of the extended borough were first beaten in the Mayoralty of Mr William Hornbrook in 1899, and, before the end of his year in office, the first sod of an electric system of tramways connecting the added areas with Devonport was cut at Camel's Head by Mr William Waycott, chairman of the Municipal Committee, at the request of the directors of the two companies who had obtained the powers, enabling the Council to buy at the expiration of fifteen years.

That same year, 1899, the Devonport Technical Schools' building was formally opened. Built to the design of Mr HJ Snell, the tower had a fine peal of bells presented by Alderman John James, three times Mayor of Devonport, while current Mayor, Mr Hornbrook, contributed the stained-glass window by Fouracre, depicting the development of naval architecture within the career of Sir William White, who had been a student at Keyham.

A pleasant reminiscence of the 1897 Diamond Jubilee Celebration at Devonport (when the foundation stone of the building had been laid) was the activity of Alderman John Rider, who was elected a member of the Corporation in the first year of Victoria's accession and continued to sit uninterruptedly, including nine times as Mayor.

1899: Camel's Head bridge lovingly known as the 'Switchback' and later, 'Shakey Bridge' as it moved when traversed and was only fit for pedestrians.

Late-Victorian Fore Street, prior to the arrival of the tram.

Amalgamation *Chris Robinson*

Blighted by pockets of poverty it may have been, but Devonport was nonetheless still one of the most important towns in the South West and although it had long since been eclipsed by Plymouth as the biggest town in Devon and Cornwall, with a population of around 80,000 it was still a significant player locally and nationally. Meanwhile, taken together, the Three Towns – Devonport, Stonehouse and Plymouth – made a formidable conglomeration.

Following the Parliamentary Tramway Act of 1870, the Plymouth, Stonehouse and Devonport Tramways Company became the first such company in Britain, and their tramline – which ran from Derry's Clock (Plymouth) to Cumberland Gardens (Devonport) has been described as the *'grandfather of all legitimate tramway companies.'* The route opened on Monday, 18 March 1872, and was a single track with eight passing-places along its 1.9 mile length (it was officially one mile and 74 chains, there being 80 chains to a mile). Two years later the route was extended deeper into Devonport, taking in Fore Street and Marlborough Street, adding just over half a mile to the length of the route; a route that was serviced by eight tram cars and some 78 horses.

Known locally as 'green trams' on account of their pale green livery – which had a white lining – the trams were pulled by two horses each of which were required to do around 10–12 miles a day (about two complete circuits). Negotiating the 1-in-11 incline of Devonport Hill would require two extra 'trace' horses and no standing passengers – 'straphangers' – were permitted as the trams went up or down the hill.

Above (left and right): *horse trams, having traversed Ha'penny Bridge, Stonehouse, start the long haul up Devonport Hill.*

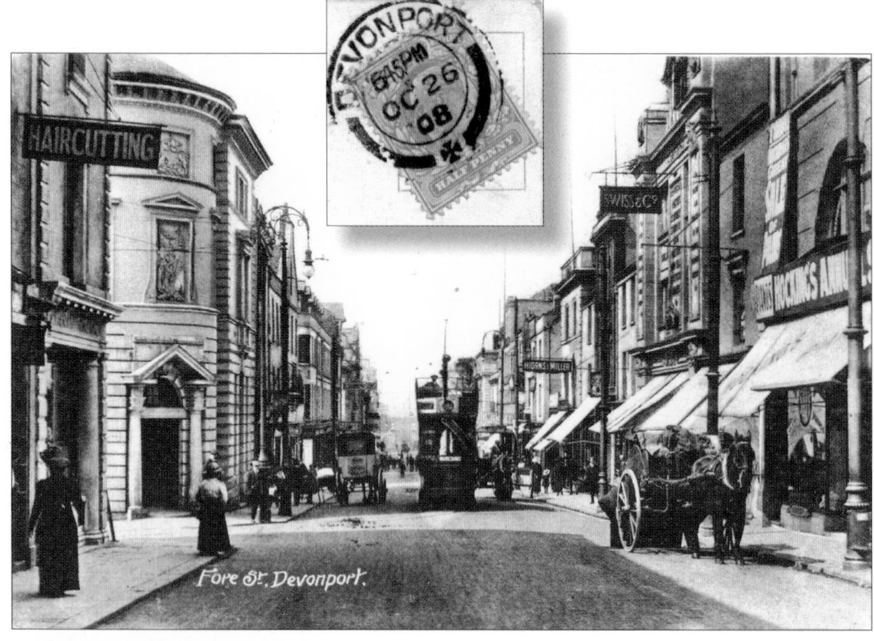

Top: *Fore Street with the Post Office on the left.*

Left: *The Devonport and District Tramways badge.* Above: *Fore Street with its new electric tram service.*

The service settled down to run daily between 8.30am and 10.30pm and was a huge step forward in the provision of public transport in the area Everyone over the age of three had to pay full fare and the maximum charge was threepence for travelling from any part of Plymouth to any part of Devonport – although you could save a ha'penny if you were prepared to sit outside. There was no service on Sunday mornings, but otherwise the trams ran every five or ten minutes.

In 1882 a more ambitious steam-tram enterprise was started under the auspices of the Plymouth, Devonport and District Tramways Company Limited. Although the steam initiative soon faltered the new company was given permission to develop seven lines, three of which were to service Devonport and in time the company became the dominant local provider as Plymouth Corporation Tramways in 1892. However, despite going 'electric' seven years later, they showed little inclination to include Devonport in their early plans and so it came to pass that in 1898 the Devonport & District Tramways Company was formed and was granted powers to create five miles of track within the borough.

Bearing the magnet-and-wheel crest of the British Electric Traction Company (who were behind the operation), the Devonport company used electricity produced by the Devonport Corporation power station alongside Stonehouse Creek. The twenty-odd American-built trams which went straight into service in 1901 were painted chocolate brown and cream and the drivers and conductors were instructed not to make *'disparaging remarks about the management of routes, or about the Officers of the company'*, nor were they to *'enter into unnecessary conversation with the passengers,'* or *'to make signs, motions or signals of any kind to men in charge of other cars'*.

As the service entered its second year there were a number of incidents and accidents, two of them – one fatal – involved a failure to be able to stop vehicles: one in Albert Road; the other, more serious, coming down from Stoke Village past the back of the recently erected Technical Schools building. The third accident was also in that vicinity, occurring when the No. 8 tram was taking a corner by the London & South Western Railway Station at King's Road and was apparently derailed by a flint-stone in the tram track. A Great Western Railways horse wagon was hit in the process, but none of the sixteen passengers were seriously injured.

William Street at the turn of the century. (SWiB)

Inside Devonport Station c1890.

The Devonport & Stonehouse Railway Station was opened on 17 May 1876, somewhat frustratingly a good twenty-five years after Plymouth had been connected to the Great Western Railway network, although the Cornish Railway had built a station on their line into Cornwall off Albert Road (then Navy Row) in 1859 – it opened on the same day as Brunel's Royal Albert Bridge was opened.
The new station, just beyond the Brickfields, was contemporary with the new LSWR (London & South Western Railway) connection via Lydford and Tavistock and complemented the subsequent opening of the new LSWR station at North Road. Opened in March 1877 the new station at North Road (which was roughly where Brunel had originally wanted to site his station for the Three Towns) was shared with GWR.
Around the same time, and to the same design as the Devonport and Stonehouse building, a goods shed was erected at Friary, Plymouth, and a goods line was established beyond Devonport and Stonehouse to Ocean Quay.
Clearly the upshot of all this for the people of Devonport was an improved service and although originally a terminal station, Devonport (the Stonehouse part of the name was soon dropped) Station became a through-station and, in 1890 and just a few years after that, the facility at Ocean Quay was improved to take passengers.

The idea here was that travellers crossing the Atlantic on the many liners then crossing the ocean could be brought to land by tender and whisked up to London well in advance of those passengers who remained on board until arriving in Southampton.
The competition for trade didn't end there however, and a fierce rivalry was played out between LSWR and GWR with regard to which railway provider could get their ocean going passengers to London first from here – the former from Ocean Quay and Devonport the latter from Millbay.

The first recorded encounter was in 1904 and GWR managed to get their customers to Paddington a good nineteen minutes before the LSWR train pulled into Waterloo. Over the ensuing months the 'contest' intensified, speeds of over 100 mph were claimed and a journey time of 3hrs54mins was achieved. However, in 1906, the driver of the LSWR attempted to take 30mph curve at Salisbury at around 70mph in the early hours of the morning and the train was derailed – 24 passengers were killed, and the 'racing' stopped.

Top: *Devonport Station exterior.* Below: *Ocean Quay terminal.*

Top left: *Boats could be hired, with or without watermen.* Top right: *The Torpoint Ferry.* Above: *North Corner – five pubs and the piermaster's house fronted Cornwall Beach.*

Getting In and Out

While the train and the tram improved the access and egress into and out of Devonport there were still only the three principal routes in: Fore Street, Devonport Hill, and New Passage Hill.

The latter was the principal link between old Devonport and Keyham, Ford, Camel's Head, King's Tamerton and St Budeaux. The stretch between the Albert Gate (the entrance to Keyham Steam Yard and Ferry Road where it met the bottom of New Passage Hill) was particularly busy and, not surprisingly, was lined with pubs. This was William Street, where many a wage packet was broken into at the end of a week's work before the owner could get it home.

Devonport was in fact littered with little pubs and beerhouses, there was one on nearly every junction and street corner, and the road down to the ferry was no exception. New Passage Hill itself, however, was an exception, with part of the Gun Wharf – Morice Yard – wall on one side and Devonport Park and the Royal Albert Hospital on the other, there were no pubs or other properties lining the way, although, at the top of the hill the Marlborough Hotel was there to welcome weary travellers.

Meanwhile, for those arriving by water other than by Torpoint ferry, luxury liner, or one of the Royal Navy's many vessels, Cornwall Beach (North Corner) and Mutton Cove were the principal points of entry, and they too were well provided with licensed premises.

Top right: *New Passage Hill.* Bottom: *The Royal Albert Hospital and the Marlborough Hotel.* Above: *Mutton Cove.*

Top left: *In the kitchen. Top right: In the coffee bar.* Bottom left: *Field gun exercises.* Bottom right: *Jack as a telegraphist at the barracks.*

HMS Vivid

Outside the old town, but nonetheless very much a part of Devonport for generations of sailors, are the blocks of the Royal Naval Barracks below Camel's Head Creek. They were first occupied on 4 June 1889. These buildings provided much-needed land accommodation for men who had previously been based in old ship hulks after being paid-off from a commissioned boat. They were laid out, as much as possible like a ship's mess deck: each barrack block had four barrack rooms with accommodation – 'that is to say for hanging that number of hammocks' – for 125 men. The idea was that 'when Jack is not wanted at sea, he is better off in a building of this nature than in some obsolete hulk where space and light are minimal.

Further blocks were added in the following years and in 1891 a grand ball was held here in honour of the Commander-in-Chief, HRH the Duke of Edinburgh (Prince Alfred). Some 1,200 guests attended and between them consumed, amongst other things, 576 bottles of champagne, 540 bottles of spirits, 3,000 bottles of soda and 6,800 oysters.

The clock-tower at the entrance was added in 1896 and the impressive wardroom was completed seven years later.

Although for the greater part of its history the complex has generally been referred to as the Royal Naval Barracks, Devonport, it was initially known as 'Vivid'. HMS *Vivid* was the name of the Commander-in-Chief's yacht, and that was the name worn on 'inmates' cap bands until 1934.

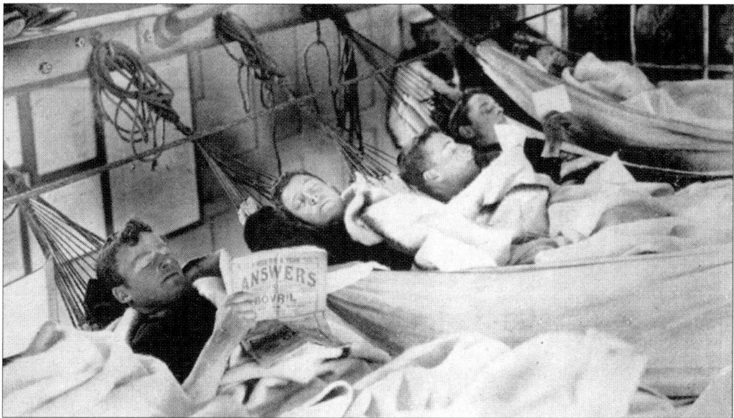

Above: *Jack in his hammock 1906*. Top right: *HMS Drake*. Right: *The Clock-tower.*

On 1 January that year the Admiralty approved the new name – HMS *Drake* – and on 24th of that same month some 3,000 cap ribbons were changed. The change had arisen from a suggestion made the previous year by the then Commander, Jack Egerton, at what was the first of many annual Drake Dinners.

However, although the name of Drake became official for the Barracks from that point on, throughout the 1920s and 1930s another name was more commonly used to describe the barracks.

On 1 October 1911, Alphonso Jago was appointed Warrant Instructor in the Cookery, where he remained until his death in 1928. During that time Mr Jago was responsible for a major change in the serving of naval nosh. The change involved a move away from eating in messes and towards eating in dining halls. It became known as the general mess system and was officially accepted in 1922. The system spread rapidly throughout the Royal Navy and it earned 'Vivid' the nickname 'Jago's Mansions'.

17 June 1905: the long metal hull of the 15,000-ton Hibernia *is about to hit the Hamoaze, where we see one of the last of the great wooden warships, HMS* Impregnable *sitting here behind the* Circe*, a training hulk that was built at Devonport in 1827.*

Aggie Weston

An even more popular name among naval personnel than Jago, however, was that of Agnes 'Aggie' Weston. A great friend of the sailor and a great supporter of temperance, Aggie Weston paid her first visit to Devonport in the early 1870s and quickly proved so popular that a deputation was made imploring her to open a temperance house close to the Dockyard gates. This she did in 1876 offering 'Coffee, Comfort and Company' ... all for penny.

So popular did this institution become that similar enterprises were opened in Portsmouth, Portland and Sheerness. Furthermore, it wasn't long before the Devonport experiment was expanded, firstly by the purchase of a second, neighbouring building and then, just over ten years later, by the purchase of the whole of the Fore Street/Edinburgh Road corner site, leading to the opening in the late 1880s (around the same time as the Naval Barracks were first occupied) of what became in 1892, thanks to a Royal Warrant from Queen Victoria, 'Agnes Weston's Royal Sailor's Rest'.

Designed by HJ Snell, the building cut an impressive silhouette to the south and east as sailors passed through the Dockyard Gates and 'Aggie's' won a special place in the hearts of naval personnel far and wide. Miss Weston herself was accorded full naval honours at her funeral in 1918 and was buried in Weston Mill Cemetery.

In addition to the main building there was also an offshoot, 'The Homeward Bound', an altogether more modest, but no less valued premises, just outside the Albert Gates of the Keyham Steam Yard (which itself had opened a little over twenty years earlier). Opened in 1878, the Homeward Bound stood on the corner of Albert Road and William Street.

Aggie Weston's, left, looking down Fore Street towards the Dockyard Gate

Top: *from inside the dockyard gate.* Above: *from outside the gate.*

Review of the troops, looking across towards Devonport Railway Station, before the construction of the Technical Schools which were begun in 1897.

Another War for the Troops

Of course, while the public perception of Devonoprt was inextricably linked to the Dockyard and the Royal Naval Barracks, there was much more to the town than that, and within the lines especially, the two big barrack complexes of Granby (Royal Artillery and Army Service Corps) and Raglan (Infantry) meant that this was every bit as much a Military town as a Naval one.

Covering a large and commanding 11-acre site overlooking the Brickfields, Raglan Barracks sported a very impressive parade ground. Indeed it was put to a wide variety of uses over the years – an estimated 15,000 turned out on Whit Monday 1888 to witness the eleventh annual Plymouth Cycling Club rally, '10 races, 78 entries!' But first and foremost this was a military base, built to accommodate 'two entire regiments of the line, or 2,000 men, and 80 officers'. The site had its own laundry drying closets, cooking places and two limestone fives' courts.

As to the barracks themselves, it was said that the buildings were originally earmarked for India but due to some kind of mix-up they ended up here. Whatever the truth, these flat-roofed, yellow brick buildings did look a little odd in Devonport, particularly with its seemingly incongruous verandas (a word which is itself of Indian origin), which, with their fancy ironwork, ran along the length of the men's quarters.

Home to some famous regiments, and in October1899, when the Boer invasion of Natal and the siege of Mafeking kick-started the South African War, the 1st Battalion of the Oxfordshire and Buckinghamshire Light Infantry were resident here, together with the 2nd Battalion of the Devon and Cornwall Light Infantry under Lieut-Col W Aldworth.

By December 1899 both battalions had been deployed to South Africa – and kitted out in khaki for the first time (at long last the military had come to understand the importance of not being too conspicuous). The following February both units took part in the successful battle at Paardeberg and although the DCLI lost their commanding officer, Aldworth, and 55 other officers and men, some 4,000 enemy were captured.

A by-product of the European scramble for Africa, this was the first war to have been reported almost as it happened in the British press. Courtesy of recent developments in land telegraphy and deep-sea

Top: *2nd Battalion Gloucestershire Regiment on parade, 1896.* Middle: *Bayonet practice, 1896.* Bottom: *Outside the Mount Edgcumbe Inn, Mutton Cove.*

HMS Doris*: The crews of the* Doris *and the* Barossa *falling in for reception at Devonport.*

cables, schoolboys across the Three Towns were able to plot the movements of our troops, with coloured flags and war-maps issued by the newspapers, including the newly instituted *Western Evening Herald* (1895) which substantially increased its circulation thanks to its coverage of what became known as the Boer War.

Notwithstanding early setbacks, the relief of first Kimberley, then Ladysmith and then Mafeking (an event that took on undue significance thanks to the attention it received in the press) and the eventual British 'success' in South Africa, there was a high price to pay.

The concentration camps were desperately inefficient - it was estimated that around 4,000 disposed women and 16,000 children died during the encounter, while Boer losses in the field were reckoned to be around 5,000. The number of British troops lost in action was ostensibly similar, albeit around the 6,000 mark. However, it is claimed that a further 16,000 men died from wounds or sickness in the course of the eighteen-month-long action, many of them with families in and around the Three Towns.

A great number of those who survived injury and amputation were treated at the Military Hospital on the northern bank of Stonehouse Creek, as throughout 1901 and the early part of 1902 casualties from the front in South Africa were shipped here.

Curiously enough, although the South African War was primarily a military affair the Royal Navy also had a significant role to play, and not just in the transportation of men and machinery. Indeed, while the men of the Oxford and Bucks Light Infantry and the DCLI were mustered at Paardeberg under General Sir Forestier-Walker, an urgent signal was sent out to the Commander-in-Chief of the Navy's Cape Command, requesting as much help as could be made available. Immediately the C-in-C, Vice-Admiral Sir Robert Harris, whose flag was then flying on HMS *Doris*, put together a naval brigade made up of every spare officer and rating, whom he then dispatched the 800 or so miles to the front line with 200 Royal Marines.

Eight months later, when the *Doris* returned to Devonport, the crew had with them a Boer pom-pom gun that they'd taken as a trophy from the battle. This trophy, they decided, should be mounted and presented, at their expense, to their baseport town, Devonport, as a memorial to their eleven colleagues who were lost in that action. On Saturday 27 February 1904 that memorial was unveiled by Vice Admiral Harris and Admiral Sir Edward Seymour the then C-in-C, at Devonport.

Top: *Military Hospital, Devonport*. Middle: *View of the grounds*. Bottom: *The Doris gun*.

Top: *King Edward VII and Queen Alexandra at the launch of HMS Queen.* Bottom:. *The biggest ship in the British Navy up to that point, HMS Queen was designed by a Devonport boy, Sir William White, who had started his career in the Dockyard.*

The Queen is dead, long live the King

Just as Her Majesty's forces were preparing for battle in South Africa a bulletin was read out at the gates of Osborne House, Victoria's residence on the Isle of Wight: it said, quite simply, *'the Queen is slowly sinking'*. It was four o'clock on the afternoon 22 January 1901. A little over two hours later, the 81-year-old ruler breathed her last and her beloved son, Bertie, the Prince of Wales, became King Edward VII.

Happily for the Three Towns, before the new sovereign had officially celebrated his coronation he and his Queen, Alexandra, came down to the area for a three-day visit.

On arriving at a densely crowded King's Road (re-named in honour of the royal visit), the King was introduced to the Mayor of Devonport, Edgar Leest, by Lord St Levan. *'The outburst of enthusiasm from the crowds packed on the hillside was extremely hearty and unanimous, and seemed to impress their Majesties,'* as a silver casket with the official introduction was presented to the King.

In his formal reply the King said: *'It has interested me much to see the vast dockyards, arsenals, and barracks of Devonport, which are of such importance to the strength and welfare of my naval and military forces, and give employment to so many inhabitants of the town, which has grown rapidly around them.'*

He added, *'I pray heartily that your municipality may continue to grow in efficiency and prosperity.'*

The following day, Saturday 8 March 1902, Queen Alexandra, with the King at her side, launched the dockyard's latest warship:

'The Queen looked radiant as she advanced to name the ship,' ran one contemporary report. *'She raised the bottle once and flung it against the bow of the ship, but failed to break it. A little more vigour in the second instance was successful. The wine ran down over the steel plates; the Queens said, "I name this ship the* Queen*. God speed her and bless all who sail in her".'*

A little over a year later the son and daughter-in-law of the royal couple (who incidentally celebrated their 39th wedding anniversary on their visit here), blessed the area with another royal visit.

The 38-year-old Prince George, Prince of Wales, and Princess Mary made history when they arrived in the West Country as their journey on the *Cornishman Express* set a new record for the fastest long-distance run ever accomplished – Paddington to Plymouth in 234 minutes and 45 seconds.

As it transpired, this royal visitation started in the Royal Duchy where the Prince was the guest of Lord Falmouth. A week or so later, on 23 July 1903, the Prince and Princess made a tour of the Dockyard, surveying the work on the Keyham Extension and launching the *King Edward VII* battleship, named after his father who had laid the keel plate on his visit the previous year.

'You no doubt realise,' said the Prince, when he addressed cadets at the Royal Naval Engineering College, *'that the British Empire could not exist without the Navy, and also the supreme necessity for the efficiency of every part of this service. The machinery department of his Majesty's ships is of vital importance. I am sure that each one of you will do his best, remembering that in the hour of trial the very existence of the Empire may depend upon the efficiency of a single individual.'*

Four years later the Prince was back to open the massive new Keyham complex which extended out over 114 acres, much of it reclaimed.

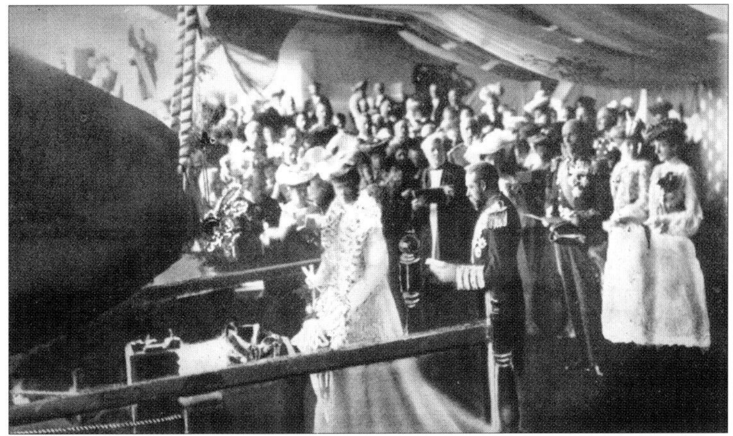

Top: *The Prince and Princess of Wales at the launch of* King Edward VII. Middle: *Cutting the cord.* Bottom: *17 June 1905 the launch of* Hibernia (SWiB). Above: *Devonport dresses up for the royal visit.*

The Prince of Wales, accompanied by the Princess, formally opened on 21 February 1907, the north dockyard extension at Devonport, proceeding into the dock on board the Admiralty yacht Vivid. The surrounding ships are seen saluting. The 35-acre basin is entered by a lock 750ft long and capable of admitting the largest man-of-war afloat.

The Biggest Docks in the World

The Keyham Extension did much to enhance Devonport's national and international reputation. The colossal project had involved almost 3,500 men and had led to the development of a new residential area at Weston Mill. All told it had taken ten years to complete and it incorporated over two million cubic feet of Cornish and Norwegian granite and over 200,000 tons of cement. It also saw a great deal of material taken from the beaches of Hallsands and Beesands on the South Devon coast, a move by the contractor that ultimately undermined those villages and saw many of the houses there swept away.

Notwithstanding all that, this was the greatest extension in the Yard's 200-year history, it had also effectively doubled the size of the Devonport facility, being more or less equal in area to the existing Keyham Yard and the original Dockyard together.

With the new housing at Weston Mill and the greater than ever before employment prospects in the Dockyard now, Devonport Town Council decided to gear up for an extension of its town boundaries. Following Plymouth's example they began by appointing a full-time Town Clerk – AB Pilling.

Within a very short time parts of St Budeaux and Weston Peverell had been brought within the Devonport boundaries and the Corporation had taken over gas and water works and created an electricity plant. It was as if the King's prayers for greater prosperity and efficiency for the Borough had been answered.

But, there were dark clouds on the horizon. The fact that British warships were getting bigger seemed like good news, but the revolutionary *Dreadnought*, the fastest battleship the world had ever seen, launched at Portsmouth in 1906 unwittingly sparked a major arms race around the world. The gauntlet was thrown down to other naval powers, notably the Kaiserliche Marine (German Navy) and their response was immediate.

Devonport played its part when the largest and most powerful battlecruiser to have been built in the port – the *Indefatigable* – slipped into the Hamoaze on 25 February 1909.

However, as Germany's imperialist ambitions became increasingly obvious in Europe, so tension in the Three Towns escalated. The local situation was exacerbated when Plymouth launched a bid to secure the Amalgamation of the Three Towns.

Top: *9 May 1910, Mayor of Devonport, Alderman Littleton, reading the proclamation of King George V.*
Middle: *Fore Street decorated for the Coronation, June 1911.*
Bottom: *Brickfields 1912, King's Birthday review.*

Top: *Devonport Fire Brigade c.1904*
Above: *Happiness is a walk in Devonport Park.*
Right: *A typical period-piece, picture postcard.*

Amalgamation!

It was with some degree of reluctance that Devonport Corporation entered into the Amalgamation of the Three Towns in 1914, indeed they spent thousands of pounds fighting the proposal; however, there was undoubtedly an inevitability about the whole affair. Plymouth had first floated the idea back in 1835, and again in 1888, when they petitioned to become the capital of South Devon County. The idea was re-introduced in 1902, by Sir Joseph Bellamy, addressing an assembly in Stonehouse Town Hall ... but nothing came of it.

Five years later, when the King and Queen paid a royal visit to the area, Admiral Sir Lewis Beaumont, the newly arrived Commander-in -Chief, pointedly invited Sir Charles Radford, the Mayor of Plymouth, to lunch on the Royal Yacht, but not William J Moon, the Mayor of Devonport. Consequently, Mayor Moon and his wife boycotted the Royal visit and his townsmen were conspicuous by their absence during the Royal processions.

It was becoming increasingly obvious that something needed to be done and encouraging ballots on the issue in 1913 prompted a Local Government Board enquiry in Plymouth Guildhall in January 1914. Plymouth's first witness was their town clerk, but it was the man who followed him onto the stand who held the key.

Major-General AP Penton was the Officer in Command of South West Coastal Defences and his view was that:

'In peacetime the organisation of the Three Towns into three distinct bodies does not affect us much ... In wartime it is an entirely different question. You would have the fortress commander having to go to three different bodies ... In fact if I was fortress commander here in wartime I should have to go to the three chief civil magistrates and say "One of you must represent the civil community".'

As it transpired the inquiry lasted another four days and, less than three months later, a Provisional Order was made to unite the towns - a move that Stonehouse had no objection to. Devonport Corporation however was not finished yet and it brought the matter to a Commons Committee. After nine days' deliberation the Committee confirmed the original decision on 1 July 1914, just three days after the assassination of Franz Ferdinand in Sarajevo (Bosnia) had upset diplomatic relations in the Balkans.

Still the Devonport Corporation refused to give up and persuaded

their constituency MP, Sir Charles Kinloch-Cooke, to block the bill in Parliament. However, a whip had been arranged by other local MPs and the bill was passed on its third reading on 21 July.
One week later, with German backing, Austria-Hungary declared war on Russia, and yet still the disgruntled men of Devonport refused to let go and lobbied the House of Lords.
In the event, the Bill received Royal Assent on 10 August 1914, by which time Germany's violation of Belgian neutrality had prompted what had long seemed inevitable: we were at war with Germany and troops of the British Expeditionary Force were being mobilised for deployment in France. But back in the 'Three Towns', Major-General Penton was now in the happy position of only having one local authority to deal with.
The Mayor and Corporation of Devonport though were less happy and had it not been for the war their efforts may have not have been so hopeless. But if anyone was in any doubt as to the long-term impact of the new arrangement it would very soon become clear.
The estimated population of the united Three Towns was said to be 213,759, and amalgamation meant that the new Council was now responsible for two waterworks, two electricity works, one gasworks, many miles of tramways, two markets and three Town Halls. Sir Thomas Baker, who had been elected Mayor of Plymouth in 1913 became head of the new body and remained in office for the first year or two of the war. He was succeeded, by a former mayor of Devonport, and resident of Nelson Villas (No. 2) Colonel John Goldsmith. The appointment, however, did little to halt the slide of power and influence away from Devonport.

1914: the last ever meeting of Devonport Borough Council.

Top: *Marching down to the Torpoint Ferry with the Royal Albert Hospital and Marlborough Hotel on the skyline.* Middle: *Wounded soldiers driven to hospital in style, Major General Penton on the left.* Bottom: *Salisbury Road School serves as a makeshift wartime hospital.*

The Great War

When war was declared on 4 August 1914 most Britons relished the prospect, the news was greeted with cheering and a wave of excitement swept the nation. Devonport was no exception and, as ever, the prospect of war brought the inevitable anticipation of an increase in activity in the Dockyard – more jobs, more ships, more overtime ... more money.

As the soldiers marched from Raglan to King's Road Station en route to the frontline in France and as Fleet Reservists from around the Three Towns were called up, so there was an air of imminent successes to celebrate. The reality, however, soon suggested a very different scenario. Within 36 hours HMS *Amphion* had been lost and before August had come to a close the British Expeditionary Force had been forced to retreat from the Belgian town of Mons to the Somme in Northern France

On Sunday 30 August the first hospital train pulled into Friary Station full of wounded soldiers from the front. A mixed fleet of buses, cars and ambulances was on hand to whisk the men off to temporary hospital accommodation at Salisbury Road School. It was a grim portent of what was to come, as soldiers and sailors came back battered and bruised ... although many never came back at all.

The men of the Fleet Reserve, men who had already served their country, were the first to be called up by the Royal Navy. Invariably they were sent out in ships that came from the fleet reserve – the older, outdated and most vulnerable vessels in the Navy:

'Every one lost produced a large Plymouth casualty list. The Battle of Jutland at the end of May 1916, in which the Royal Navy lost fourteen ships and 6,274 men, hit the port desperately, for five of the lost ships, and at least four of those badly damaged, were Devonport-manned. There were crowds outside the newspaper offices for hours awaiting the casualty lists, and for weeks after the streets seemed full of black widows' weeds.

Every battle in France too, with its infinitely larger casualty lists, hit the town, but none like the Battle of the Bois de Buttes in May 1918. The 2nd Devons, long-since robbed by the long war of their regular soldiers, and made up of wartime soldiers, went down to hopeless odds with Colonel Anderson-Morshead of the old Plymouth merchant family, dying with them, revolver in one hand and hunting crop in the other'. [Crispin Gill]

Back at home there was little to do except wait. Street lights were dimmed to a ghastly, ghostly bluish glow and sea-facing windows were screened, although the prospect of ship or submarine attack was considered slight. London may have been in range of aeroplane and zeppelin attacks but Plymouth was well outside the danger zone.

No German battleship ever approached the port and allied shipping passed safely in and out of the harbour. Indeed one of the most spectacular sailing convoys of all time entered the Sound in October 1914. With a cargo of some 25,000 Canadian troops, some 33 liners arrived after an eleven-day crossing of the Atlantic. They had been bound for Southampton but U-boat sightings off Cherbourg and the Isle of Wight prompted a change of plan.

The influx of troops from the Commonwealth did little to change the tide of events in Europe however. The casualty lists got longer, the first battle of the Somme saw over 600,000 British and French deaths and around 650,000 German casualties. It was *'in terrain absolutely barren, in personnel disastrous'* observed Churchill.

While the British may have lost some tactical advantages of surprise in their early unveiling of the tank in this land encounter, at sea the German U-boats continued to visit major losses upon our shipping.

In April 1917 alone, a thousand Allied vessels of one kind or another were lost; after that the adoption of the convoy system helped bring the figure down to a few hundred, but the U-boat scourge was still a huge problem and it was what brought America into the war.

Suddenly there were *'swarming flotillas of little ships in the Sound, flying the Stars and Stripes' – Mr Henry Ford's mass-produced submarine chasers flitting into the Channel and back at all hours of the day and night'.* [Walling]

Meanwhile the Dockyard had a major part to play in the development of decoy ships, 'Q-ships' as they became known, innocent-looking, but heavily armed, merchant vessels designed to lure U-boats to the surface and then take them out.

These were heady days in the Yard. Earlier in the conflict Winston Churchill, as First Lord of the Admiralty, had ordered battlecruisers *Inflexible* and *Invincible* to the South Atlantic to reinforce the British contingent looking for the German fleet. The men in the Dockyard here worked night and day to get the ships readly. On being told the ships would be fit to sail on 13 November, Churchill ordered that they should set sail on the 11th and if the work was not finished then *'the Dockyardsmen should be sent away with the ships to return as opportunity may offer'.* And so they were.

Clockwise from top left: HMS Vanguard, *a Devonport-based battleship that blew up (apparently due to faulty ammunition) while anchored in Scapa Flow in 1917 – over 800 crew were lost. HMS* Amphion, *sunk by a mine in the North Sea less than two days after war had been declared. HMS* Pathfinder, *sunk by a torpedo off the coast of Scotland, September 1914. HMS* Highflyer *which 'performed the magnificent feat of attacking and sinking the armed liner* Kaiser Wilhelm der Grosse.

King George V presenting decorations on board HMS St Vincent, *June 1917.*

Top: *HMS* Warspite *in the dockyard.* Bottom: L9 *one of the early submarines.*

Work, Work, Work.

Ironically the Great War saw the launch of the last battleship to be built at Devonport - the *Royal Oak*, in November 1914. But there were other classes of vessel under construction as well; with the oiler, *Ferol* preceding the *Royal Oak* and the cruiser *Cleopatra* also slipping into the Hamoaze soon afterwards.

Then, over the course of the next two or three years the Yard's first locally built submarines, excitingly called *J5, J6, K6, K7* and *J7* were all built under covered slipways, with King George V and Queen Mary witnessing the launch of the first two.

Building work in the Yard wasn't just restricted to floating objects either, for it was during this time that one of the Yard's best-known harbourside structures appeared - the massive Cold Store depot. Capable of housing some 5,000 tons of meat, it was erected for the Ministry of Food at a cost of £53,000.

All of the above spelt unprecedented employment opportunities as there was also an enormous amount of ship repair and renewal work to be done at Devonport.

At the outbreak of war there had been approaching 14,000 men working in the Yard. At the peak of the hostilities there were over 20,000 (a number that, due to the exigencies of war, included quite a few women). Over and above the sheer number of jobs, wartime bonuses had in many instances, doubled wages. There had been plenty of overtime and in almost every instance, there had been absolutely no danger ... and no need to forsake the comforts of life at home. By contrast, those men who went into the Services were not nearly so well paid, what's more many paid the ultimate price and many more ended up on the sick and wounded lists. Life at the Front was appalling, life at sea was better, but there was little home leave. The contrasting situations of those on active duty and those in the Yard *'was to leave a bitter taste in many mouths long after the end of the war'*. [Gill]

However, that didn't stop many of the men in the Yard complaining that their rates of pay were not as good as those in the private sector: typically around 39/- a week for Admiralty engineers as opposed to between 43/- and 48/- a week outside. More problematic still, however, was the inevitable round of redundancies after the Armistice of November 1918.

In 1921, after much heated debate, the Government decided to reduce the working week by seven hours in a bid to preserve the numbers of those in work. However, by the end of the year a two-phase increase saw the hours go back to first a 42-hour-week and then a 47-hour-week (including Saturday mornings).

Those Post War Blues again

However, without a war, or at least the threat of war, to drive production the situation was bound to be unsustainable.

The boom-time increase in population, coupled with a desire to sanitise certain areas, had prompted a need for new housing: Duke Street, James Street and Morice Square all saw new developments prior to 1919; while Tamar Street, John Street and Cornwall Street all saw redevelopment in the 1920s and 1930s and in 1927 the Admiralty had a new development (174 houses) created for men and their families who had been forced down here due to closures at Pembroke and Rosyth Dockyard – hence the name of the new road: Pemros Road.

However, as the twenties progressed, employment statistics in Devonport Dockyard were not making happy reading, and as the peace settled so numbers dropped: the peak of 19,000–20,000 soon fell to 15,837. By 1925 it had dropped to 11,436 and then, in the year Pemros Road was laid out, the number of dockyardies dropped to where it had been at the start of the Great War, 10,854.

The gloom didn't stop there though and suddenly another 800 men were sacked in a matter of just a few weeks and *'men who had regarded the dockyard as their career were being discharged'* [Gill].

Hand in hand with the lay-offs from the Yard, of course, came the decommissioning of thousands of service personnel – soldiers, sailors and marines. Small wonder therefore that Devonport, which traditionally relied on the Dockyard and the Services to keep many of its shops, pubs and places of entertainment ticking over, was starting to feel the pinch as the twenties progressed.

The discharges of dockyard workmen, causing discomfort and agitation, prompted many schemes for substitute industry, all of which came to naught. Plans for devoting a part of the dockyard to commercial ship building, plans for using some of the docks and wharves as a terminal for ocean liners, and many other projects, were discussed and abandoned. The dockyard did a little 'repayment work' – building or repairing on contract terms for private owners – but the figures of unemployment rose steadily until, at the nadir of depression in the early 'thirties, there were close on 10,000 insured out of work [Walling].

Devonport still had its big shops; Tozer's (Draper's and House Furnishers in Fore Street, Marlborough Street, Princes Street, Tavistock Street and Morice Street), HJ & EA Boold's (on the corner of Market Street and Tavistock Street) and JB Love's (dominating one side of Willes Street) – later Garratt's ... *'but none had the gloss of the Plymouth stores. The eclipse was showing, even in the 1920s'* [Gill].

Top: *Marlborough Street looking west.* Middle: *Marlborough Street, looking east.*
Bottom: *JB Love 's impressive Emporium in Willes Street.*

The Hippodrome, Princes Street, with programmes and playbills from the Theatre including one of the first talkies to be shown in Devonport, in 1930.

Life Between the Wars

There was a similar story in the entertainment provision for the town: Devonport was not slow to have its own cinemas, The Tivoli (Fore Street), the Electric (Fore Street), the Coliseum (St Aubyn Street), and the Morice Town Picture Palace, all opened between 1909-14. Sadly the Coliseum burnt down shortly afterwards – fire was always a hazard with nitrate film stock; the Morice Town Picture Palace went the same way in 1931, while the Tivoli closed in 1939, presumably, in part, on account of the opening of the state-of-the-art Forum in Fore Street the previous year.

More enduring was the Alhambra Theatre (formerly the Metropole), in Tavistock Street, which doubled as a cinema for a number of years in the twenties and early thirties. It had been the opening of this venue, and that of the Hippodrome in Princes Street, that did for the old Dock Theatre back in 1899.

Both the Metropole and the Hippodrome were 'earthier' than the Grand Theatre and Theatre Royal in Plymouth, with the Hippodrome *'presenting revues, musicals, and, of course, variety. Gracie Fields made a very early appearance there when she was completely unknown, and so did the young Jack Train. Talent concerts were the vogue and in the early days of the Hippodrome the legendary long hook was pushed forward from the prompt side to pull off those who did not please the patrons in front'* [Harvey Crane].

Jack Train, incidentally, was a comic entertainer and former Regent Street schoolboy from Plymouth who became nationally famous via various radio series, starting with Tommy Handley's ITMA (It's That Man Again).

With seating for about 2,000, the Hippo (as its roof proclaimed) was relaunched in December 1929 as a cinema, screening MGM's Broadway Melody – the world's first 'talking' musical. At the end of the thirties the Hippodrome became part of the County Cinema circuit.

Around the same time a large site that included the former Princess Street Chapel was purchased by a Welsh-based firm with the 'intention of building a kinema'. They placed a tiled façade over the top of an earlier, Victorian, Fore Street frontage and the following year, 1938, the Forum Cinema was opened.

PROGRAMME—ONE PENNY.

THE DEVONPORT
Alhambra Theatre
TAVISTOCK ST., DEVONPORT.
Telephone—DEVONPORT 385.

Proprietors: THE PROVINCIAL THEATRES SYNDICATE, Ltd.
Joint Managing Directors:
MR. JOE COLLINS & MR. JACK GLADWIN.

Director and Secretary ... Mr STANLEY WATSON
Resident Manager ... Mr. ARTHUR C. KNIGHT

Twice Nightly: 6-30 :: 8-45.

POPULAR PRICES (inclusive of Tax).

BOXES. to hold 4	STALLS	CIRCLE	PIT STALLS	BALCONY
8/-	1/6 & 1/-	1/3 & 1/-	6d.	4d.
BOOKED FREE			NOT BOOKABLE	

Reduced Prices for Children to all parts except Balcony, at all Matinees, and at Evening Performances other than on Bank Holidays and Saturdays.

Booking Office (Next to Theatre). Open Daily 10 a.m. to 10 p.m.

WHY NOT BE ON OUR PERMANENT BOOKING LIST? AND HAVE YOUR SELECTED SEATS EVERY WEEK.

Advertising Contractors—... Co., Ltd., ... Charing Cross Rd., London W.C.

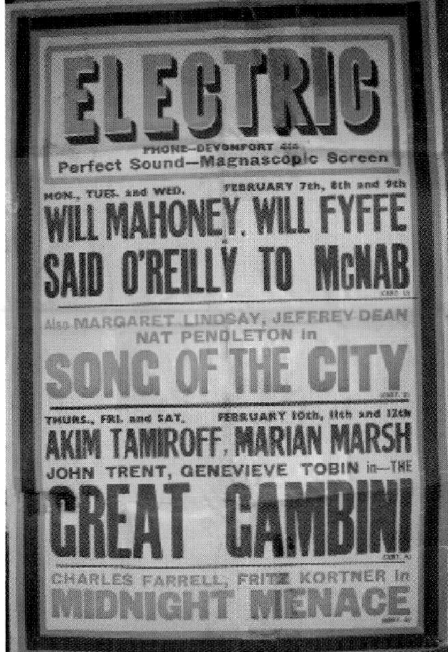

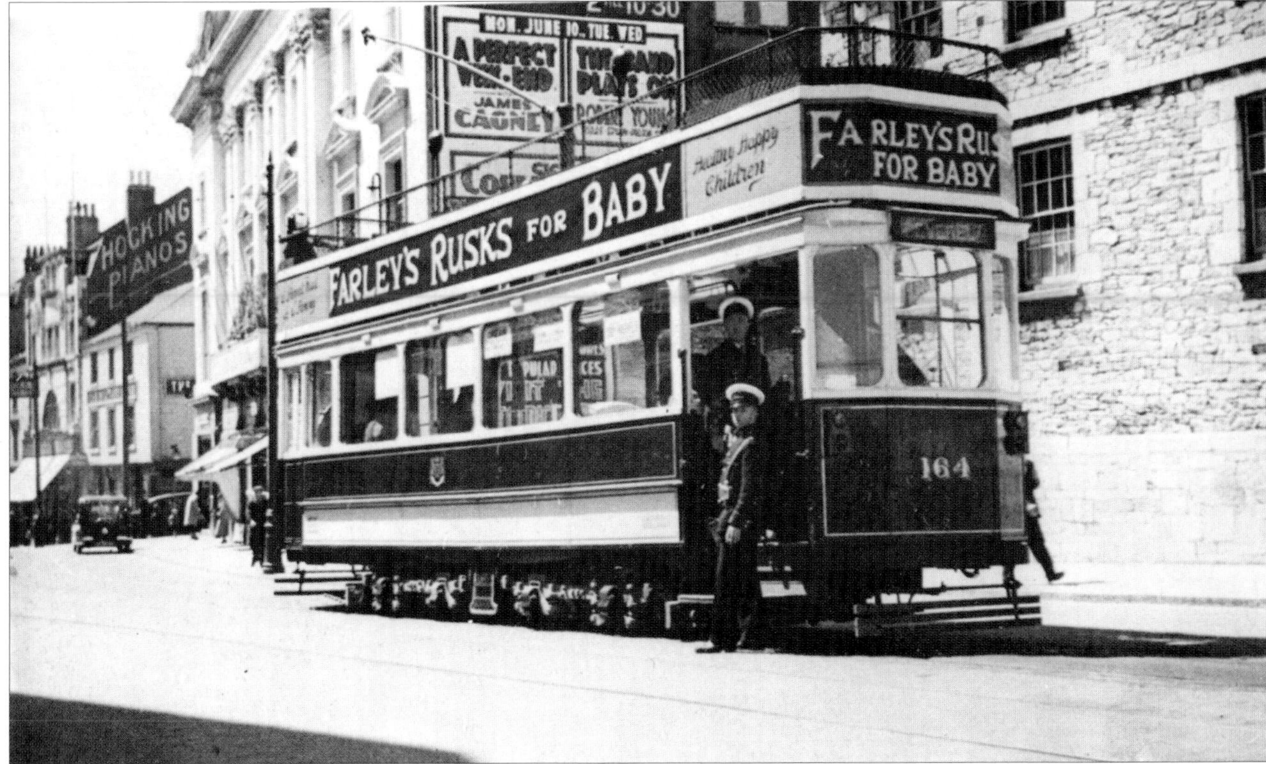

Clockwise from top left: *The Alhambra, Tavistock Street and bill; the Tivoli and Electric (behind the tram) both in Fore Street, and Electric poster.*

August 1938: the newly built Forum Cinema – standing directly opposite the Victorian Post Office – opens its doors for the first time.

Away from the heart of Devonport there was also the Ford Palladium (the former, late-Victorian Theatre Metropole), in St Levan Road; the short-lived Star or Assembly Hall Cinematograph Theatre at Camel's Head and the 750-seater State in St Budeaux. The latter opened with a showing of 'That Certain Age', the latest vehicle for the popular actress/singer Deanna Durbin, on Thursday16 November 1939, two months after war had been declared.

Carnival Time

Clearly the phenomenal growth of cinema had a major impact on the way people spent their leisure time and the situation in Devonport was duplicated across the Three Towns and the country as a whole.

The fate of Devonport Carnival was truly symptomatic of the bigger picture, both in relation to the impact of the 'new' form of entertainment and in relation to the falling fortunes of Devonport itself.

In the twenties the annual carnival was something that all Three Towns celebrated and the Civic Week procession would run through Devonport, Stonehouse and Plymouth. Great numbers of people would be involved and even greater numbers would turn out to support the occasion, with monies collected going to alleviate the suffering of the large numbers of unemployed in the area. The local theatres and cinemas provided much of the organisation and one of the great figures at the centre of the festivities was Putty Philpott, a larger than life character (quite literally – he weighed in around twenty stone) who had retired from the Navy and had been the landlord of the No Place on Eldad Hill and, before that, a doorman at the Palace Theatre in Union Street.

It had been from the Palace that for years a pram derby had been staged, local mums racing around a circuit that took them through Stonehouse, Devonport, Stoke, Peverell, Mutley and Plymouth city centre.

By the late twenties, however, the enthusiasm for the events across the Three Towns was declining a little and Devonport decided to go it alone – but even here it was becoming more and more of a struggle and 1936 saw the last of the Devonport Carnivals, notwithstanding an attempt to revive the proceedings in 1938 (and one or two much later, post-war efforts).

Top: *Pembroke Street celebrates c1935*
Bottom: *Putty Philpott - Carnival King.and George Drake drive through Devonport.*

Sport and Recreation

Around the same time as Plymouth was losing its taste for some of the more parochial pastimes it was actively trying to re-invent itself as a tourist destination and while Devonport has never particularly seen itself in that light, it wasn't long after the improvements began on the swimming facilities at Tinside that work began on the provision of dedicated facilities in Devonport. Within a few years of the end of the Great War, the Mount Wise Open-Air Sea Water Baths were opened in Bullock's Dock. Almost immediately the Devonport Swimming Association was formed, with local lad Reg Bossom one of the most tireless coaches and leaders.

While Tinside was primarily a leisure pool, the Mount Wise facility, being a more regular, rectangular shape, more readily lent itself to swimming events and by the end of the thirties the venue had become home to a large number of swimming galas and competitions, including National, County, and Area Championships.

Another extremely popular activity between the wars was rowing: *'Just about every church club, including the YMCA and the Royal Engineering College at Keyham, had one or two boats and on Saturdays the various clubs could be seen going out of the Hamoaze into the Sound. If the tide was rising they would make their way up the Tamar'*. [Roger Watkins]

Typically, a club – and there were many – would buy a 26ft Cutter or a 27ft Whaler that the Naval Stores Department had decided was no longer worth maintaining. Boats would be sold at auction, and having acquired one, clubs generally had no shortage of young-manpower to put the craft in fine working order.

Competition was fierce and regular regattas pitted young Naval recruits against various organisations of local lads, both before and just after the war.

Top: *Swimming at Mount Wise,* Middle: *1923 'The opening of Devonport's new swimming bath at Bullock's Dock'.* Left and bottom: *the new pool.* Right: *Schoolboy coxswain Fernley Tranter collects a trophy on behalf of the Morice Town rowers c1946.* Below: *Devonport YMCA junior boat Aurora full of members c1932.*

Another popular pursuit, particularly among the pugnacious, was boxing and Devonport had a thriving club with one of the brightest stars of the interwar era – the former York Street schoolboy, Len Harvey. Len fought for the British welterweight title in 1926 while still 18 and was held to a draw by Harry Mason. In 1929 he took on Alex Ireland for the middleweight title and in the seventh round became British Champion with a knockout.

After losing on points to Marcel Thil of France for the World middleweight title, he successfully challenged Eddie Phillips to take the British light-heavyweight title and then beat the unbeaten Jack Preston to become British Heavyweight Champion. In 1939 he gained British recognition in the world heavyweight championship at Harringay Arena when he beat his old adversary Jock McAvoy.

Devonport Motor Cycle Club, was another very popular organisation, for those who could afford to forsake shanks' pony and public transport and experience the freedom of the country roads. Most people, however, spent their leisure time locally, and for the majority that meant Devonport Park, Sparrow Park, next to the Albert Road Gate, Mount Wise or the 'New Park', which opened in 1932 (the year after Central Park), at the end of Richmond Walk. A pleasant spot overlooking the water with swings, a roundabout and a merry-go-round, the site was requisitioned by the Admiralty at the end of the decade. Meanwhile the other end of Mutton Cove was cleared of much of its ramshackle properties and warehouses in 1937 to make the area generally more accessible.

Bottom left: *Devonport Boxing Club in the early twenties.* Below: *Len Harvey.* Top right: *Devonport Park bandstand, 1928.* Middle: *'Robin's' Park, Mount Wise, Mercia and Bernadette Kay with their grandmother.* Bottom: *Mutton Cove.*

Pembroke Street c1930.

Ringing the Changes

As the universal depression of the twenties deepened over Devonport it became a *'common sight to see youngsters waiting for men to leave the Dockyard at the end of the day and ask them, "Any lefts, Sir?" whereupon the man asked may have produced from his bag a sandwich or a couple of biscuits for the lad. Money was scarce; there were innumerable one-parent families due to the father being killed during the War - also many men returned unable to work due to injuries or lack of work. Soup kitchens were set up at various points in the town and something like a pint of soup could be had for tuppence'*. [Roger Watkins]
The ramifications of the economic situation were widespread. It was difficult to halt the general decline of the housing stock but a programme of building new flats went some way to alleviating the problems.

In 1936 Cornwall Street, probably the oldest street in Devonport, was compulsorily purchased and families, many of whom had been there for a very long time, were moved out to newly built properties in St Budeaux. Meanwhile, the old three-storey houses facing the street were pulled down and new council flats erected in their stead, the pubs fronting Cornwall Beach at the bottom of the street were kept, but almost everything else was cleared away, including the Duke of Cornwall, the William IV and the Princess Royal. The latter had actually closed its doors back in 1924 and was an early casualty of the post-war recession.
Overall, within the confines of the Lines there had been a hundred or so pubs in old Devonport at the end of the Great War, however a third of them had gone by the end of the thirties, including four in Queen Street, three in Pembroke Street and a couple in Cumberland Street. It seems that compensation was paid in almost every instance suggesting that all the closures were part of redevelopment projects, but certainly none of them were replaced.

Top left: *Princess Royal, Cornwall Street.*
Top right: *Marlborough Hotel.*
Right: *1930 Ada Parrell and Hilda Tofts, Fore Street.*

Looking across to St Aubyn's Chapel and Raglan Barracks from Devonport Column. Inset l–r: *St Stephen's, St Paul's (Morice Square) and St Aubyn Chapel.*

Distinguished Visitors

There was no shortage of famous faces dropping in on Devonport between the wars: as well as our own Royal family, Marie, the Queen of Roumania made more than one appearance. Her father, the Duke of Edinburgh had been Commander-in-Chief here in the 1890s, just before she married King Ferdinand, and Marie, who was a great friend of Lady Astor, was always happy to recall the three years she spent living at Mount Wise as a teenager.

Another celebrated individual who spent his early years in and around Devonport was Robert Falcon Scott, who was born at Outlands, Milehouse in 1868. Tragically defeated by the elements in 1912 in his quest to reach the South Pole, in 1925 the memorial to him at Mount Wise was unveiled. His son Peter was here for the official ceremony, together with Commodore of Naval Barracks, CWR Boyds, who had been with Scott on an earlier expedition.

Twelve years earlier, Field Marshall Paul Methuen (Lord Methuen), was on hand for the unveiling, in Devonport Park, of the memorial for the 2,000 Devonport men who lost their lives in the Great War.

Although the air hung heavy with the sense of loss, few there on that day could have imagined that all too soon the country would be involved in another war of global proportions. This time, however, not only would it bring more work and, inevitably, more heartache, but it would also, for the very first time, bring war to Devonport itself.

Top left: *The All Blacks at the Rectory 1935.* Middle: *Queen of Roumania in Fore Street.* Right: *Lord Methuen unveils Devonport War Memorial.* Above: *Scott Memorial, Mount Wise (inset) Peter Scott lays a wreath on his father's memorial.*

Clockwise from top left: *Navy Week advertisement; Navy Days display; Keel laying of HMS* Leander; *HMS* Rodney *during Navy Week, 1930.*

Peace in the Meantime

At the end of the Great War one of the celebrated Q-ships, the *Hyderabad*, and two German U-boats were brought into the port for all to see. The *Hyderabad* was berthed at Millbay for a couple of weeks before coming into the Dockyard and then moving up to Torquay. Some 3,000 people visited the *Hyderabad*, with proceeds going to naval charities.

While the Dockyard and the Royal Navy employed a very large number of men who were very familiar with the life and the layout behind the Dockyard Walls, for most people access was somewhat restricted. However, towards the end of August 1928 a new event was instigated – Devonport Navy Week – which was soon being billed as: 'The Most Attractive Event of the Year in the West Country'.

Every year, around the August Bank holiday, thousands would flock to Devonport: families and friends, sons and daughters, wives and lovers anxious to see the great grey floating warships that their loved ones lived on for so many months a year – or even years at a time.

The Field Gun Crew would put on a special show and there would be gymnastic displays on a grand scale.

The band would play and there would be guided tours of selected ships. The big guns of HMS *Rodney* always attracted great interest, as did any of the big new ships.

There was an interesting situation regarding new ships as the twenties came to a close: early in 1929 the First Lord of the Admiralty, Lord Bridgeman, declared that work should begin in the Yard on HMS *Northumberland*. However, little more than preliminary work was under way when Prime Minister Ramsay Macdonald, who had been re-elected in the summer of 1929, announced 'big cuts' in the naval programme. Work on *Northumberland* and her sister ship *Surrey*, was suspended and orders were cancelled on 1 January 1930. A few months later when Lady Madden, launched HMS *Exeter* at Devonport, there was speculation that it may be *'years before a similar scene is witnessed at Devonport'*.

As it transpired, less than twelve months after these big naval cuts had been announced the European situation became such that the Government was prompted to reconsider its decision and on 8 September 1930 the keel was laid in Devonport of HMS *Leander*, the first 6-inch-gun cruiser to be built since 1918 and also the first single-funnelled cruiser to enter service in the Royal Navy. Viscountess Cantelope laid the keel plate and twelve months later, *Leander*, which, when fully manned, had a complement of 570, slipped into the Hamoaze.

The launch of the *Leander* marked the dawn of one of the most active ship-building decades that Devonport had ever seen; up until the completion of HMS *Exeter* only half a dozen other ships had come out of the Yard in the twenties – *Frobisher* (1920), *Olna* and *Nassa*, both oilers (1921 and 1922), *Adventure* (1924), *Cornwall* (1926) and *Devonshire* (1927).

Admittedly the *Hastings*, *Penzance* and *Fowey*, all launched in 1930, had been laid down earlier, but then followed in quick succession: *Bideford* (1931); *Orion, Falmouth, Milford, Weston* (1932); *Grimsby* and *Leith* (1933); *Apollo, Lowestoft* and *Wellington* (1933); *Londonderry* (1935); *Birmingham, Aberdeen, Fleetwood, Hebe* and *Sharpeshooter* (1936); *Leda, Seagull* and *Gloucester* (1937) ... and *Bramble* and *Britomart* (1938).

The Dockyard played a significant role in Britain's bid to keep up with the arms race initiated by Germany as, one by one, cruisers, destroyers, patrol sloops, minesweepers and the like slipped into the Hamoaze, cheered on by the men who had helped build them, by visiting dignitaries ... and often crowds of excited schoolchildren.

Of course, it wasn't just more ships that the Admiralty now wanted, there was also an appetite for bigger ships, and bigger ships necessitated bigger docks. In 1924 the entrance to No. 5 basin had been widened to 125 feet and four years later there was a proposal to do the same thing for No. 10 basin, which was then just 95 feet wide. As the process involved a not inconsiderable amount of upheaval and inconvenience, at what was a very busy time in the yard, work wasn't actually started on this move until 1936 and took several years to complete.

In 1937 a most unusual event occurred in the Yard when HMS *Apollo*, launched here just three years earlier, arrived in port with the mortal remains of the former British Prime Minister, Ramsay MacDonald.

MacDonald's pacifist stance had been popular in the twenties. In 1924, he had been the first ever Labour Prime Minister, albeit briefly (from January to November), but, during his second spell in office, from 1929, his reluctance to stand up to the threat of Hitler drew increasing criticism from many, including Churchill. The Labour leader resigned during the Great Depression, but was persuaded by the King to lead a cross-party Parliament and was re-appointed on the same day, 24 August 1931, as leader of the National Government.

However following a decline in health in 1933–34, MacDonald was eventually forced to resign altogether, in May 1935, and take the token post of Lord President, which Stanley Baldwin, who assumed power in his place, himself vacated (Baldwin had twice been Prime Minister in the twenties).

At the general election later that year, MacDonald lost his seat, but was back in Parliament the following year after winning the Combined Scottish Universities seat at a by-election. His health though, both physical and mental, broke down again later that year – hence the decision to take the South American cruise. Unfortunately he never quite made it, and on 9 November 1937 a radio message was sent out from the liner sailing in Caribbean waters to announce his death from a heart attack. MacDonald's body was taken to the next scheduled stop in Bermuda, where, after lying in state overnight in the Anglican Cathedral in Hamilton, his coffin was taken to HMS *Apollo* at anchor in the Great Sound, for transportation back to England.

With *Apollo*'s flag flying at half-mast and MacDonald's coffin draped with a Union Jack, the body was brought ashore at Devonport.

Top: Apollo*'s keel laid.*
Right: *HMS* Exeter *launched, 1929.*
Above: *Ramsay MacDonald's body arrives in Devonport.*

Battered and bruised, HMS Exeter *returns triumphantly to Devonport.*

War Comes To Devonport

October 1938 saw the Lord Mayor, Alderman Solomon Stephens, invited, as the head of the civilian community, to a dinner that was attended by some 200 naval officers. It was not an altogether joyous occasion. On the last day of September the Prime Minister, Neville Chamberlain had come back from Munich with Hitler's signature on a document that promised that Britain and Germany would *'never go to war with one another again'*.

Chamberlain was very pleased with himself but our naval officers were not so sure and the *'grave anxiety of the Services, which knew what was bound to happen, soon seeped into the general consciousness. They could not speak* coram publico, *but they contrived by degrees to inspire the city with their sense of urgency'*. [RAJ Walling]

Admiral Sir Reginald Ernle-Erle-Drax was the current Commander-in-Chief at Devonport and had been for three years, however his term here was coming to an end and while he had been doing his best to alert those he came into contact with, as to the impending crisis, he took the opportunity, at this dinner, to spell out the *'near prospect of war, of the country's unpreparedness for it, and of the need for rounding the citizens to a sense of realities* (ibid).*'*

Furthermore, after the dinner the Admiral (a veteran of the Great War) and still on active duties (he was about to go to Moscow on an important mission), gave the Lord Mayor a paper setting out and expanding his view of the situation in order that Alderman Stephens might fire up the local authorities and prepare the City for what looked to be inevitable.

That said, *'nobody then realised, for it was inconceivable, that within a year the City would be but a hundred miles from enemy aerodromes instead of four or five hundred miles away'*.

So wrote Robert Walling in *The Story of Plymouth* written at the end of the 1940s. Walling was editor of the *Western Independent* throughout the war years, his father had succeeded Henry Whitfeld as editor of the *Western Daily Mercury* and in turn Robert had become the first ever editor of the *Western Evening Herald* when it first hit the streets in 1895. So he knew his city and those who shaped it – indeed he had been appointed editor of the *Western Independent* by Lord Astor when Astor bought the title back in 1922.

Even when war was eventually declared, on 3 September 1939, Walling later observed that *'The usual naval precautions came into force. A number of anti-aircraft guns were manned – not nearly enough sites nor big enough guns as it proved. But it seemed quite unlikely then that the town would be more deeply disturbed than in the War of 1914 except possibly by a few marauding aeroplanes which could be shot down by British marksmen. That dream was an astronomical distance from reality …'*

Reality Bites

Britain and France had both made certain pledges to Poland, and when, on 1 September 1939, German forces breached the Polish frontier an ultimatum was served. Hitler, however, refused to withdraw his troops and when, two days later, the ultimatum deadline passed, we found ourselves at war with Germany once more.

It wasn't long before the consequences of the situation were being felt in Devonport. On Saturday 16 September the aircraft carrier *Courageous* left the Dockyard with four destroyers in support. The following day, in the mouth of the English Channel, an enemy submarine was detected and two destroyers were despatched to find it. Unfortunately the submarine, *U-29*, managed to fire off three torpedoes at *Courageous* two of which hit home and sank the veteran craft within 15 minutes. Launched as a light battle-cruiser in 1916, *Courageous* had been converted to a carrier in Devonport Dockyard between 1924 and 1928 at a cost of over £2million. Devonport-manned *Courageous* was the first battleship to be lost in the Second World War and 518 men, including the captain, were lost with her.

The loss created hundreds of widows in the city, and given that many of the men were reservists and therefore older and more often than not married, hundreds of fatherless children too.

The first British naval casualty, HMS Courageous. *Contrary to a contemporary British newsreel that claimed that the U-boat that sank her could never have withstood the subsequent bombardment from the supporting destroyers,* U-29 *survived the war, at least until scuttled by the Germans in May 1945.*

Within a fortnight the newly appointed First Lord of the Admiralty, Winston Churchill (who had previously held the post 25 years earlier), had paid a visit to Devonport.

The King, too, was here before the end of the year, by which time another Devonport-built ship, the *Royal Oak*, had been sunk by a U-boat (*U-47*), again with great loss of life.

It was not all doom and gloom however and on 13 December a hunting party of three British destroyers, tracked down the infamous *Graf Spee* which had been causing havoc in the Atlantic and which had already sunk nine Allied merchant vessels. Famously described as a 'pocket battleship', because constraints imposed by the post-Great War treaty of Versailles meant that the Germans couldn't build anything bigger than 10,000 tons, the ship was a state of the art warship. Having been welded rather than riveted, thereby saving *weight and materials, and sporting pioneering radar equipment, the Graf Spee* was eventually trapped in the River Plate by HMS *Ajax*, HMS *Exeter* and HMS *Achilles*. Deeming his position to be hopeless, after a fierce battle, the German Captain, Hans Langsdorff, opted to scuttle his ship. Three days later, wrapped in an Imperial flag, Langsdorff took his own life.

Meanwhile, battered and bruised, first *Ajax*, and then *Exeter*, made their way back to Devonport. Both were given tremendous receptions, although, as a Devonport-manned ship, the welcome home for *Exeter* was particularly rapturous. Arriving in Plymouth Sound on 15 February, more than two weeks after *Ajax* – on account of having to be patched up in the Falkland Islands – *Exeter* was greeted by cheering crowds, with Churchill himself taking the salute as she passed the Commander-in-Chief's headquarters at Mount Wise. The Admiral of the Fleet, Sir Dudley Pound and the Chancellor of the Exchequer, Sir John Simon, were also on hand to honour the ship's company.

At the Dockyard itself many of the men that greeted her there had worked on the construction of the ship a decade earlier. Churchill was one of the first on board and *'in glowing phrase he told the crew how the news of the action off the River Plate had come home to the country as "a flash of light and colour on the scene", and pictured the shades of Drake and Raleigh and the Sea Dogs hovering over that home-coming to Plymouth.'* [Walling]

Ready or Not

The first of the big, bloated, silver barrage balloons had been floated above the city in May 1939. Small RAF units were responsible for each of these monsters designed to deter enemy aircraft and suddenly the prospect of an aerial attack, although still thought to be unlikely, seemed a little more serious. Indeed later that month the *Western Evening Herald* warned its readers that this City was indeed a likely target.

And yet still there was a shortfall in the appointment of Air Raid Wardens, with more than 1,000 still needed out of a recommended total of around 3,000.

The city had been divided into two control zones, Plymouth and Devonport, and within that into 440 sectors, each to be manned by six wardens housed in a variety of premises – private, public and business. The Devonport control centre was in the basement of the Market.

Gas masks were issued, public and domestic air-raid shelters were erected and sandbags were placed in front of public buildings and phone boxes, windows were criss-crossed with tape to reduce the potential bomb-blast impact, and, after the invasion of Poland, householders were required to blackout their windows.

At the same time street lights went out across the city and white stripes were painted on lampposts, kerb stones, steps and any other unlit street furniture or features.

However as the first few months of the War passed uneventfully on the home front, the Government felt comfortable with reducing the Civil Defence provision. The Home Office called for the number of first-aid posts to be cut in half.

Marlborough Hotel with windows blacked out, note the blacked out phone box, too and the white stripes on the kerb and lampposts.

Meanwhile the Chief Constable of Plymouth, George Lowe, suggested to the Emergency Committee, in line with Government thinking, that there should be a significant reduction in the City's Civil Defence establishments and faced with a proposal from the Ministry that the number of ambulances on standby be reduced to 34, the Emergency Committee went one step further and dropped the total to 30.

The Commander-in-Chief of the Western Approaches, however, was not happy and he wrote to the Secretary of State requesting better defence provision. The reply suggested that Plymouth, of all our naval bases, would get more warning of air attack than any other and further, that *'it has been decided that an adequate defence against probable risks can be provided by balloons alone'* (quoted in Gerald Wasley's Blitz – *An Account of Hitler's Aerial War over Plymouth*).

The Message Hits Home

Above: *17th Battalion Devonport Home Guard.*

And then on 10 May 1940, a week after the Allies had been forced to pull out of Norway, Germany invaded Belgium and Halland. With overwhelming aerial support from the Luftwaffe, the German military machine pushed across the borderlines: after eight months the so-called 'Phoney War' had now ended. Within another seven weeks the Allies had been crushed, and over 1,000 ships, about 800 small civilian craft, had evacuated over 330,000 troops from Dunkirk.

Prime Minister Neville Chamberlain had been dismissed by a senior Tory, Leo Amery, with the words Cromwell had used before in the Commons three hundred years earlier, 'You have sat too long for any good you have been doing ... In the name of God, go!'

Churchill, who had been appointed in his stead (Clement Attlee, the Labour leader, saying he was not prepared to support Lord Halifax), described Dunkirk as a 'miracle of deliverance'.

Meanwhile, back home, a few weeks later some 80,000 French troops (who had got away after Dunkirk and before the German advance to Finistere) were re-embarked at Millbay for a journey back to France and a continuation of the fight with the Allied forces on their home soil. Two days later a large contingent of Canadian troops also left from Millbay to join the fray. However they didn't even get out of the Sound, as news of the fall of France saw them return, along with thousands of British, French and Belgian refugees.

Within five days of the cease-fire in France the wailing notes of the air-raid siren sounded across the city in earnest for the first time. Nothing greeted the sound of that sickening lament but with the Germans now in France, Plymouth, it appeared, was now vulnerable.

A week later the switch at Greenbank police HQ was flicked again and the this time undulating tones of the strategically placed sirens (the Devonport one was in Ker Street), was followed by the doleful drone of enemy aircraft and the first bombing raid on the city. Three lives were lost on the Corporation Housing estate at Swilly.

The following day, a sunny summer Sunday, saw a second day-time raid, this one over Cattedown. Six people were killed.

Monday brought another raid: *'This time early morning at Devonport. Four bombs were dropped in the vicinity of Morice Square and Marlborough Street. There was one death, Mr. Slee, butcher, who was killed in his shop when the building was demolished by a direct hit. Three other persons were seriously injured and seven slightly injured. These bombs dropped within a few yards of the Royal Albert Hospital, but the building sustained little damage. One bomb penetrated the Royal Sailors' Club, Morice Square, from roof to basement, exploding in the kitchen, and wrecking the dining-room above, which half an hour before had been crowded with sailors having breakfast before reporting to their ships. There were no casualties in this building. Another of these bombs wrecked a dwelling-house, but the only casualty was a woman, who was dug out of the debris and taken to hospital. There was extensive damage from the blast in Marlborough Street.*

There was now no longer any question in anyone's mind as to the vulnerability or remoteness of Plymouth as far as air attack was concerned. Plymouth was bang in the front line' (Pat Twyford – local journalist and War Correspondent for the *Western Morning News* and *Evening Herald*).

Slee's Butcher's shop, Marlborough Street, 8 July 1940.

Just before these incidents, on 3 July 1940 there was an unfortunate incident in the Dockyard. As the French had laid down their arms the British Government asked its French counterpart if they would allow the French fleet to sail into British ports so that it didn't come into German hands. However, the terms of the Armistice saw control of the French navy passed over to the Germans. Thus it was that those French vessels that were already in Devonport and Portsmouth (two warships, two battleships, two super destroyers, two other destroyers, six torpedo boats, seven submarines and a number of smaller craft) were boarded by Royal Navy personnel and taken over.

Everything went relatively well apart from the crew of the *Mistral* who tried to scuttle their ship and a tragedy on board what was then the largest submarine in the world, the *Surcouf*. Accounts vary as to how the events unfolded but officers on both sides died in a short, heated exchange, that occurred when the submarine was boarded at 5am of the morning after the French crew had been cordially received at Devonport.

The Tension Builds

As the German presence settled across France so the pressure on mainland Britain intensified. Across the Battle of Britain summer of 1940 as the RAF doggedly resisted the challenge mounted by the Luftwaffe so the plight of the ports became increasingly uncomfortable. The ability of British scientists to interfere with the navigation beams that the Germans were using to guide their planes across the country meant that the Luftwaffe were tending to concentrate their efforts on coastal targets rather than industrial centres in the heart of England.

The sirens sounded over the Three Towns 240 times before the year was out and there were 26 actual raids, and yet by the time the King and Queen came to visit the area in March 1941, there had already been a dozen more attacks.

Arriving at Millbay Station at 10.30am, the royal couple undertook a whistle-stop, pre-lunch tour of the Marine Barracks, Naval Barracks and Dockyard. Lunch was had at Admiralty House and the afternoon was spent touring Plymouth, where to date most of the damage had been done, and then tea was taken with the Lord Mayor, Lord Astor, and Lady Astor at Elliot Terrace. Despite the itinerary having been a closely guarded secret it had been a great flag-waving, morale-boosting time, although there were those who were concerned that such a visit might make Plymouth an even greater target.

Top: *The* Surcouf, *the French submarine in Devonport Dockyard.*
Below: Bomb damage outside the Gypsy Tent in Albert Road.

Blitz

And so it proved as, for whatever reason, the Luftwaffe decided to visit the greatest night of bombing thus far on the City. Plymouth City Centre bore the brunt of the attack, and before they could fully appreciate what had hit them, the onslaught was repeated the following night. Some 338 citizens were killed in the two attacks, 20,000 properties were destroyed or damaged and a rough estimate of the.damage done in the two raids was placed at not less than £100,000,000.

Remarkably there was little devastation outside Plymouth but *'people were, however asking the question "Will Devonport experience the same awful fate?" By comparison that end of the city, at least, the business part, was almost unscathed. We had been told that "Haw-Haw", the renegade William Joyce, who was well remembered in Plymouth as one of Mosley's Blackshirts, had declared over the German radio that Devonport's turn was to come'*. [Twyford]
And come it did.

Top left: *King George VI and Queen Elizabeth visit Devonport.*
Top right: *Plymouth Guildhall and Post Office the morning after.*
Above: *Catherine Street, Devonport with Aggie Weston's on the left.*

22 April 1941 Pat Twyford

Last night there commenced another series of appalling raids, and until the end of the month the city was to pass through yet another terrible ordeal which was to test the spirit, the endurance, and the courage of its citizens to the limit. These new raids caused all the greater apprehension, because we still had the all too vivid memory of the events last month.

It now seemed that the Nazis were determined to finish their fiendish work. Their March attacks had left the city with its heart bleeding, business premises which had been household words in the Westcountry heaps of smouldering ruins, lovely public buildings and churches mere blackened shells and fire-scorched husks, hundreds of once happy homes piles of blasted plaster, stone and timber strewn with grim relics of the home comforts, and an awful trail of dead and injured. Yet Plymouth had emerged from that with courage still high, and was beginning to heal her gaping wounds when these next blows were hammered on her broken body.

It was about 9-30 last night when the sirens wailed their warning, and from then until 3-30 this morning it was, in very truth, "hell let loose". Death and destruction rained down once again from the starlit heavens. We knew the stars were there, but we could not see them for the dust and the smoke. The flashes from guns and bursting bombs, and the lurid glare of the terrible fires blotted them out of vision. The beast was again loose to pour out his total warfare on a civil population.

The raiders' tactics were very much the same as those employed a month before – a vanguard of planes dropping thousands of flares and incendiaries, which turned night into day and set the beacon fires to illuminate a target area into which successive waves of bombers dived and released their loads of destruction. I was told that the majority of these bombers came in at a height of about 20,000 feet, and then dived to about 5,000 feet to release their bombs. At that height and in that glare their targets must have been easy. The din was terrific. The glare from the fires could be seen from all parts of the Westcountry. People outside the city, on the faraway hill-tops, in the distant towns and villages, watched that fearful glare, fascinated and horrified. Poor Plymouth!

And poor Devonport too. While Plymouth suffered again this time Devonport shared the pain.

High explosives close to the Royal Albert Hospital, Devonport, necessitated the patients and staff being evacuated.

Another unlucky western-end target was the Corporation Gasworks at Keyham, which received several direct hits and where fires were started. It resulted in the undertaking being put out of action for some time, as far as the provision of gas for public consumption was concerned.

Among the military objectives where damage was done were the Royal Marine Barracks, the Royal William Victualling Yard, the Royal Naval Hospital, the Royal Dockyard, Mount Wise, Raglan Barracks, Granby Barracks, and the Royal Naval Barracks. The full extent of the damage to the Services' establishments, and the casualties among Services' personnel in the port and garrison, was not revealed for security reasons, but the most tragic of their incidents was at the Royal Naval Barracks, where there was a direct hit on the petty officers' block. The killed were stated to number about eighty.

Pat Twyford's contemporary recollections make grim reading, but there was worse to come.

Top: *Marlborough Street. Middle: George Street smoulders.*
Above: *Sorting out the mess in Fore Street..*

23 April 1941

Yet another nightmare; practically a repetition of the previous night's raid. Again the raid started about 9-30, and went on with devilish intensity for six hours. It would seem that the Hun was determined not to leave anything of Plymouth standing.

The procedure was much the same – showers of incendiaries, followed by wave after wave of bombers diving down on the flaming city. If anything the raid was heavier than on the previous night, and hardly a section of the city escaped the widespread destruction caused by fires and high explosives.

On this night the enemy raiders certainly fulfilled the threat of "Haw Haw" that "Devonport's turn is to come". Devonport and Stonehouse did, I think, receive the worst of the mauling. The whole of Fore Street, the shopping centre of the western end of the city, was laid in ruins, with one or two small exceptions. The adjacent areas of Catherine Street, Tavistock Street, Marlborough Street, High Street, and Queen Street were all embraced in the welter of destruction. Famous buildings like the Royal Sailors' Rest, known the world over, the Welcome, the Central Hall, Electric Theatre, Alhambra Theatre, the Belisha Hall, the Hippodrome, and others, were totally destroyed.

Another dawn came today, revealing an even more agonising picture. There seemed to be a seething rage and hatred in the breast of every citizen. Haggard, begrimed, weary to the point of dropping, they were still gritting their teeth, and their one earnest appeal seemed to be summed up in the phrase "Let them have it back for this". It was utterly impossible not to feel and express the spirit of revenge for this wholesale destruction of life and property.

On this day there was yet another pitiful addition to the homeless, the bereaved, and the distraught, and it was at once apparent that gigantic organisation would be needed to deal with the emergency problems of shelter, feeding, and general welfare.

In my diary for this night I see I made this comment: "Again the already tired-out and heavily-pressed Civil Defence services worked heroically. There will be 'inquests' and criticisms. But let us take the big view. There was splendid courage".

Left: *Marlborough Street/Fore Street junction, note the signs for Tozers and Coombes.*
Above: *Fore Street from the Dockyard gates looking east.*

Aftermath Ron Radford

There was another attack the following night and a further two before the month was out. It was estimated that no fewer than 750 enemy aircraft had taken part in the April raids on the city. The number of civilians killed was just under 600, although many were reported missing, no trace of them having been found ... *'they were simply buried under two tons of debris or blown to pieces.'*

Thousands had escaped the night-time horrors by trekking out into the surrounding towns, villages and countryside, only to confront the full horror on their return in the morning:

We had spent the night sleeping on Bere Alston railway station because Lord Haw Haw had warned the citizens of Devonport that their town was going to be destroyed.

We came back next day and the heart of Devonport was gone. Everything was either burning, standing as a shell, or completely flattened. Our house and shop was a flat pile of bricks. The Auxiliary Fire Service were playing a hose, with very little water pressure, on the smouldering ruin. I remember my mother asking the firemen if there was anything she could save and they told her it was just a pile of hot ashes.

All we had were the clothes we were wearing and the little money mum had in her purse. She sat on the edge of the pavement and cried.

We slept a few nights at the Royal Albert Hospital. My brother was a porter there and cleared several incendiary bombs from the roof during the raids. Eventually we moved back to Granby Street. A small block of three houses behind the Hippodrome had somehow survived the bombing and we moved into one of them.

There were happier days then, even though the war raged on. When the Americans entered the war, they arrived in what remained of Fore Street and built a small town of Nissen huts up and down both sides of the street. From now on the cry over their loudspeakers "Now hear this" would echo around the area.

Best of all, they brought chewing gum, chocolate and ice-cream with them and generously handed them out to all the local children.

They asked permission to use the civilian shelters. I think arriving from the peace of America, to the ruins of our town, was a culture shock. In the early days they were more worried by the sirens than we were.

Devonport from the Column – Catherine Street with Aggie Weston's is in the middle distance on the left, while Devonport Market dominates the right of the view.

Two more views from the Column after the arrival of the Americans.

The Dockyard at War Pat Twyford

During the five years and eight months of the European war Devonport Royal Dockyard, by virtue of its geographical position and its first-class facilities, became Britain's No. 1 Naval Repair Establishment. Throughout hostilities it was commanded by Vice-Admiral Sir Arthur N Dowding as Admiral Superintendent.

There was only a limited amount of new construction on the slipways at the South Yard, including some submarines, but the definite Admiralty policy was to utilise to capacity the great resources in repair, maintenance, and 'modernisation'.

In all these directions the Yard accomplished much with an industry which worked right round the clock, and if ever the word 'impossible' had elimination from Britain's war-time vocabulary it was in connection with some of the jobs done here – not only in the actual character of the work but also in working against the clock.

Only at the end of the European operations was it possible to lift the veil on the activities and tell something of the contribution which the Devonport Dockyard 'matey' made to victory.

Throughout the war that much-maligned individual had worked behind the high walls of security. The fighting services had their spots of limelight; the Dockyard just carried on, but, as the Navy will tell you, it delivered the goods.

Now, too, it is also possible to give something of the picture of damage which was caused by German high explosive and incendiary bombs on this big, vulnerable target. It was never comparable with the exaggerated German claims – Devonport Dockyard was very far from being put out of action.

It was in the heavy raids of March and April 1941that the heaviest damage was done at both the South and North Yards.

Among those very old buildings at the South Yard there was ready material for disastrous fires. The Mould Loft and the ancient Ropery were among the burnt-out buildings on what I might call the working side of the Yard. But there were also two other scenes of notable destruction. That lovely terrace of houses which for generations provided the official residences for the Admiral Superintendent and the principal officers was gutted almost from end to end. Only the two end houses were repairable. The Dockyard Church was also destroyed.

Antiquarians were glad to know that the Scrieve Board, that 150-year-old building, with its single-span roof of 103 feet, in which so many of the famous ships built on the nearby slipway had been modelled, was saved by the magnificent efforts of the then voluntary fire-watchers. There were fifty incendiaries on that roof, but they were grimly tackled and beaten out.

At the North Dockyard where, of course, the 'shops' are much more modern, there was a considerable amount of damage to roofs. Men and women worked in "tin hats" to protect them from falling debris, as roofs were being repaired, and were provided with clogs as protection against glass on the floor.

The increase in Dockyard personnel for the war was not as large as in the last war, something about 15 per cent. But the manpower problem was one of the big headaches. This was no 'umbrella' for the unskilled man. Many hundreds of the young labourers were called to the fighting services, and labour was diluted with many women. They were largely employed in cleaning up the yard, but in the skilled trades they did splendid work as welders and drillers.

This man-power problem was intensified by reason of so many of the skilled men going to establishments overseas and in the north, while scores of the best men of the foreman type went on overseeing duties with the big Admiralty contracting firms.

Top left: *The Terrace before the bombing.* Right: *The bomb damaged Terrace.*

Most of Britain's best-known warships, from the modern *Anson, Howe, King George V,* and pre-war battleships down to the smallest craft, were at one time or another at this Dockyard during the war. Ships had to be constantly 'modernised' to keep them equipped with the latest scientific devices, sometimes when they were but a year or two old. Others had to be refitted. It was, however, in repair work to ships damaged in action, by mines, torpedo, or aerial torpedo, that the record of Devonport Dockyard makes proud reading. Take as an example Admiral Lord Mountbatten's destroyer *Javelin*, which was brought back to the Dockyard with both bow and stern just masses of twisted metal. The damage was so extensive that you just wondered how on earth the middle kept afloat. But it did, and the Dockyard did a wonderful job of 'ship surgery'. They fitted a new bow and a new stern. And there were many other ships where the craftsmen of the Dockyard showed equal skill. Rightly, too, there was a measure of pride in these achievements.

As one remembers this enormous contribution to the war effort, it is gratifying also to know that the Admiralty are – at any rate, at the time of writing – attaching so much importance to this Westcountry establishment that they are planning extensive extensions in the post-war reconstruction of the city. Much that was familiar in pre-war Devonport will vanish with the 240 acres that they are acquiring from the residential and business area that lies adjacent to the Dockyard from the Naval Barracks to Mount Wise. From these definite indications there is the bright prospect of Plymouth's assured future prosperity.

Above: *Women at work - "in skilled trades they did splendid work as welders and drillers."* Left: *HMS* Terrible *being fitted out. Launched in 1944 she was the only aircraft carrier to have been built and completed in a Royal Dockyard. The cruiser,* Trinidad *and six submarine were also constructed at the Yard during the war.*

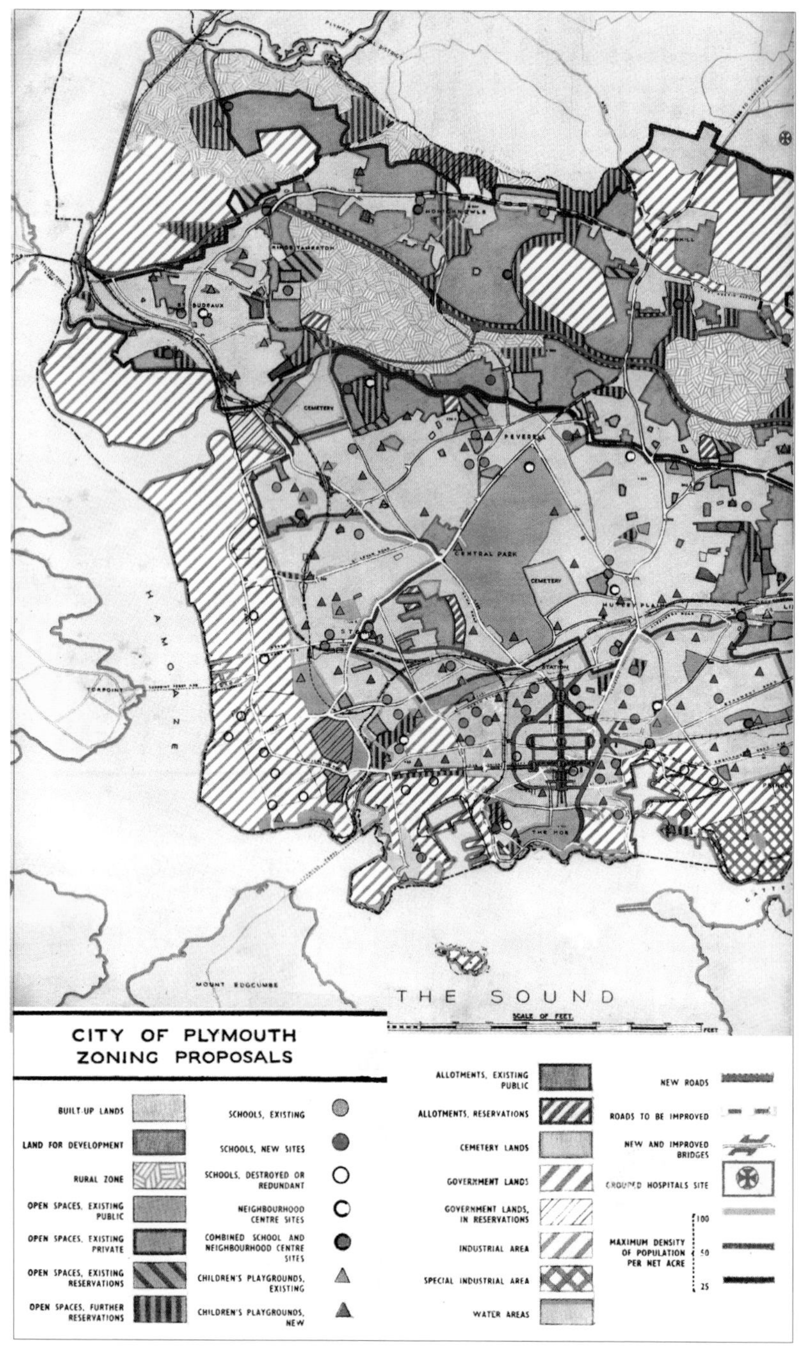

The Plan for Devonport

Twyford's assertion that the Admiralty were looking to take over some 240 acres of pre-war Devonport was largely supported by the authors of the Plan for Plymouth – Professor Patrick Abercrombie and the City Engineer, James Paton Watson. The two had been engaged to work on proposals for rebuilding the city soon after the Minister of Works, Lord Reith, had visited the area in July 1941. Lord Reith advised the Council to go ahead, boldly and comprehensively, with good planning *'and bank on getting financial help'*.

Paton Watson had already been in office for some years, while Abercrombie was one of the most distinguished town planners of his day. Abercrombie's involvement was almost certainly thanks his connections with the wartime Lord Mayor, Lord Astor, and although one of the key visions of the Plan – Armada Way – was clearly a Paton-Watson idea (he had been intent on finding a better link between the railway station at North Road and the Hoe since he first arrived in the city in 1935) the overall plan, which was completed in July 1943 and published the following year, was very much a joint product.

However, the Plan for Plymouth was very much just that – a plan for Plymouth – Devonport and Stonehouse were somewhat sidelined. The reason for that, certainly in Devonport's case, was that the Admiralty's idea of swallowing up some 240 acres of dockside land made it difficult for the authors to formulate any clear proposals for the site, unlike Plymouth City Centre, where the intention was to completely clear over 70 acres of land and build an all-new commercial centre: a centre, moreover, that would include businesses forced out of Devonport, as one obvious consequence of the fact that *'Plymouth's most important occupation, the Dockyard, requires more room'*.

'This,' said the authors, *'must be a first consideration in the Plan'*.

They argued that *'Plymouth was already an important Shopping Centre for Devon and Cornwall and was ripe for complete reconstruction which could and would doubtless have been undertaken without the tragic happening which has precipitated this work.' 'The elimination of the secondary main shopping centre at Devonport, also destroyed, but not to be rebuilt owing to the requirements of the Dockyard, will lead to the concentration of a greater area of shopping floor space in the new Plymouth centre.'*

In contrast to Plymouth's pre-war centre with 550 shops of varying size, Devonport's sub-centre, at Fore Street, had 110 retail shops spread over 6 acres and one acre devoted to banks and offices: *'34 of the shops, however, were branches of Plymouth businesses or multiple shops.'*

'If,' they argued, *'Devonport is not rebuilt, many of the smaller shops will, no doubt, set up around the nucleus of a sub-centre which already exists in the middle of the residential area of Stoke and in the vicinity of Ford House, where it would serve the shopping needs of Ford and Swilly areas. Many with the distribution of population envisaged no longer being required in Plymouth, would follow the drift of the population into suburban areas, thus it will not be necessary to provide accommodation in the new centre for the whole of the shops that were at Devonport.'*

In other words, not only did the planners not think it necessary to rebuild Devonport's shopping centre, they didn't even think they needed to provide sites for Devonport's pre-war shops in the bright new Plymouth City Centre.

It seems fair to say, however, that not everybody bought into this version of the future and the authors were therefore forced to acknowledge that there was *'some justification for the request to have included in this Report a possible alternative layout for the reconstruction of the Devonport business area, as circumstances might render abortive the Admiralty scheme for the expansion of the area of the Dockyard to the extent indicated. If this should be so, consideration will have to be given to the planning of the Devonport, Morice Town and Keyham areas, and the reconstruction of the flourishing Fore Street shopping area.'*

With this in mind the planners made the assumption that while the Admiralty would still require about 20 acres on the edge of South Yard, at least the Granby and Raglan barrack sites would become available. Central to this vision would be another pivotal, Armada Way-style principal axis, a new Morice Street, which *'would be continued in a straight line to Mutton Cove, forming a tree-lined avenue from the centre to the waterside, at points on which it would be possible to obtain glimpses of the estuary with Mount Edgcumbe in the background.'*

Housing a community of roughly 8,000 where there had been 14,000 south of Fore Street before the war, *'drastic reconstruction'* was envisaged as the area *'is almost entirely "blight", although previous slum clearance has produced some good examples of three-storey flats, in Clowance and Prospect Streets.*

'Foulston's Guildhall in Ker Street, and Devonport Column are, of course,

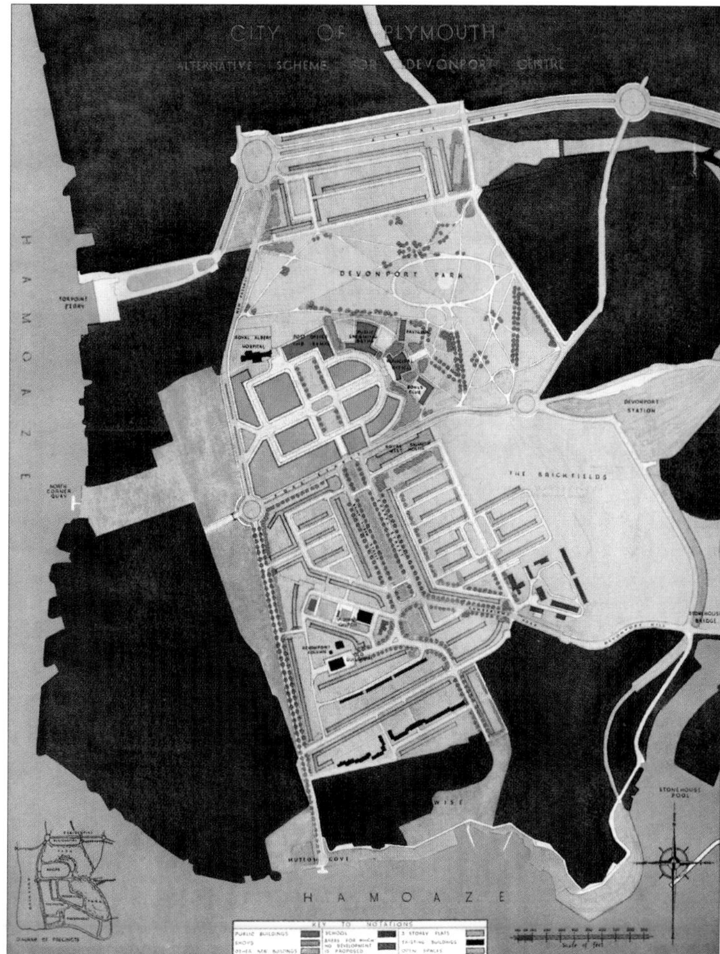

The last page of the 1943 Plan for Plymouth – the alternative for Devonport Centre.

retained, and form a focal point of the redevelopment.'

Meanwhile, they concluded: *'the community of interest, for shopping alone, between Devonport and the population of East Cornwall would justify the re-creation of this shopping centre. In addition, the population of Stoke, Ford and St Budeaux, who find employment in the Dockyard, would continue to be attracted to his centre.'*

It's seems strange that this logic didn't apply to the main scheme.

Fore Street after the war, looking down towards the old Dockyard Gates, with Woolworths and Barclay's Bank in the middle distance beyond the Nissen huts, with the Midland Bank nestled between Burton's and Marks & Spencer in the foreground on the right.

The Dust Settles

Nissen Huts, Hangars and Prefabs: Top: here a former Harrowbear hangar is deployed as a temporary home for Central Hall, Fore Street - opened in May 1950. Middle: Fore Street from just outside the old Dockyard wall looking east. Bottom: American type prefabs in King's Road.

'The Future of this city, and particularly the Devonport area, is dependent upon the maintenance of a Grand Fleet, the necessity for which is bound up with the political and international picture structure of the Allied Nations in the years after the war. He would be a bold person who would be dogmatic on such a subject with world events and conditions changing as they have done during the past few years.'

So wrote the authors of the Plan for Plymouth, two years before the Second World War came to an end. However, it could have been written 20 or even 120 years earlier. The big difference was that 120 years earlier the man in the street exercised little influence on the way the world turned, now, however, the country was altogether more democratic and in the first post-war General Election, in August 1945, just days after the Japanese surrender, Labour leader Clement Atlee, who had been No. 2 to the Conservative Winston Churchill in the wartime coalition Government, became Prime Minister as Labour scored a landslide victory.

Labour's plans for a welfare state with a free national health service, together with proposals to nationalise the railways and the coal industry had brightened the bleak post-war picture.

Victory had been achieved but 420,000 British servicemen and 60,000 civilians had lost their lives, as had nearly 300,000 American

servicemen, 13 million from the USSR, 3.5 million Germans and 3.6 million Japanese.
In addition to the human fatalities, hundreds of thousands of Britons had lost their homes or had major rebuilding work to undertake, countless businesses, entertainment places and pubs had disappeared forever. The cost of rebuilding and repairing the nation was daunting as was the problem of feeding and fuelling the nation. Food, tobacco and petrol imports were, of necessity, being reduced. The American government had just pulled the plug on the Lend-Lease arrangement whereby Britain had been importing food from the States without down payments in cash. British production was mainly being directed abroad to help pay for our imports, but due to the pressures placed on industry during the war, our exports were running at around half the pre-war level.

The war had been won but Britain was bankrupt. Rationing was here for the foreseeable future as the outlook for the next few years was not a particularly rosy one – and it was even harder in those places that had suffered at the hands of the Luftwaffe. All these ingredients influenced the outcome of the election. For the first time in Plymouth's history neither a Conservative nor a Liberal MP was returned as Lucy Middleton won Sutton, Bert Medland took Drake and Michael Foot defeated the sitting Conservative member, Leslie Hore Belisha.

It had been the unemployment situation in the Dockyard after the First World War that had really kick-started the Labour movement locally. Jimmy Moses, the leader of the Shipwrights' Union in the Yard, had been a member of the last Devonport Town Council back in 1914 and was part of the new amalgamated Plymouth body. Bert Medland was another dockyard man, he led the Engineers' Union and by the end of 1923 both he and Moses had been made Aldermen. Another dockyardie, Harry Mason, was also elected to the Council, along with a railwayman, RR Oke.

In 1926 following the election of another half a dozen or so Labour councillors, Jimmy Moses was created Plymouth's first Labour Mayor. Three years later he was elected MP for the Drake constituency, and became Plymouth's first Labour MP.

Hore-Belisha, by this time, had been returned as the Liberal MP for Devonport: he was a minister in successive governments throughout the thirties – most famously as Minister of Transport in the mid-thirties when he introduced the driving test, traffic lights and what became known as the Belisha Beacon. Later, at the War Ministry, he introduced conscription and became a great reformer of the army.

Meanwhile, back in the Mayoral seat, Harry Mason stepped into the chair once it looked likely that the war was about to end – Lord Astor being more than happy to step down after his extended stint. At the end of his year, Mason became leader of the new dominant party in the City Council: *'and as was only to be expected, Labour took the chairmanships of most of the important committees, like Reconstruction (Mason himself), Finance (Alderman H Wright), Housing (Bill Miller), Education (Councillor Neil Bradley) and Transport (Alderman Louis Hodge).'* [Twyford 1949]

Top: *Sir Clifford Tozer with Leslie Hore-Belisha.* Inset: *the new 'Belisha' beacons.* Bottom: *Lucy Middleton and Michael Foot electioneering.*

Next Seven Years In Devonport

Sketch map showing areas in the Devonport Dockyard extension scheme which are expected will be acquired within the following years: A in 1952, B in 1953, C in 1954, D in 1955, E in 1957, and F in 1958.

Vanishing Devonport

For all the grand plans for Plymouth City Centre, however, the first priority had to be housing: 15,000 to 20,000 homes were needed urgently *'to make up the leeway of the lost years and to make good the war destruction and with thousands of its citizens scattered like refugees over the countryside, all eager to return to the city'* (ibid).

The situation in Devonport, however, was aggravated by the indecision of the Admiralty over their intentions. After early indications that they would want to acquire some 240 acres of dockside land after the war, they eventually asked Plymouth City Council if they would acquire 182 acres. However, three years later and with little activity in the meantime, they announced that over the next twelve years they would require just 154 acres. The following year they cut that almost in two and said that 78.5 acres would suffice: then, in March 1955, the Admiralty released 17 acres of that allocation: *'the reduction being thought due to modern warfare's need to avoid excessive industrial concentration.'* [Lt-Cdr Ken Burns, *The Devonport Dockyard Story*]

In 1957 they surrendered a further 10 acres, which brought the total space they were looking to enclose to just over 50 acres –. and by then that process of enclosure was already underway, as a long, unattractive and foreboding wall had started to take shape, putting most of Fore Street and all of Catherine Street, Tavistock Street, Edinburgh Road, York Street, Sydney Street, Market Street and most of Cumberland Street and Duke Street, out of sight and out of reach.

A similar exercise south of Keyham Yard consigned William Street, Mooncove Street, and much of Charlotte Street disappear. At the same time, as part of the drive to rehouse those who were destined to remain in Devonport, plans were set in motion to

Top: *Surviving shells in shell-shocked Devonport.*
Middle: *The wall takes shape around the corner of Duke Street and James Street.*
Bottom: *Looking northwards across Fore Street with York Street School in the foreground.*

Devonport from the air in 1949 with Marlborough Street running left to right towards St Pauls Church, its tower still standing on St Morice Square.

Looking north across Devonport Park

remove those pre-war, congested 'blights' that were seen as unsightly blots on the Devonport landscape. Ultimately, it seemed, this pincer movement on the part of the Admiralty and the Local Authority would mean that little of pre-war Devonport would survive. What the enemy hadn't razed the plotters and planners would, as a brave new town, albeit one with comparatively few shops, facilities and places of entertainment, would spring up in its stead.

Again the pub story speaks volumes: Fore Street alone saw most of its public houses wiped out in the war: the Golden Lion, Lifeboat, Military Arms, Prince George, Thomas's Bar, Two Trees and two separate Wine Vaults. Others in the old part of the town also went in the raids, and in the period leading up to the building of the wall, and the redevelopment of the Pembroke Street area, another forty or so Devonport hostelries were lost and not replaced.

However, significantly, Aggie Weston's Royal Sailor's Rest was kept going. It re-opened soon after the war in the building formerly occupied by the United Services Home for Girls, the old Orphanage at the top of Albert Road. The Orphanage itself moved to Newquay during the war – and stayed there.

The site of the pre-war premises however was cleared early on, as was Willes Road, while Edinburgh Road was closed and the site was made ready for the construction of a new Gun-Mounting Store.

By 1950 a few single story buildings – laboratories for Dockyard use – had been erected in Charlotte Row, while in Fore Street the Manager Engineering Department had occupied Burton's (one of the group of three buildings surviving in that stretch), the Manager Constructive Department had taken on a single-storey building just outside the Fore Street Gate.

Gradually Fore Street was cleared and earmarked for different Dockyard uses. In 1954 signs started appearing here and there: between Fore Street, Chapel Street, Cumberland Street and Catherine Street, their stark message: Keep Out – Admiralty Property.

Meanwhile, time was called on various wartime survivors, like the Elephant and Castle, Post Office Inn, Volunteer Inn, Butcher's Arms, plus Chaplin's Pickle Factory, and the Union Savings Bank – although the latter was to be rebuilt in the New Welcome Building in the surviving section of Fore Street.

Certainly not everyone in Devonport was prepared to give up on the old town. Speaking earlier at a meeting of the Devonport Mercantile Association in December 1951, the City Engineer, James Paton-Watson, told members that any proposals by the Association concerning the trade development of Devonport would be favourably considered by Plymouth City Council. *'The Admiralty,'* he said, *'decided in the early days to proceed on the assumption made in the original Plan for Plymouth – the practical elimination of Devonport.'*

Royal Albert Gate with the remains of William Street still standing on the far left.

Work begins on the new road through Devonport Park

'There had,' he added, *'been a great deal of suspicion that the early proposals of the Admiralty were too bold, but he thought everything possible should have been done to compel the Admiralty to adhere to its original decision.*

'In altering its boundary the Admiralty has left the city with an almost insoluble problem. Devonport has been segmented into three areas – the Pembroke Street area, a portion of the business area which is too small to do much with, the reduced area at Albert Road, and odd shops left in the north.' [quoted in the WEH 5 Dec 1951]

Looking at what needed to be done first, however, Paton Watson said that the first proposal was to create a small neighbourhood unit in the Pembroke Street area, but before that could be brought to fruition, 4,000 people had to be removed from the area and rehoused.

The City Engineer also pointed out that road traffic had multiplied ten times between 1919 and 1938, and further, that business traffic since 1938 had doubled. A new road was needed, he said, *'and the only satisfactory route is from the top of Chapel Street, through the Barracks, across Devonport Park, and along Garden Street into Albert Road. I don't think it will be long before it is carried out,'* he added.

In the event it wasn't until 1957 that Granby Barracks came down with the barrack wall in Princes Street. By which time there was precious little left of pre-war Devonport.

The new road at night.

The two florists – Hearl's and Crosley's – who had been occupying the old Devonport Market building, moved out in May 1954 – the former going to Cumberland Street, the latter to Ordnance Street. That same month Marks & Spencers closed their Fore Street premises and transferred their staff and stock to their new Plymouth branch. Earlier that year the Plymouth Co-operative Society had cleared its tailoring shop out of Marlborough Street, and its confectionary outlet in Morice Street. Sometime later Perkin Brothers, the long-established outfitters, and specialists in school blazers, caps and badges, closed down.

Meanwhile, sections of Catherine Street, Market Square, Market Street, James Street and Duke Street were closed off and the bulldozers started clearing large parts of James Street and Mount Street. St Paul's Church, Morice Square was demolished as a number of once-prominent landmarks were removed.

Slowly the rebuilding began. A new Barclay's Bank was built in Marlborough Street, to replace the lost Fore Street premises while in Fore Street itself the new Welcome Building was joined by a new Central Hall and a new Railway Hotel (re-christened the Ark Royal by the time it was opened) was erected on the site of its pre-war counterpart. Sadly, though, the planned streetscape here was destined not to be fulfilled.

The commitment to housing had to be greater. In May 1957 Messrs Laing started building new flats at the back of Marlborough Street and the Corporation commenced work on the new road from the heart of the old town to Albert Road.

The other, western, side of Marlborough Street, saw little action though, and twenty years after the publication of the Plan for Plymouth a report was published for the area which still blamed the *'uncertainty remaining after the war as to how much land in Devonport would be required for Dockyard extensions'* for the *'atmosphere of dereliction and decay'*.

It continued: *'Several gaps remain in the shopping frontages of Marlborough Street. Elsewhere in the area the bombed sites are often used for car parking by Dockyard employees and others, and for illegal dumping of rubbish.'*

And therein lay another problem – there was nowhere near enough parking to serve the demands of residents, dockyard workers and the business community.

Top: *The Ark Royal, as built.*
Below: *The Railway Inn, as planned, by architect Frank Weemys*

Consequently, among the various proposals put forward in that 1964 document were: a four-storey car park, adjoining South Yard Gate, for around 240 vehicles to be built by the Ministry of Defence (which now incorporated the Admiralty); accommodation for 96 cars on the west side of Marlborough Street and abutting the east side of an improved Morice Street, plus a further 30 spaces along New Passage Hill and garage accommodation for 253 cars (one per dwelling) for the proposed residential development.

The housing scheme in question was to be made up of three 15-storey tower blocks, three 4-storey blocks and one of 2-storeys: *'The tower blocks will be linked by car parks, the roofs of which will be landscaped as amenity space for occupants of the flats.'*

Completion of the scheme was envisaged in 3–5 years, *'depending on the phasing of the work.'*

That work involved *'all the existing shops and public houses* (including the Two Triangles and the Lord Hood) *situate in the area west of Marlborough Street to Queen Street'* being demolished *'with the exception of the Boot Inn'*. *'The existing shops and public houses in Marlborough Street are adequate'* said the Report, *'to serve the needs of the new residential development.'*

The proposals also required the displacement of more than 60 families who were currently living in the 40 or so pre-war 'dwelling units' that were still standing and still occupied (there were eight that were empty).

Marlborough Street area, Devonport Report 1964

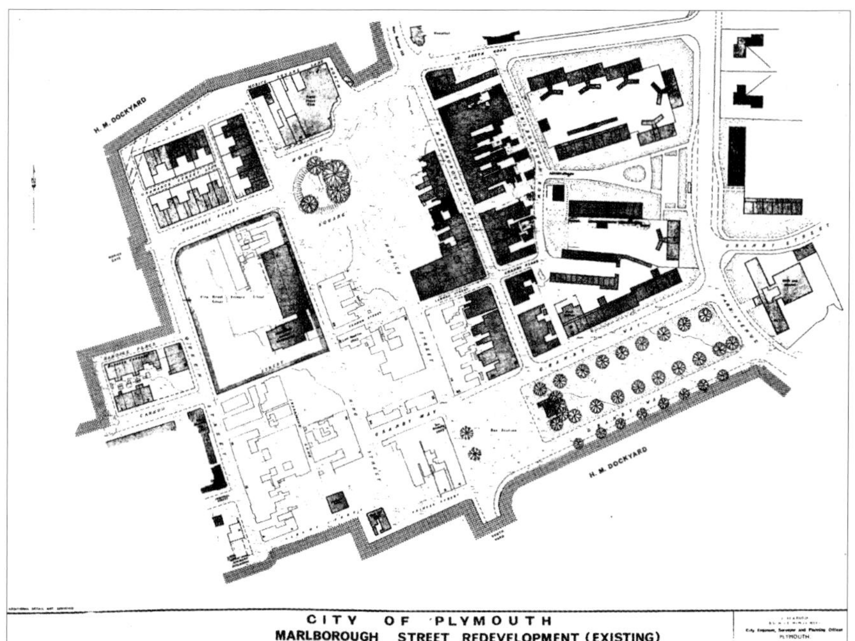

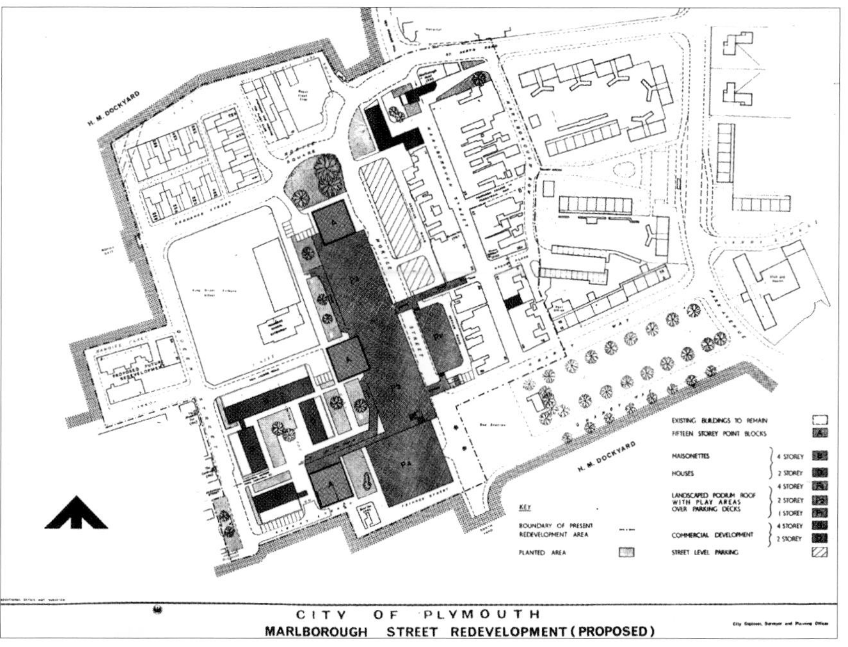

Apart from those surviving bits of Marlborough Street and Fore Street and one or two other isolated buildings and blocks, notably at North Corner, there was not much of nineteenth-century Devonport left outside the Dockyard wall above Fore Street, and certainly precious little that was deemed to be of value – apart from No.10 Morice Square which was on the Supplementary List of Buildings of Special Architectural or Historic Interest.

South of Fore Street the situation was not vastly different: Foulston's Town Hall, Column and Egyptian building were safe, but the southern side of the street, an impressive residential block also credited to the celebrated architect, was bulldozed after an impassioned campaign to preserve it, supported by Stanley Goodman and the Old Plymouth Society.

The Blitz-surviving churches of James Piers St Aubyn were also pulled down: St Mary the Virgin, in James Street, which had survived unscathed, went in 1959, again despite protests – the church council secretary, Henry Gendle arguing that it should be preserved on account of its history, structure and architectural beauty. At the same time St Stephen's, in George Street, the tower of which had survived although the body of the building had been left a shell, also came down. As did the church of St John the Baptist, in John Street, which had been damaged by enemy action but converted as a community centre, was also razed.

The rationale was that the ecclesiastical needs of the area could now be served by St Aubyn Church in Chapel Street and so the parishes of St Stephen's, St Mary's, St Paul's and St John the Baptist, were merged into one, and the Reverend JH Jones, was appointed to oversee the newly merged congregations.

Meanwhile, the opportunities for those residents who were left to carry on congregating in the various pubs of the parish was diminishing spectacularly around the Pembroke Street redevelopment area too.

Among the many casualties: the Duke Street Inn, Bakers Arms, Foresters Arms (Duke Street), the Impregnable (James Street), the Albion, Rose and Crown, Himalaya (Pembroke Street), the White Swan (George Street) and the Volunteer (Chapel Street).

All in all, whereas there had been over 100 pubs within the confines of old Devonport at the end of the First World War, within 20 years of the end of the Second World War that number had dropped to just 21 *'two of which possess eating facilities'*.

Top: *The doomed Foulston flats in Ker Street.*
Bottom: *St Mary's comes down, 1959.*

Baker's Arms

Himalaya, Pembroke Street

The Albion

Time is called at the Victory Inn, Gloucester Street

Duke Street Inn

Rose and Crown, Pembroke Street, inset: the interior.

Clearly there were deemed to be enough, however, as there was no talk of replacing any of them.

There was a similar stance taken towards shopping facilities.

'It is proposed that despite the new housing envisaged in this area (which would bring the number of residents up from 4,000 to over 5,500) no further shops should be provided, and that convenience shopping in the Mount Wise area should be served only by the existing shops in the George Street/Duke Street area ...' [City of Plymouth 'South Devonport Report' 1966. South Devonport here being old Devonport] ... *'the area surrounding the South Dockyard and its Extension and within the ring of open space composed of Devonport Park, the Brickfields and Mount Wise'.*

There were, at the time, 50 shops in the South Devonport area, two-thirds of them in the Marlborough Street area:

'By far the larger of the two, it is already acting as a district centre and attracts shoppers from a wide area beyond South Devonport.'

There was, however, a noticeable divide between the two shopping centres, the reality of the Dockyard Extension and surrounding wall was the *'loss of a series of north to south road links'* but all was not lost, as *'the Development Plan provided their replacement by the improvement of Chapel Street.'*

Improvement? It may have been widened, but in what other sense could it possibly be regarded as having been improved? Walking alongside the wall was like walking along the perimeter of a prison and almost as gloomy for those on the outside as it was on the inside.

Ron Johns' parents had a shop near the Brown Bear: *'When the wall went up trade dropped about 75% overnight. The business was restyled as a coffee bar – with the Beatles a permanent fixture on the jukebox. Soon afterwards it became a late-licence night club – Rovaro's.' However even that wasn't enough to keep the business afloat and before long Rovaro's relocated to the Barbican and became Ronnie's.*

Chapel Street, Devonport, 9 December 1966

of private ownership went all too often hand in hand with a lack of ongoing care and repair for the built environment.

Nor did it help that the post-war planning for Devonport was not overly family-friendly. There was too much one-bed, or bed-sit, accommodation and too much high-rise development.

The authors of the 1966 Report for the area were well aware of these short-comings: *'It will be noted that no further one-bedroom and bed-sitting accommodation is proposed for South Devonport, though it may be desirable to include a few old persons' bungalows if the need arises.'*

But how much 'damage' had already been done?

'Probably the most significant factor requiring a fresh examination of the Marlborough Street area has been the change of opinion arising from greater experience of the social and economic consequences of very high-density housing schemes. Broadly it can be said that not only is the cost of high-density building very high per dwelling, but it provides accommodation in a form which is not generally desired by the majority of families which Councils have to house.' The report continued: *'There is little doubt that flats, especially in high blocks, are far from ideal for families with children, particularly young children.'*

And then after citing advice of the Ministry of Housing and Local Government, they noted that: *'Conditions prevailing in Plymouth and especially in South Devonport are not such as to require or justify very high-density building.'*

olling ship. St then n the bold vered large there , the iralty) ouses *nd of rland* had lack

Top left: Devonport's new tower blocks.
The new flats fronting Ker Street and Duke Street with a new high rise block further down Duke Street.

Top left: *The new flats in Pembroke Street.* Top right: *The pre-war Corporation flats in Cornwall Street c.1966.* Middle: *Devonport Secondary Modern School off Devonport Park, opened 9 September 1963.* Bottom: *Mount Wise School,*

Such fine sentiments didn't stop the high-rises happening, however, and having built them the best had to be made of them.

Otherwise the new flats at Devonport weren't all that different to the pre-war developments. The star-shaped blocks, popular across the city (there were more on the Barbican and at Pennycomequick), were reminiscent in all but overall shape to 1930s Corporation flats – like those in Cornwall Street. Other pre-war blocks to survive were those at Duke Street, Mount Street, Clowance Street and Prospect Row.

Clearly the need to press on and provide accommodation was keenly felt, as were the financial constraints that overshadowed all these projects, it was nevertheless disappointing that so much of the architecture was flat, featureless and utilitarian, and not designed to be appealing aesthetically and therefore affording some potential to be cherished and respected.

Equally uninspiring were the new schools that were being hastily erected around the city and South Devonport was no exception. At the time of compiling his 1966 Report, City Planning Officer, CC Gimingham, noted that there were five schools serving the area: Mount Wise (J,M & I – Junior, Mixed and Infants); Ker Street (I), Cornwall Street (J from Ker Street); King Street (closed temporarily) and St Joseph's Roman Catholic Primary at Mount Wise. Some 800 children were currently being catered for and the plan was to raise pupil numbers to 1,000 but to rationalise the school and have just Mount Wise (J,M & I) serving Pembroke Street area; King Street (J,M & I) serving the Marlborough Street area, and Raglan Barracks (J,M & I) for the new housing to be built on the old barracks site. There was also the new Devonport Secondary Modern School on the north side of Devonport Park.

The new arrangements spelt the end of Ker Street School and Cornwall Street School, with the latter being earmarked as a potential Youth Club once the new educational facility in King Street had been completed.

Youth Clubs, at this time, were seen as important social centres and there were several dotted around South Devonport – the Dockland Settlement at Bluff Battery, the Johnston Memorial Hall in Clowance Lane: there were meetings here every evening as well as being the base for Devonport Amateur Boxing Club. There were also Youth Club meetings three evenings a week at Methodist Central Hall – the Welcome – in Fore Street, plus scout and guide evenings.

In addition to these social centres the old Guildhall in Ker Street, which was now owned by the Corporation, was used as a Folk Club. Meanwhile, the Forum Cinema had been converted to a Bingo Hall and 'teenage' dance hall known briefly as the Key Club. The club had moved across from the Barbican and opened with top rhythm and blues band Georgie Fame and the Blue Flames. Later, mod-rockers, the Who, played there (all in all, however, the Key club era lasted less than a year, and the club moved on to Exmouth Road. Other facilities, also existed, like the Fleet Club, and the Salvation Army Red Shield Club at Granby Way, but were mainly used by service personnel.

Apart from a branch library in Duke Street (the main Naval History Library moved out of Mount Wise to go to the Central Library in 1962) and the 21 remaining pubs, that was about it for Sixties entertainment in South Devonport – a far cry from the pre-war days when the community had its own cinemas, theatre, more than 70 pubs and a large number of churches, big and small dotted around the community.

The once-proud town looked nothing like either of visions of it that had been proposed in the 1943 Plan for Plymouth, indeed 20 years on it had become a relatively unfocused, soul-less and sprawling Council estate. The majority of the indigenous population doubtless would have defended it and made the most of it, but there was little or no reason for the rest of Plymouth to visit, particularly as the opening of Central Park Swimming Pool had meant that Plymouth schools no longer had to endure the vagaries of the British weather and stage their swimming galas at Mount Wise, although for many there was little alternative to the Brickfields when it came to sports day – whatever the weather.

Plymouth College sports day, Brickfields, 1964

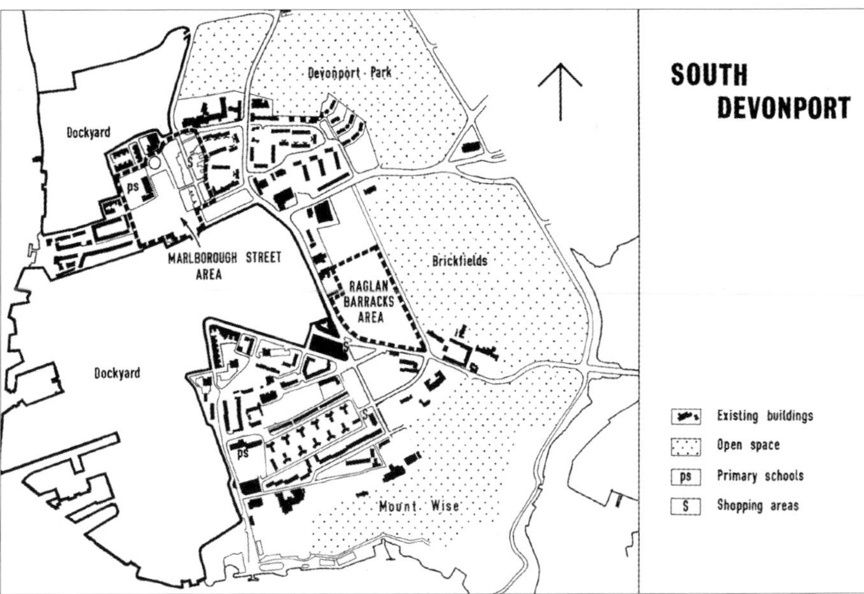

Top: *The new Naval Stores building, opened in February 1963.* Below: *South Devonport in 1966.*

Ghost Town?

As if to emphasise the idea that there was no real reason to venture into the heart of old Devonport the passenger service to King's Road Station ended on 7 September1964, along with the link between St Budeaux (Victoria Road) and Devonport Junction. Seven years later – 7 March 1971 – the last goods train pulled out of King's Road and the station closed altogether. Of course these closures were not exclusive to Devonport as Dr Beeching's axe cut rail services right across the country. Some 3,000 (roughly half) of all British stations (and around a quarter of the rail routes) were lost in the ten years following the publication of Richard Beeching's report *The Reshaping of British Railways*.

The intention was to stem the losses incurred in the wake of the expansion of road transport and business and private vehicular traffic. Only viable stations and routes were kept and clearly King's Road was not deemed to be one of them.

In an unrelated but adjacent development the tidal creek just south of the station was filled-in the year after King's Road closed – the events weren't entirely unrelated as much of the infill material came from redundant British Rail buildings and bridges (some came from the Dockyard as it was being redeveloped too). This removed a 'stinking mud flats' situation and afforded extra sporting facilities for the schools – Devonport High School for Boys and Tamar – that had moved into neighbouring blocks of the old Military Hospital in the 1940s (although thanks to the war the move was not entirely smooth or seamless). The infilling of the creek up to Millbridge did, however, curtail certain of the boys' sailing activities.

Meanwhile, by the end of 1974 only odd traces of the erstwhile King's Road Station remained as the main buildings and tower block of the newly created Plymouth College of Further Education were opened on the old railway site. The influx of students, teachers and support staff had an uplifting effect on the area and in a not entirely coincidental development one or two of the local pubs experienced an upturn in their fortunes. The Ark Royal in Fore Street and the Old Chapel on the corner of George Street and Duke Street became popular live music venues, while the Swan Hotel at North Corner, which had recently been closed, was, in 1975, re-invented as a real ale pub and another live music venue.

Top: *Summer of 1964, the 11.47am Exeter Central to Plymouth via Okehampton.* Middle: *8 March 1968, the Duke of Edinburgh passes through on his way to open the Maritime College.* Bottom: *1965 Devonport King's Road (all this page Bernard Mills)*

Left: *The new College of Further Education.* Above: *April 1963 Stonehouse Branch Line and Creek, looking up to Devonport High School for Boys. (Keith Holt)*

On the Other Side of the Wall

As might be surmised from the prevarication over the extent of the Dockyard extensions, work in the Yard after the war was not as abundant as it might have been. With the conclusion of hostilities the order for the aircraft carrier, *Polyphemus* was cancelled as was the completion of the patrol boats *Ace* and *Achetes* after their launches in March and September 1945.

It wasn't until June 1953 that a new warship was built at Devonport: a new air-type direction frigate, the *Salisbury,* was the first all-welded vessel to be put together in the Yard. Six years later HMS *Plymouth* slid into the Hamoaze and was followed by *Tartar* in 1960, *Cleopatra* in 1964, *Danae* in 1965 and *Scylla* in 1968. Six frigates in 15 years – a stark contrast to the first 14 years of the twentieth century when the Dockyard had turned out ten battleships, two battlecruisers and three cruisers.

The situation was not destined to improve either, as the *Scylla* was the last warship to be built at Devonport. In 1979 the big, pre-war cantilever cranes on either side of slip No. 3 were cut down. Over the next two years seven more cranes were similarly removed, the last survivor, crane No. 308, being sold to a firm in Sheffield for scrap in 1981.

Such is not to suggest, however, that work in the Yard dried up altogether, indeed whilst there was not enough to sustain the immediate post-war peak of 21,000 dockyard workers, Devonport became a major centre for the conversion into and refitting of, aircraft carriers. *Furious, Glorious, Courageous* and *Hermes* were all big conversion jobs, while the *Eagle* and the *Ark Royal* were regularly in for refits, the former arriving for a four-year 'modernisation' in 1960 – the project costing £30 million and employing 3,000 men, and the latter also undergoing a £30 million refit from 1966 to 1969.

Of course it wasn't just the ships that were undergoing modernisation, the Dockyard itself was undergoing major changes. New Central Offices were built on part of the William Street site between 1964 and 1966 and, as part of the restructuring, the building of a wall around this new extension was taken as an opportunity to move the gate to Keyham Yard from the bottom of Albert Road and the Dockyard clock was moved from one western tower into the one nearer the road.

Top: North Yard. Bottom: HMS Salisbury, the first all-welded ship to be built on a prefabricated principle. Inset: Navy Days programme, 1966.

An historic day: 8 August 1968 – the last warship to be built in Devonport – HMS Scylla – is launched.

Around the same time an overhead road link was established between this new part of the Yard and Morice and between Morice Yard and South Yard. Vehicles no longer needed to go out of the Yard to get from one part to another and thus the internal transport situation was hugely improved. The demise of the old Dockyard train was hastened by these developments, thereby drawing a line under a system that had served the yard one way or another for over 100 years, and which at its height had some twenty miles of track in constant use. At one time or another some 70 locomotives had been employed on the internal railway – a railway that had links to the national network and, underground, between all three yards.

Up until its closure the system had also provided a free passenger service throughout the Yard, across the whole of the twentieth century, and had boasted six classes of accommodation from general labourer through to Principal Officers and the Admiral.

A restricted rail service, for the transportation of goods, continued to operate for some years (until 1982) but the passenger service was replaced by coaches initially, and then, from December 1969, by six double-decker buses (four for Dockyardies and two for naval ratings).

The changes weren't confined to the physical environment either. In October 1966 a new post was created – General Manager for Devonport Dockyard: 54-four-year-old Captain Horace Gerald Southwood was appointed and tasked with forming a new management structure, similar to that recently implemented in the three other Royal Dockyards.

Southwood's period of tenure also saw a commitment expressed in 1968–69 to modernise and redevelop Devonport: Devonport henceforth became a base for Type 21 and 22 frigates. The Navy Minister, Dr David Owen, who was also then the MP for Plymouth Sutton, also announced that Devonport was to become an operational base for nuclear submarines and for the docking, refitting and refuelling of said submarines.

The following year, 1970, Devonport Dockyard was re-designated Devonport Naval Base, and, in April, Vice Admiral Anthony Griffin was appointed as the newly instituted role of Flag Officer, Plymouth (superseding the old Commander-in-Chief position) and a few months later, he was also made Superintendent of the Dockyard bringing the two roles together for the first time since the Yard began.

Top: *Mount Wise.* Middle: *The Ark Royal returns.* Bottom: *March 1963 The last Dockyard train. (Bernard Mills)* Opposite page: *HMS* Decoy *passes Mount Wise, 1962.*

D106

Top: *May 1980 Prince Charles opens the Submarine Refit Complex pictured above.*

Complex Arrangements

Among the other initiatives brought in around this time was the decision to accept female apprentices. In 1970 advertisements were placed and they generated sixty enquiries: in the event however, only nine girls completed application forms and only seven of them sat the entrance examination. Of those seven, six passed but four of them changed their minds about going into the Yard, which left just two, one of whom failed at the interview stage ... so then there was one! Happily, having passed the interview, she was offered a place, subject to attaining certain grades in her school GCE 'O' levels. Sadly she did not attain the grades and so no girls joined that year. The following year 14 girls (out of 21) passed the exams and eight took up apprenticeships, alongside that year's entry of 230 boys.

The Sixties generally had seen something of a fall overall in dockyard numbers, as *'employment in the shipbuilding sector declined from 56% to 41% of manufacturing employment in the Plymouth travel-to-work area between 1961 and 1971'* (Bishop 1991). The trend, however, was reversed in the 1970s as three of the biggest developments in many years were undertaken with the construction of the massive, three-hangared Frigate Complex (opened by Dr David Owen on 23 September 1977), the Fleet Maintenance Base, off Weston Mill Lake (opened by the Prime Minister, James Callaghan, on 21 April 1978), and the nuclear Submarine Refit Complex at the top of North Yard (opened by HRH Prince Charles on 23 May 1980).

Hailed as being the *'best submarine refit facility in the whole of Europe'* the latter was dominated, visually, by a £2.5 million crane and a nine-storey (four of them below ground) submarine support building.

The Frigate Complex meanwhile transformed the Dockyard's ability to work on ships whatever the weather, while the facilities for connecting ships docked in the Complex to electricity supplies, air conditioning, and sewage disposal, meant that it was possible for the ship's company to live, eat and sleep on board throughout the refitting process.

The massive doors of the Complex rise to a height of 160ft and are in four sections, each capable of independent action so that top section can be lowered to allow for natural ventilation.

Other, smaller-scale Seventies developments in the Yard included a new restaurant facility (1971) a 169-metre long Pipe Shop (1975) and a Medical Centre (1979).

Foreign Secretary and Devonport MP David Owen opens the Frigate Complex – 1977.

Plenty of Action

The fact that there was a great deal of construction work taking place in the Yard did not mean that everyone was happy behind the wall - far from it: a mass one-day stoppage took place across the general workforce in August 1969 and eight months later the Dockyard's first recorded case of industrial action at officer level occurred when 68 instructors walked out in protest over pay. The men wanted to be rewarded the same as civilian instructors which essentially meant that they wanted an extra four pounds per week - they eventually got it.
In 1972 there were more strikes over pay culminating in a week's action in September that brought the Yard to a halt.
Towards the end of the Seventies, Civil Servants at the Naval Base also staged a walk-out, affecting work on various refit programmes and in June 1979 the Yard was again almost brought to a standstill.
Once again these issues weren't confined to Devonport: nationally it was a time of great industrial unrest, the miners strike in 1972 had prompted a power crisis and precipitated the necessity of a three-day working week. Growing dissatisfaction also ousted Conservative Prime Minister Edward Heath but the situation didn't ease and inflation rose to a record 25% per year.
The situation in Ireland was also overheating and a succession of IRA bomb attacks in England and Northern Ireland led to the banning of Servicemen wearing uniform outside of Naval or Military bases. A generation of Britons had grown up knowing only peace in Europe and now domestic troubles were causing heartache, as race riots too flared up in London, Liverpool, Birmingham and other major cities - but not Plymouth.
Notwithstanding these home-grown issues, the need to equip a large Army, Navy and Air Force was deemed to be receding and in 1981 the Secretary of State for Defence, John Nott, announced massive cuts in defence spending the net result of which was that Chatham would close, Portsmouth would become a minor repair yard, leaving just Rosyth and Devonport, with Devonport designated the *'undisputed home of the Royal Navy with enough work to keep the Yard fully employed for many years to come and with a probable addition of 1,500 staff - some of whom would be transferred from Chatham and Portsmouth.'* [Burns]

All Hands on Deck

Among the many proposals contained in John Nott's review was the intention to withdraw HMS *Endurance*, Britain's only naval presence in the South Atlantic. This was believed by some to send out the wrong signal to General Galtieri, who, in December 1981 had become acting President and head of the military junta that had been governing Argentina since 1976. The regime was struggling with an economic crisis and civil unrest over human rights issues, and so an attempt to reclaim land in the South Atlantic that Argentina had long regarded as its own was deemed to be a good move, emotionally and politically and an excellent diversionary tactic to boot.
Thus it was that on 19 March 1982 60 hired Argentinian scrap merchants landed, illegally, on a flimsy 'metal-collecting' pretext, on the tiny island of South Georgia, which lies some 800 miles to the south-east of the Falkland Islands.
Having landed they raised the Argentine flag. Britain was incensed and, suspecting British mobilisation, Galtieri ordered the invasion of the Falkland Islands to take place on 2 April. Diplomatic negotiations failed to remove the Argentine host and on 5 April an armada assembled at Portsmouth bound for the South Atlantic.

The men of HMS Ardent *wave a fond farewell as they set sail for the South Atlantic. Sadly the ship was sunk in Falkland Sound on 22 May, 22 of the crew were lost.*

Media attention focussed on Portsmouth, but Devonport was a hive of activity as ferries, container ships and roll-on/roll-off vessels were converted into aircraft transports and support ships. Men worked long hours, a month's work was done in just over a week as decks were strengthened and makeshift landing platforms were welded into place. Weapons and supplies of all kinds poured into the yard as work continued around the clock.
In all, the conflict lasted 74 days, the Argentine surrender being signed on board HMS *Plymouth* on 14 June.
Several ships had been lost, including the Devonport based *Ardent*, *Antelope* and the container ship *Atlantic Conveyor*: 255 British servicemen had died, along with 649 Argentinian soldiers, sailors and airmen and three Falkland Islanders.
There was a day of rejoicing in July as thousands massed for a welcome of tears and cheers. Two thousand men rode in a coach convoy, creating the biggest traffic jam that the city had ever seen. In November, Prince Andrew led a huge parade and spectacular fly past and the Crown in Stonehouse was renamed the General Moore in honour of Major-General Jeremy Moore who had accepted the Argentine surrender.

The anticipated security in the wake of both John Nott's Defence Review, and the Falklands War, was not immediately apparent. In 1984 Peter Levene, advisor to the Defence Secretary, Michael Helsetine, recommended that private companies should take over the management of Devonport and of Rosyth Dockyards.
The following year Michael Hesletine was in the Plymouth, determined to privatise the Dockyard: *'I am not getting value for money'*, he said, *'and I will get value for money'*.
In 1986 12,000 Devonport Dockyard workers walked out in protest over the proposed privatisation of the yard, nevertheless, in 1987, the Government leased Devonport Dockyard and its facilities to Devonport Management Limited (DML) who lost little time in shedding 3,000 jobs.
In the meantime, Devonport-based frigate HMS *Broadsword* went into the Yard for a major nine-month refit after its return from two months' service in the Gulf with the Armilla Patrol.
Work, however, was by no means plentiful, and two years later it was announced that the Dockyard had won a contract to build a fleet of eleven steel yachts that DML had been contracted to produce for the British Steel Challenge – the Round-the-World race – a race that the acclaimed yachtsman, Chay Blyth was organising.
Meanwhile, the submarine *Opportune* completed its refit – it was the 28th Oberon and Porpoise class submarine to be refitted in the yard.

City of Plymouth
Welcomes home the Task Force
OFFICIAL PROGRAMME:
50 pence

Fighting Talk

1990 saw DML win its first Royal Fleet Auxilliary refit – on the *Grey Rover* and then, in August of that year, the country once again found itself involved in a theatre of war following Iraq's invasion of Kuwait. The move was condemned internationally and the United States, Saudi Arabia, Egypt and the United Kingdom joined in the military operation to expel the Iraqi forces.

On a morale-boosting exercise, Prince Charles and Lady Diana visited Devonport Dockyard meeting staff involved in preparing ships for the war zone in the Gulf. By the end of February 1991, what was to become known as the First Gulf War, was all over.

In July HMS *Brave*, then the longest-serving Gulf War ship, returned to a hero's welcome. Later in the year there were more than 20 ships on show at Navy Days, including the very latest Type-23 frigate, HMS *Marlborough*.

The big issue in the Dockyard however was jobs and DML were shedding them at an alarming rate, not just as part of a cost-cutting exercise but also because there was simply not enough work coming into the Yard.

Hence the high-profile campaign, backed by the *Evening Herald*, to secure the Trident contract for Plymouth rather than Rosyth. Devonport MP David Jamieson went to 10 Downing Street armed with a petition signed by thousands, a 25lb pasty and a group of Dockyard workers. The 'Battle of the Dockyards' became a major topic of debate and great was the relief for DML boss Mike Leece and his workforce, when, in June 1993, the Defence Secretary, Malcolm Rifkind, announced in the House of Commons that Devonport had been selected to refit Britain's Trident nuclear submarine fleet.

But for some it was already too late.

In his chapter on Defence, The Dockyard and Diversification (in *Plymouth: Maritime City in Transition*, 1991), Paul Bishop noted that in *'1947 21,000 workers were employed at the Dockyard'* adding that although *'the post-war period saw a gradual decline in employment, the Dockyard remained the largest employer in the area. By 1981 15,535 workers were still employed in the shipbuilding sector, almost entirely accounted for by the Dockyard.'* However, by 1987 that figure had dropped to around 12,000, 11,000 of whom were employed in the Yard. By 1994 the stark reality was that over

Top: *Prince Charles and Lady Diana visit Devonport Dockyard 1991*. Middle: *Devonport MP David Jamieson accompanies Dockyard workers to No.10 Downing Street.* Bottom: *DML boss Mike Leece celebrates success in the battle of the dockyards.*

'Hunter killer' HMS Trafalgar enters No.5 basin. Inset: Navy Days poster reflecting the admission of women into the Royal Navy in the early 1990s.

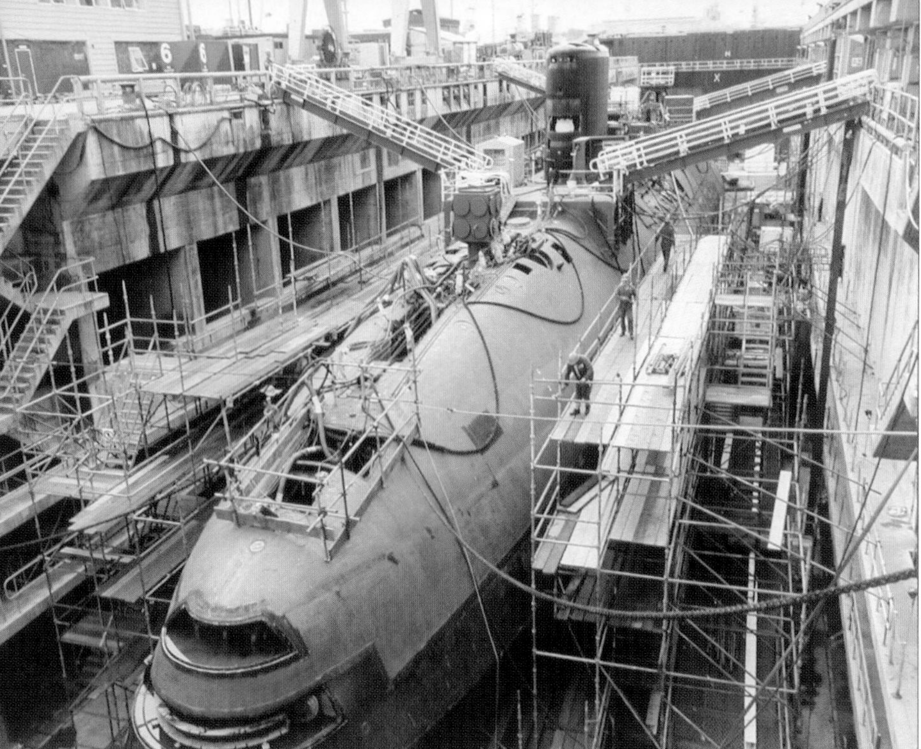

Top: *HMS Ocean sails into the Hamoaze.* Bottom: *Refitting a nuclear submarine. This is a complex and time-consuming process. Submarines also need interim servicing, then, at the end of their working life, a period storage afloat while the radioactivity in the defuelled reactor plant decays to sufficiently low levels, this may take 30–50 years.*

the seven years he had been in post as Managing Director, of the privatised Dockyard, Mike Leece had been forced to implement some 8,000 job cuts, a task he found both difficult and upsetting. True the company had won a contract to refit ten yachts that had taken part in the 1992 Challenge race and had a deal to build another five for the 1996 race, but it simply wasn't enough, there was just too little surface ship work. The departure of HMS *Illustrious*, the Navy's most advanced warship, didn't help.

Of course these statistics represented only a part of the story. The thawing of the Cold War – the process of 'perestroika' – had allowed the Western world to enjoy something of peace dividend when it came to Government spending, however, for Plymouth, and particularly for Devonport, the economic and social consequences were dramatic.

Back in the late-thirties there were over 121,000 naval personnel compared with around 40,000 (including 2,000 voluntary reserves) in the mid-late nineties. Thus, it wasn't the size of the Dockyard that was crucial to the local economy for, without the ships, and without the sailors, the amount of disposable cash feeding the local money-go-round was fast dwindling. Pubs, pasty shops, newsagents, clothing stores all felt the pinch and while there were various initiatives – some funded by central government – to the north and east of the city to attract industries and create employment, that was of little use to those Devonport businesses that depended on the passing pedestrian for their survival.

Over and above the submarine contracts, work continued to trickle into the Yard: in 1995 DML won a £20 million contract to design, procure and install new chilled-water systems into Trafalgar Class nuclear submarines; in 1998 the Glasgow-built, Devonport-based HMS *Ocean* was commissioned and in 2002 the Duke of Edinburgh came down to open the new Vanguard-class submarine refit facility and the first Trident submarine arrived at Devonport – but by then the number of people working there dropped to under 5,000.

To give the matter some perspective, to merely pay the wages of an extra 10,000 workers at a modest average wage of around £20,000 per annum then with all the national insurance contributions and pension allowances well in excess of £200 million needs to come from somewhere, every single year, and that's without any operating costs or materials.

Ownership

Such figures underline the importance of major contracts to the yard and the total value of the Vanguard contract was reckoned to be in excess of £1 billion which, it was said, would guarantee work in the area for at least ten years.

Arrangements in the Yard, however, are by no means as straight forward now as they have been for the previous 300 years. When DML bid the Yard they were owned by two companies – the long-established American construction and shipbuilding concern Brown & Root and British-based Vickers Design & Projects. In 1987, when DML acquired the contract, that ownership shifted and Balfour Beaty and the Weir Group both bought a 30% stake in the business and Barclays de Zoete Wedd a little over 10%.

Seven years later the electronics Giant GEC acquired VSEL (Vickers Shipbuilding and Engineering Ltd) and withdrew their interest from the DML consortium prompting the Ministry of Defence to persuade Brown & Root to take a 51% controlling interest in the Yard, which they did and then promptly bought the Yard for £40.3 million.

Brown & Root in turn were a subsidiary of the American-based international oil and energy giant Halliburton, which, in 1998 acquired the MW Kellogg Co (originally US power plant specialists) and merged it with Brown & Root (creating KBR which, thereby, interestingly became the largest non-union construction company in America). Eight years later Halliburton decided to float KBR on the stock market – a move that the MoD were less than happy with, on the grounds that they thought it might make DML a little unstable.

The following year, 2007, Halliburton announced that they were prepared to sell the DML group and a number of major players in the global defence industry appeared interested, including, so it was rumoured, BAE Systems (British Aerospace, successors to a number of well-known aircraft, warship and defence electronic companies). The Ministry of Defence, seemingly supported this initiative as they were keen to combine with the existing submarine production facilities of BAE.

However, in the event only two bids were forthcoming: one from the Carlyle Investment Group, and the other from Babcock International (the British-based company which had, in 2002, switched its focus from Engineering to Support Services. Over the next few years

Babcock absorbed a number of other companies, including Service Group International, Turner and Partners, and the Alstec Group (a nuclear and airport services operator). On 28 June 2007 they added DML to their portfolio as part of Babcock Marine Services. in a deal that was worth £350 million.

Since then Babcock (who also have interests in Rosyth) have taken over International Nuclear Solutions Plc (August 2007), Strachan & Henshaw (April 2008) further strengthening their nuclear and submarine support activities, and, in September 2009, UKAEA (the United Kingdom Atomic Energy Authority), leaving the MoD – and the rest of the world – in no doubt as to their expertise in the world of nuclear energy. Crucially, perhaps, for Devonport, as the company themselves point out, the acquisition represented *'a significant extension to Babcock's existing nuclear skills by bringing proven capabilities in waste categorisation, decommissioning of high hazard facilities, encapsulation and storage of hazardous materials and transportation of waste, which are applicable to both the civil and military sectors.'*

Regeneration

The major changes affecting the Nuclear and Submarine programmes of course tend to focus on North Yard – the area above 'old' or South Devonport, all of which has tended to render South Yard itself increasingly redundant – currently barely half the yard is needed by the Navy, while Mount Wise has, for some years now, been surplus to requirements.

Of course one consequence of this was to decimate even further the potential employment opportunities in South Devonport, making living in the area all the more difficult for men and women with families to support. Having said that much of the post-war housing arrangements conspired against that anyway, the emphasis being firmly on flats rather than houses. Although, when the first phase of building on the Raglan Estate was opened on 15 May 1976, it was as married quarters for naval personnel.

Nevertheless, with the Devonport skyline dominated by its the three great tower blocks, flats were very much the order of the day and when the Roman Catholic church of St Michael and St Joseph at Mutton Cove was demolished to make way for a residential development, that development was a further 48 flats.

Interestingly enough, the replacement for the Victorian church, St Joseph's, which was built on part of the old Raglan site, was extremely basic – it cost just £250,000, a figure that takes on some sort of significance when you consider that the previous year, 1984, saw a grant of £100,000 awarded towards the restoration of Devonport Guildhall (it was at the time the largest urban grant to have been awarded west of Bristol).

There was a further housing development on the Raglan site (Raglan Gardens) in the 1980s and, in common with most of the other, post-war developments in Devonport, there was little attempt to acknowledge the heritage of the area, save for the retention of the original Raglan gatehouse (which still stands empty). It was as if the planners were quite happy for this once proud town to become little more than a relatively ill-equipped social housing estate with a bleak future.

May 1976, the Raglan Estate is opened. (South West Image Bank)

he heart of Devonport with the MOD Storage Enclave dominating the view.

Above: *Inside the Plymouth Naval Base Museum.*
Left: *the hangman's cell.*
Below: *HMS* Plymouth, *the ship upon which the Argentinian surrender was signed, and which was berthed, for a while, in Millbay Docks. Sadly it did not prove to be a viable tourist attraction and there was insufficient funding available from the City.*

No Past? No Future!

An oft-repeated plea for Devonport has been that of establishing a major Naval Museum in South Yard. Portsmouth set up their Historic Dockyard Museum just before the First World War, and the attraction consistently attracts over 400,000 visitors a year (over 500,000 in 2005 when the bi-centenary of the Battle of Trafalgar was celebrated). Indeed HMS *Victory* was voted the second best historical attraction in the UK a few years ago (by UKTV History viewers) and is a key part of Hampshire's tourist industry which is worth well over £2 billion per year. Portsmouth's Museum also benefits from having Henry VIII's favourite ship, the *Mary Rose* and HMS *Warrior,* Britain's first iron-hulled, armoured warship.

Devonport undoubtedly has the potential for an impressive museum of its own, and stored within the yard's original collection of artefacts – the Adelaide Gallery – was the flag under which Nelson fought at Trafalgar. However, all was lost in the Great Fire of 1840 and although there was a suggestion to set up a proper museum in 1914, soon after the Portsmouth initiative began, the idea was quietly forgotten over the next few, war-dominated, years.

It wasn't until 1969 that Stanley Greenwood, a long-time employee of the Naval Stores Department, realised the long-held ambition and Plymouth Naval Base Museum was opened – on 28 April 1969. Officiating, Dr Basil Greenhill, Director of the National Maritime Museum at Greenwich, said 'There are few places with a greater maritime history than Plymouth'.

Reg Blackett was the attraction's first curator and visitors to the North Yard used to form long queues outside Albert Gate morning and afternoon. In December 1969 it was reported that 1,500 people a week were being given conducted tours around the dockyard and visiting the duty ship; there were also pre-booked visits from organised groups and schools.

The Museum moved twice in the 1970s and currently occupies the former Cashier's buildings. Tours of the Museum include visits to the various listed buildings in the Yard, among them: the ropery; the old hangman's cell; and, until recently, the decommissioned submarine HMS *Courageous*. However, despite numerous feasibility studies and the sterling efforts of a team of volunteers (managed for many years by Commander Charles Crichton), the Museum has never really received the support, financial or otherwise, that would really put it on the map nationally and internationally, and give Devonport something to be really proud of – and be a major driver in the local economy.

Things Can Only Get Better

As it was, throughout the 1980s and 1990s the indigenous Devonport economy seemed to be in free-fall. Worse still, all the usual social indicators were in free-fall too as crime (against persons and property) was increasing (at Mount Wise it was double that of the rest of PLymouth), drug abuse was spiralling out of control, as were certain of the area's younger element – cars were regularly vandalised and set on fire. Meanwhile, the rates for teenage pregnancy were the highest in Plymouth, and the pass-rates, at GCSE level, at Parkside School were the lowest in Plymouth, indeed they were among the lowest in the country!

It was around this time that I approached City Bus with a view to running a regular open-top tour bus around historic sights of Plymouth: the Hoe and the Barbican, Mount Wise, Devonport Guildhall, etc. The response was, on the whole, very positive, but we were told the company would not be prepared to take the buses into Ker Street and the Mount Wise areas as they feared that stones would be thrown at the vehicles and they were not prepared to risk damage to either the buses or the sightseers. As it transpired, a national tour bus operator (Guide Friday) took on the task locally, but needless to say they didn't include Devonport on their routes.

Another incident I recall from the early 1980s was the landlord of the Swan at Cornwall Beach recounting how a couple of very young boys swaggered into his pub one day and informed him that they had keys for all the lockable rooms in the building! It was said, incidentally, that the pub had closed in the mid-1970s, prior to its reincarnation as a real ale pub, amid rumours of it being associated with one of the oldest professions – the same one that had kept the Lock Hospital at the top of the hill in business for many years.

For most Plymothians such stories were off their radar as they had little or no reason to visit the area and the local papers were not then as keen to report such day-to-day miseries. For those residents living in the middle of it all though it could be hellish: *'sheer bedlam – car burning, youths running riot and nobody wanting to get involved with anything at all'*, was how one resident described it.

'When built in the 1950s the new council-owned flats were sought after, tenants who moved in considered themselves fortunate. But by the late-1980s ... the flats stopped being sought after. Pembroke Street had degenerated, it had become an inner city area that nobody wanted to live in.' [Lizzie Cook, devonportonline]

Power to The People

Feeling abandoned and neglected, a number of the Pembroke Street tenants decided it was time to make a stand. Thus it was, in 1987, that they formed a residents' group to try and tackle the various problems.

'The big opportunity came in 1991 when the group applied to take part in the Government's 'Estate Action' programme. They successfully secured £5.1 million of funding, using it to upgrade both the homes and the environment of the estate. Community meetings were carried out, reports were written, and plans devised.'

The flats now, *'not only look good, they are also pleasant to live in, and safe, with security at the entrance to each block. In 1994 residents took over management of the flats themselves – by forming an Estate Management Board (EMB). The entire site is maintained regularly by the tenants, via their Board, from an office at 102 Pembroke Street.'* [Cook]

Pembroke Street: Before and after the redevelopment. New Gate (Pembroke Street)

Never-Ending Story?

Ultimately it was the degree to which the Pembroke Street initiative regenerated the community spirit that was the key to their success: *What made Pembroke Street a 'community', a successful community, was their actions in going beyond the physical upgrade. They don't just cut grass and sweep the road, what they do is carry out a range of community-based activities focusing on community wellbeing: basically they look after each other, everyone plays the good neighbour. If someone is ill and they live alone, the EMB team ensures their shopping is done, if an elderly person cannot walk to the chemist, the team ensures their prescription is obtained. If someone requires household maintenance of some sort, there is a maintenance team on hand to help. The aim, and it's been very successful, was to reduce isolation and enhance the quality of life for tenants. The values held at Pembroke Street are all about caring, about social inclusion, being morally accountable and holding high ethical standards. These are the things that have made it a community.'* [Cook]

The Pembroke Street story doesn't end there, however: since becoming fully operational the Pembroke Street Estate Management Board have come to play a major role in the regeneration of the area as a whole, indeed, in some respects, the country as a whole.

In 1995–6 the Pembroke Street scheme won several awards, including a British Urban Regeneration Award and an Abercrombie Architecture Award. The PSEMB's work attracted attention nationwide and was one of those bodies singled out in the paper *Putting Back the Pride*, a report conducted by the Joseph Rowntree foundation at the request of the Department of the Environment, Transport and the Regions (now the Department for Transport, Local Government and the Regions).

In Devonport, near Plymouth, the residents of the Pembroke Street Estate played a leading role in the Estate Action-funded refurbishment of their estate; this led in turn to the formation of a Tenant Management Organisation run by the residents and employing several of their number. But the project also encompassed a wider vision which included the economic transformation of the surrounding Dockland areas.

Clockwise from top left: *The street team. The old flats. The new flats. (Pembroke St EMB) Pembroke Street address list - 13 blocks of flats housing 450-500 people.* Inset: *A typical house sign. (Cook) Visitors from Cornwall learn from a resident. (Pembroke St EMB)*

Top left: *New houses around James Street.* Bottom left: *View across James Street from Tavy House.* Bottom right: *New housing and the old column .* *(Images from Plymography)*
Top right: *South Yard – ripe for redevelopment.T*

Top: *Cornwall Street is cleared for redevelopment. (webrarian.co.uk)*
Above: *Cornwall Street today.*

The Changing Face of Devonport

While the Pembroke Street initiative had been hugely impressive, it had, at the end of the day, only addressed the practical problems of a very particular part of Devonport. However, what it had also done was to give people locally the belief that they could instigate change themselves – with a bit of help from central Government of course.

Thus it was that a local consortium was formed in March 2000 - the 'Devonport Five' – to bid for £48.7m from the Government's New Deal for Communities (NDC} programme.

Devonport, they said, *'is a distinct and diverse community, which exhibits all the signs of multiple deprivation and exclusion. The scale of deprivation revealed in our baseline information shows a growing gap between Devonport and elsewhere; the way services are currently provided can clearly be seen to be failing the residents of Devonport. Our community is determined to take action to achieve a much greater influence on what happens in the area to address the issues of poor educational performance, (significantly below that of both Plymouth and the whole country), poor basic skill levels, unemployment levels (at twice the average for Plymouth), low levels of economic activity, an average income of under £8,000 per household, poor housing conditions, very poor health and high levels of crime.'*

Their submission was supported by a whole raft of statistics that made for dismal reading and reflected badly on the city as a whole, but at least now that the plight of Devonport was being better articulated more people seemed to be taking notice.

In February (2001), the *Evening Herald* (Plymouth's daily paper) started a campaign to rid the community of the greatest blot on the landscape, the one that had divided and depressed the community – the Dockyard extension wall.

'Bring the Wall Down' was the cry and a letter to that effect was sent to the Prime Minister, Tony Blair, and to the Defence Secretary, Geoff Hoon. The following month Hoon replied and promised he would work hard to find a solution.

In April 2001 it was announced that Devonport had been awarded £48.7 million from the NDC programme which in turn heralded the biggest social regeneration programme Plymouth had ever seen, and for Devonport it opened the door to a more sensitive and satisfactory schedule of work and initiatives than those that were put in place after the war, spearheaded by a wider consortium - Devonport Regeneration Community Partnership - with local residents and community representatives in the majority. Indeed it heralded a new dawn for the old town and one which would at last see it largely freed from the shackles of social housing (which had accounted for up to 80% of the accommodation in places), in favour of a more balanced approach where at least 50% of the housing was privately owned.

On top of all this, also in April, Hoon's successor as Defence Minister, Lewis Moonie, pledged that the wall would come down, a statement that he followed later in the year with a study into the feasibility of redeveloping the whole of South Yard storage enclave.

In May 2002 Moonie announced that the whole of that part of South Yard (that part appropriated by the Admiralty in the fifties) would indeed be handed over to the people of Devonport by the end of 2004.

In the meantime, a number of other projects left the drawing board: Plymouth City Council, in 2001, decided it was time for the pre-war and post-war Council flats at Pottery Quay, to be rebuilt. The work, which was said to be worth around £10 million, was to be overseen by the Guinness Trust, in conjunction with the Westcountry Housing Association and Midas Homes, and was to be carried out in two phases, ultimately providing a mix of rented and shared ownership affordable housing.

The demolish-and-rebuild approach was also taken at Ker Street, where all the flats were of post-war construction.

The MoD's decision to release the South Yard storage enclave created new possibilities for Ker Street. Previously it had been somewhat restricted in it's interconnections with the wider community, now, with a clean sheet, planners could see opportunities to allow access to the north and south, rather than just along its east/west axis. The Council offered the site, subsequently christened 'Evolve' to a team made up of Devon and Cornwall Housing, Midas and Westco Developers.

During 2006/07 residents were 'decanted' and in June 2008 78-year-old Philip Coombe, who had been living in the Ker Street Bull Ring development since it had opened in 1962, was afforded the opportunity to start the demolition process.

Overall, the new proposals promised more houses with gardens (60%) rather than flats (40%), and more privately owned properties.

Phase 1, on the north side of the street, was partially opened on 11 July 2009, with local swimming star Sharon Davies MBE unveiling a new three-bedroom, three-storey home (available for £144,950).

Top two images: *the old flats at Pottery Quay come down. (Barry Kinsman)*
Below *them we see the first of the new properties.*
Top left: *The old Bull Ring at the bottom of Ker Street. (Plymography)* Left: Crowds cheer the beginning of the demolition process. (Simon Gomery) *Post-demolition the sign boards go up.* Above: *the first of the new Ker Street houses. (Plymography)*

Tamar, Tavy and Lynher – the three tower blocks, before and after their makeover. (Plymography)

Phase 2 of the work was twice the size (129 new homes as opposed to 62) and involved building over part of Mount Street – the old east-west route through to Mount Wise, and the widening of Pembroke Lane to provide a new east-west access route. Both phases of work were frustrated by the fall out surrounding the recession that blighted the country at the time of the development and both were supported via the Government's Kickstart funding (£601,000 towards Phase I and £1,450,000 towards Phase 2).

James Street and Bennett Street saw similar programmes of redevelopment, and the three big tower blocks, Tamar, Tavy and Lynher, were reclad and 'softened' with red, blue and green finishings respectively (the colours being those of the Devonport Field Gun Team). However, the project that dwarfed all of them was the one that covered the South Yard storage enclave and which was christened by the developers Redrow: 'Vision':

The Old Market Square. The River Tamar. An impressive eco lifestyle ... If you've been searching for a place to live which offers the best in contemporary living, surrounded by nature, look no further – Devonport has it all.

Vision is our very latest development, featuring more than 450 new homes, shops, offices, and community facilities. The exciting mixed-use neighbourhood boasts a stylish collection of 1-, 2-, 3- and 4-bedroom homes, built to the highest standard. With specific attention to achieving high eco standards, this superb range of homes isn't just more cost-effective to run, it will also have a less negative impact on the environment.

Set in a suburb of the marvellous maritime city of Plymouth, to the far south west of Devon, Devonport boasts a truly enviable position.

Wind the clock back 100 years, to pre-amalgamation Devonport and the prospect of this once proud town being described as a suburb of Plymouth might have had one or two members of the Devonport Borough Council spluttering over their cornflakes, but sadly this was the new reality, and at least it is true to say, from a location perspective, that Devonport does boast an enviable position. To date, however, the realisation of the Vision has been more difficult than first envisaged.

Having been commended for Housing Project of the Year, in the *Mail on Sunday*'s British Home Awards in 2007 – the year the digger moved in on THAT wall, the scheme has stuttered and struggled in the face of the recession.

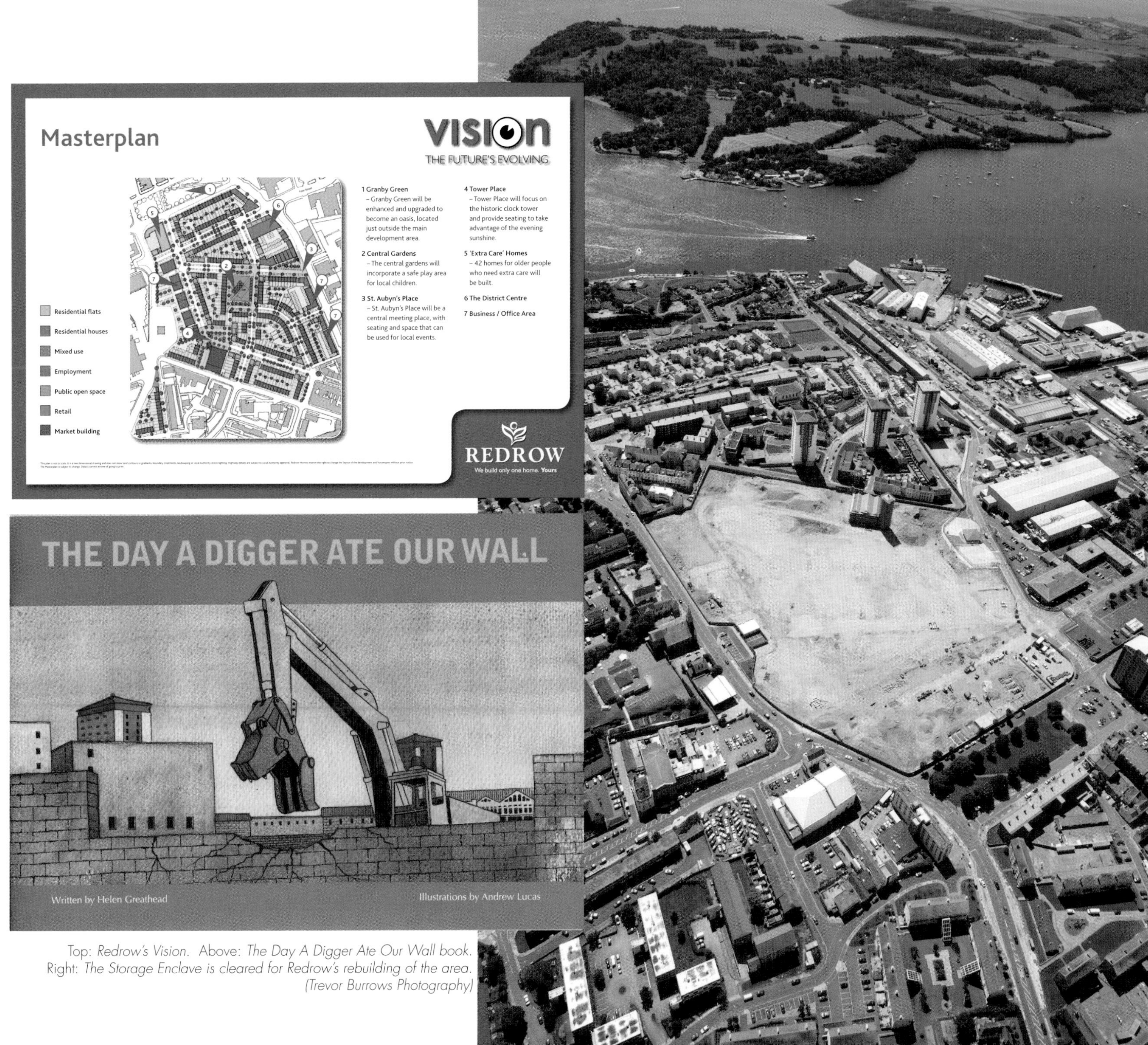

Top: *Redrow's Vision*. Above: *The Day A Digger Ate Our Wall book.*
Right: *The Storage Enclave is cleared for Redrow's rebuilding of the area. (Trevor Burrows Photography)*

In the summer of 2008 the first residents moved in to the row of 17 new houses off Granby Way. Hailed as a 'significant milestone' in the transformation of the South Yard enclave, the Area Director of English Partnerships, David Warburton, said that the *'scheme has been some time in the making and will be a few years before the entire project is completed.'*

Shortly afterwards, a scheme to help first-time buyers, particularly key workers like teachers and nurses earning under £60,000 a year, was made available for around fifty homes in the Vision scheme. However, the recession continued to squeeze the building industry and in May 2009, Devonport Councillor Nicky Wildy said the site was *'becoming an eyesore'*.

Welcome, therefore, was the news, early in 2010, that, thanks to Housing Minister John Healey, Redrow's Vision scheme has secured a KickStart grant of nearly £3 million – 50% of which would need to be repaid, but at least it gives the developers, here and elsewhere, a hand to get the site back up and running (across the country some 22,500 homes were potentially affected).

'This is good news for the City,' said Plymouth Sutton MP Linda Gilroy. *'Not only will it mean a key affordable housing scheme gets back on track, but part of the deal means that Redrow must provide schemes for local labour and apprenticeships.'*

Granby Way (Plymography)

Back to the Beginning

'Vision@Devonport', as it's styled by Redrow, is not the only major housing scheme for Devonport that has experienced recession-induced difficulties, there is another, equally ambitious, £60 million proposal to build 450 homes (364 open market, 84 affordable), plus offices, shop, bistro and an hotel, at Mount Wise.

This scheme, driven by Mount Wise Ltd (an offshoot of the Bristol-based company Firmac Developments) was put on the table soon after Firmac bought the site (for £5 million) from the Ministry of Defence, in 2006. Work was scheduled to start in the summer of 2007 but planning permission was not obtained until the following year by which time concerns over the design of some of the facades had further delayed things. As time passed other variations to the scheme have come and gone, including a plan for a 20-storey tower block – the proposal has been superseded by plans for three blocks of five-or six-storey flats. Meanwhile, all has been quite quiet on the 28-acre site.

Interestingly enough, if a hotel does appear on this site, it will be the first new hotel to be opened in Devonport in over 100 years (the Royal Fleet Club being the last in 1899). It is also, currently, the only hotel in old Devonport (although even that situation is changing as the building was sold in June 2010 to the Church of Scientology for about £1million, by Kailash Suri (who had bought it, reputedly for £1.5m, in December 2008). The significance of the Mount Wise proposal should not therefore be underestimated, it is, after all a long time since the area was deemed to be a suitable visitor destination, and as far as I'm aware there have been no tourist-type picture postcards of Devonport produced in over sixty years.

Mount Wise, however, with its ever-increasing potential for public access, is an important key to a new future for Devonport and the recent addition of the site into the Devonport Conservation Area (itself a relatively new concept), augurs well for the area as a whole.

Mount Wise is a truly spectacular location, however even the opening up of the old fort site (where Sir Thomas Wise built Devonport's first recorded property) and the construction of a forty-metre high, millennium lookout tower/mast there, has done little to attract anything more than the odd dog walker.

And yet Mount Wise, which was first laid out as a public park around the same time as the Hoe, in the 1890s, has the potential to be as attractive as the Hoe. At the moment its open-air pools are free to use when open in the summer season (the pools were refurbished as part of £5 million urban park

Mount Wise and Devonport. (Trevor Burrows Photography))

project at the end of the 1990s and were jointly funded by Plymouth City Council, the Heritage Lottery Fund and Plymouth Development Corporation}.

Mount Wise had been one of three sites (the others were the Royal William Yard and Mount Batten) that the Plymouth Development Corporation was set up to deal with in April 1993. The PDC only had jurisdiction over seven acres of Mount Wise, and although they perhaps delivered a little less than was hoped for, they undoubtedly improved the appearance of the area – an area that *'contains nationally important buildings, structures and significant archaeology. Some of these buildings, such as Admiralty House, are landmark buildings and are of national importance.'* (PCC Devonport: Characterisation Study & Management Proposals 2006)

Set up as the Maritime Headquarters during the Second World War, significant aspects of Mount Wise exist below the visible surface: as the Plymouth Underground Extension – a network of tunnels joining planning rooms, a communications centre, dormitories, shelter and other facilities – was constructed with an entrance through MHQ.

Mutton Cove and Richmond Walk also have their own peculiar pockets of history and herein undoubtedly lies an important element in the regeneration of Devonport.

The City Council's 2006 study identified well over 100 buildings/ structures in Devonport that are either Listed or of 'Townscape Merit'. Many of these are in either South Yard – where there are also four Scheduled Ancient Monuments (Covered Slip of c1763; the West Ropery; the Scrieve Board and No. 1 Basin and No. 1 Dock) or Morice Yard *'which remains today one of the best preserved and complete of all the Georgian ordnance depots.'*

The only problem is that access to the latter is seriously restricted and to the former, generally pretty limited. Such is not to say that over the coming years that situation might not change for the better. However, one thing that needs to happen sooner rather than later is putting into working order of a number of those currently empty historic buildings in South Yard that are currently quietly deteriorating.

As is the Raglan Barracks Gatehouse *'one of the most impressive barrack entrances and guardhouses in England – Fowke, the designer, was among the leading army architects, most famous as the co-designer of the Albert Hall.'*

Sadly neglected and standing in splendid isolation, the gatehouse sits

Top: *Mount Wise Park.* Inset: *the Millennium Mast.* Middle: *Looking South from the Mast.* Bottom: *Looking North West from the Mast.*

opposite the entrance to the main car park servicing Plymouth Albion who moved to Devonport from Peverell in September 2003. Since their arrival at the Brickfields, the rugby club have worked together with the local authority, the DRC Partnership and the Rugby Football Union, and first-class facilities, including a rubber crumb pitch, are now a feature at Devonoprt. DRCP, PCC and Sport England funded a new Brickfields Sports Centre: a multi-purpose hall that includes a fitness suite; dance/aerobic studio; clinic/consulting rooms; community meeting space; changing facilities; office space; reception area; grandstand seating for up to 1,200 spectators.

Separate funding was approved for existing facilities – via Sport England, DRCP and PCC – to improve the Brickfield's Athletic facilities and running track.

Interestingly enough, the wider Brickfields site has also now been included within the Conservation area – there is evidence that the historic Dock Lines are in a good state of preservation. Like the Grade II listed Devonport Park and Garden, the Brickfields was pressed into service in various ways during the Second World War, although more survives as a legacy of that era in the Park, with its Air Raid Shelter and the single-storey, red-brick Gas Cleansing Centre. Restoration of the latter, estimated at £60,000, was part of the successful 2006, £5.5 million bid (£3.3 million from Heritage Lottery, £905,314 from DRCP, the rest from PCC, to return Plymouth's first public park to its former glory.

Sadly, the Local Authority's attitude towards the park in the previous two decades had been similar to that towards the area as a whole: *'with the exception of a new shelter, there appears to have been a slow decline in the expenditure and consequently the condition of the park. The last park keeper, and eight out of ten gardeners, were removed in the late 1980s.'*

Happily however, that situation has, for the time being at least, been turned around and among the many features to undergo restoration are the splendid Swiss-style entrance lodge, the 1863 Napier fountain (also known as the Sea Captain's or Royal Marines Memorial); the Galatea Monument, the Sicilian Fountain, the Memorial Garden, the Lower Lodge, the Doris Gun, the park railings and pathways. Furthernore, the old bandstand has been recreated and a new play area added. It is just to be hoped now that there is an appetite (and a budget) to ensure that the excellent endeavours of the last few years are cherished and protected.

Top: *Plymouth Albion*. Middle: *Devonport Park (Plymography)*.
Right: *Devonport Park Lodge*. Far right: *The Park Pavilion (Plymography)*.

Clockwise from top left: *Ultra Violet property marking explained; talking Satellite Navigation on the Torpoint Ferry; Art in the Community at Mount Wise; Brickfields Sports Centre; cutting the first turf for the Dental School; Christmas lights in Marlborough Street. (DRCP)*

The Bottom Line

The present Park scenario is echoed across all aspects of life in Devonport today – when all the grants are spent, when all the funding is exhausted what will happen then?

The Guildhall at the top of Ker Street is currently undergoing its second major overhaul since the war, this time £1.75 million has been made available to *'turn it into a thriving creative social enterprise hub for the Devonport community and creative industries across the region'*. The initiative is being managed by the Real Ideas Organisation *('working closely with strategic partners and local regional and national organisations including DRCP, Plymouth City Council and Big Lottery')* to *'preserve the building's heritage and significance within the community.'*

It will, say the Real Ideas Organisation, *'provide everyone who visits and uses the space with the opportunity to meet people, make contacts and inspire each other in an environment that is innovative, vibrant and alive. It's about freedom to think, move and create, there will always be something going on which you can seek out and be inspired by.'*

Thinking comes from awareness and education, and over the ten years of its existence, DRCP has been doing its best to promote that process in a variety of ways to a variety of age groups. Like the 'learn and earn' programme that was introduced at late-lamented Parkside School, before it closed amid falling numbers and a degree of controversy. For a while the scheme helped drive up exam results quite spectacularly – the last results, in the summer of 2008, being their best ever.

More enduring perhaps was the breakfast club initiative at Mount Wise school. In response to pupils coming to school late and with empty stomachs, the breakfast club successfully enticed more children into school and generally earlier, helping parents to get back to work in the process.

There is also currently a Learning Together project, started at Mount Wise Primary in 2005, where the focus is on family and adult learning, and the DRCP-funded Inclusion for Youth programme, enabling *'young people between 11-25-year-olds access to support, guidance and information so that they can make informed decisions about their lives'*.

Certainly one by-product of these and any number of other initiatives that have been started under the DRCP umbrella, has been a massive drop in the rate of teenage pregnancy in Devonport – it had been the highest in Plymouth.

There has also been a marked improvement in anti-social behaviour. Again this has been helped in no small measure by the support of the DRCP for the Bobbies on the Beat scheme, but also in the efforts made to find things for young people to do, notably music and sport.

'The devil finds work for idle hands to do' runs the old adage and certainly the greater the number of real opportunities to be constructive, the less car burning, burglary and violent crime there has been in the area, indeed less crime of all kinds.

Again through a variety of initiatives, business start ups in the area have increased dramatically and the level of self-employment in the old part of Devonport is currently around 20% higher than it is in the rest of the city. There has also been a 20% increase in those earning over £220 per week.

There can be no doubting the improvements, the only question mark is over the sustainability. But as the neighbourhood becomes safer, happier, cleaner, tidier, prettier, then it is bound to be more attractive to more people, thereby encouraging the sort of social mix that has been missing since the Second World War bombing raids drove so many local shopkeepers and small businessmen and women out of the community.

Currently there are fewer shops and fewer pubs in Devonport than there have been in over 200 years. At the end of the Napoleonic Wars there were about 200 pubs in Devonport, at the end of the First World War, around 100 – clearly this situation has been mirrored in other parts of the country too, but by the end of the Second World War that figure had dropped by half again, and today there are less than 10 pubs still trading in Devonport. Remarkably now they are all either listed buildings or deemed to be of significant townscape merit, but even so some of those, like the eighteenth-century Swan at North Corner, probably the oldest pub building still standing in Devonport, and the handsomely fronted King's Arms, in George Street, are closed, while the Old Chapel is now a Co-operative supermarket.

Moreover, there is currently no butcher, no bank and no DIY or electrical goods store serving the community, but there are four fast-food outlets in Marlborough Street alone.

Envoi

Devonport undoubtedly has a great deal of heritage, but it needs jobs, it needs decent houses, decent schools, and a well-maintained and cared for social infrastructure.

The arrival of part of the Peninsula Medical School, in Devonport, Britain's first new Dental School in forty years and part of the Universities of Plymouth and Exeter, is another feather in Devonport's (and DRCP's) cap and bodes well for other institutions favouring the area in the future.

With so many schemes on the table and with so much potential for opening up this area up without the traditional Services' stranglehold – and the inevitable ups and downs of war and peace – the future for Devonport has never looked brighter. South Yard alone is bigger than some small towns, and the sooner Mount Wise, the Storage Enclave and the rest of South Yard is freed up, the sooner Devonport can settle down, enjoy the views and become the desirable location that it deserves to be.

Devonport Town Hall after its £1.5 million refurbishment in 2010. (Plymography)

Conclusion

Mount Wise, from Cremyll

Standing on the platform of the Millennium Mast today, looking out over Mount Edgcumbe, it is hard to believe that Mount Wise itself was a largely undeveloped area a little over 300 years ago.

While the Mount Edgcumbe estate has changed little in all that time (the Tudor house was rebuilt after being gutted by incendiaries during the Second World War), the Tudor house at Mount Wise, which stood on the site of the mast, was pulled down soon after work began on the creation of Plymouth Dock.

Thereafter the stories of the two Mounts could hardly have been more different, as one remained the comfortable seat of a noble family and the other became the bustling home of a royal dockyard: one surrounded by parkland, trees and deer, the other encircled by defensive lines and walls, and sea.

However, when senior members of the royal family deigned to visit, they stayed, not in the dockyard town, but at Mount Edgcumbe and apart from a brief heyday around the time of the Napoleon Wars, when money and prizes (captured 'treasure' ships) were pouring into the port, the wealthier residents, whose livelihoods depended on Dock, chose not to live in the crowded town, but in the rural areas around it.

Apart from the Governor's House, Admiralty House, and later Seymour House (and the Piermaster's House at North Corner), there appears not to have been a single substantial detached residence erected in Devonport after Mount Wise house came down, and I don't believe there are any current proposals that will change that.

In Plymouth, there were several such big houses built in the wake of the Elizabethan expansion with the money Drake and his contemporaries brought into the town. In Plymouth Dock there was no such tradition, and with most of the land in the hands of the St Aubyn estate, there was little potential, or appetite for such developments.

Hence whereas the wealthier residents, in time, moved out of Plymouth and looked to sites along Regent Street, North Hill and beyond, the wealthier Dock residents built their villas outside the lines between the Brickfields and Stoke Village, some in splendid isolation, others, like Albermarle Villas and Penlee Villas, in orderly lines, but always commanding impressive views. Meanwhile the working class overspill was catered for to the north of Devonport itself, in Morice Town, Ford and Keyham.

The significance of all this was really to make its impact after the First World War: for it was then, with the improvement in public transport, that it started to become apparent that Devonport residents were looking more and more to Plymouth for shops and services. It is true that Devonport was still well-provided for but *'none had the gloss of the Plymouth stores. The eclipse was showing, even then.'* [Gill]

After the Second World War that eclipse was obvious to all. The commercial heart of Devonport simply wasn't rebuilt and once that great champion of Devonport, Sir Clifford Tozer, had moved his stores out of Devonport and into the new City Centre, it was clearly doomed (Tozer was Lord Mayor of Plymouth 1953-54).

Apart from the Railway Tavern (it re-opened as the Ark Royal) precious few bombed buildings were replaced.

In the drive to rebuild Plymouth after the war the demolition men went mad. One local councillor even suggested that the Civic Crest be replaced by *'two bulldozers rampant'*.

The reality was that for every building that was pulled down, the government would make a grant available to replace it, and this is what fuelled the housing programme on the new estates.

In Devonport there were complaints when the Admiralty requisitioned acre after acre of the old town, effectively cutting it in two and destroying whole roads and the old street pattern. There was a similar story in Plymouth, only there the clearing of 72-acres of blitz survivors was so that a new commercial centre could arise: it wasn't to erect an imposing and depressing wall around the site and create a no-go Admiralty area in the heart of the community.

Furthermore, in Plymouth, when it came to the Barbican and buildings that pre-dated the early days of Dock, and the city centre, the cry 'enough' was eventually heeded.

The Plymouth Barbican Association was formed off the back of the Old Plymouth Society, in 1957, following the wanton destruction of the old Elizabethan Ring of Bells, and before long the situation started to turn around.

Many buildings were lost, but many were saved and, significantly, the Government Grants continued to be forthcoming, as long as the old buildings were looked after and not used for residential accommodation.

Thus a community of artists, potters, and other craftspeople – those who were prepared to pay rent for such ancient edifices – started to spring up and the area was transformed.

Had this not happened there could be little doubt that the Barbican would have ended up like a Devonport by the sea: a 1950s council estate with only the odd isolated treasure – like the Merchant's House, the Elizabethan House and the Gin Distillery – still standing once the dust had finally settled.

It is worth pointing out that in the 1943 Plan for Plymouth the authors refer to just a few ancient buildings being kept in what they called 'the Historic Precinct'. Devonport, with the Town Hall, Column, Egyptian House, Old Chapel, King's Arms, and Market, was not hugely different to that vision.

Fortunately there is still enough of interest to be found outside the Dockyard in Devonport to merit the creation of a Conservation Area, and this, together with a more sympathetic and catholic approach to building new houses across a range of price bands, may yet properly regenerate the town. Indeed, if all goes well enough, it could yet see Devonport in a better position than it has ever been. The various recent developments following the Pembroke Street initiative and the wide ranging schemes supported by the DRCP have already kick-started this process in a significant way. Let's hope that in another 90 years or so, when someone else picks up this narrative baton, there's a happy ending to record, and a new beginning too.

Devonport at night from the Mast. (Plymography)

Acknowledgements & Bibliography

The author is indebted to a variety of texts and websites, magazines, periodicals, plans and brochures as well as a number of public bodies - the Central Library, the City Museum and Art Gallery, the Plymouth Barbican Association's South West Image Bank, the Herald, Western Morning News and the Naval Base Museum. A number of individuals have also been extremely helpful, directly and indirectly and while I will almost certainly have forgotten to include everyone, mention must be made of Stacey Dyer, Peter Waterhouse, Mary Wills, Gerald Barker, Monica Twyford, Maureen Attrill, Brian Moseley, Lizzie Cook, Nigel Overton, Charles Crichton, Bob Cook, Gerry Rendle, Joan Dancer, John and Sylvia Boulden, Sally Luscombe, Andy Endacott, Dena Goves, Joe Pengelly, Richard Creber, Dave Luckham, Stanley Goodman, Terry Guswell, Audrey Hosier, Roy Westlake, Barry Kinsman, Jason Nolan (Plymography), Bernard Mills, Trevor Burrows Photography, Bryan Bailey and Steve Johnson (Cyberheritage).
On the proof reading front, Bill Bugler, Clare Robinson, Helen and Patricia Greathead, Doreen Mole, and Rob Warren have all been invaluable.

To Rob Warren I am particularly grateful as his wonderful colour washes have worked wonders in bringing so many of the early images to life, many of them are seen here in colour for the first time ever: not only do they look fabulous, they make the material so much easier to 'read' ... thanks Rob.

300 Years Devotion to Duty **Andy Endacott** 1991
A Letter From Plymouth **David Chamberlaine** Old Plymouth Society 2007
A Plan for Plymouth **Paton-Watson Abercrombie** Plymouth City Council 1943
Baseport, Devonport, Warships Part 1 & IV **Sydney VC Goodman** 1982
Days In Devonport Parts I to VI **Gerald W Barker** 1982-86
Devon & Cornwall Illustrated **Britton & Brayley** Fisher, Fisher & Jackson 1832
Devon Roads **Michael Hawkins** Devon Books 1988
Devonport Characterisation Study and Management Proposals - PCC July 2006
Devonport Dockyard Past & Present **Chris Robinson** Herald Supplement 2001
Devonport Dockyard Railway **Paul Burkhalter** Twelveheads Press 1996
Devonport Dockyard Story **KV Burns** Maritime 1984
Devonport in old picture postcards **Gerald Barker** European Library 1987
Devonport Regeneration Study Historic Buildings Jean Manco GHK 2007
Devonport Stoke and Morice Town Stonehouse & Plymouth **John Sanford** 1830
Devonport, Hail and Farewell to FS Blight Trans PI, xii 1951
Devonport, History of **RN Worth** W Brendon 1870
Devonport, Inns and Beerhouses 2 vols, **Henry Horwill** manuscript PLHL 1975
Doidges Annuals 1888-1954
Drainage of a Town, **A Hamilton Bampton**, Plymouth & Devonport 1849
Early Tours in Devon and Cornwall ed R Pearse Chope Augustus M Kelley 1968
Elizabethan Plymouth **Chris Robinson** Pen & Ink 2002
Henry Winstanley, Artist, Inventor and Lighthouse Builder, **Alison Barnes** 2003
Historic Defences of Plymouth **Pye & Woodward** Exeter Archaeology 1996
HM Naval Base Devonport, Historic Architecture of Jonathan Coad **NMA 1983**
HMS Drake Wardroom Mess 1973
It Came To Our Door **Pat Twyford** (revised Chris Robinson) Pen & Ink 2005
Kelly's Devonshire Directory also published by White & Billings 1856-1928
Lost Landscapes of Plymouth **Elisabeth Stuart** Sutton 1991
Mr Rawlinson's Report on Sewerage, Drainage, of Plymouth PD&S Herald 1853
Naval Heritage in the West Parts 1-3 **Andy Endacott** 1986-88
New Maritime History of Devon vol 1 Various Conway Maritime 1992
Ordnance Land at Devonport Western Daily Mercury 1857
Payne's Devon **Peter Hunt** Devon Books 1986
Playbill, A History of Theatre in the Westcountry **H Crane** McDonald Evans 1980
Plymouth & Devonport Church & Chapel Rowing Clubs **J & B Cusack** 2000
Plymouth & the West, Early Newspapers in, **JL Palmer** TPI vol xix 1944
Plymouth A New History **Crispin Gill** Devon Books 1993
Plymouth and Devonport Guide with Sketches **HE Carrington** Byers & Son 1838
Plymouth and Devonport in Times of War and Peace **H Whitfeld** Plymouth 1900
Plymouth Devonport & Stonehouse etc, Handbook **Henry Besley** 1864
Plymouth Dock Guide Etc **E Hoxland** Dock 1792
Plymouth in Pictures **Crispin Gill** David & Charles 1968
Plymouth In The Twenties and Thirties **Chris Robinson** Pen & Ink 2008
Plymouth In War and Peace **Guy Fleming** Bossiney 1987
Plymouth Municipal Records ed **RN Worth** Plymouth 1893
Plymouth Ships of War Lieut Cdr **KV Burns** National Maritime Museum 1972
Plymouth Steam 1954-63 **Ian H Lane** Ian Allen 1984
Plymouth Through the Lens Vols 1-6 **Brian Moseley** 1985-1993
Plymouth, 100 Years of Street Travel **RC Sambourne** Glasney Press198?
Plymouth, A History **CW Bracken** Underhill 1931
Plymouth, History of **Llewellyn Jewitt** WH Luke 1873
Plymouth, Story of **RAJ Walling** Westaway 1950
Pottery Quay Newsletter Various 2005-2008
Pubs of Plymouth Past & Present Vols 1 & 2 **Chris Robinson** Pen & Ink 1997
Raglan Barracks, Navy & Army Illustrated May 1896
Red Rocks of the Eddystone **Fred Majdalany** Longmans 1959
Risdon's Survey of Devon **Tristram Risdon** London 1811
Royal Naval Hospital Plymouth Surg Capt, PD **Gordon Pugh** 1972
Sir Wm Morice CW Bracken, Devon & Cornwall Notes & Queries vol 21 1940
South Devonport Report CC Gimingam City of Plymouth 1966
The Beauties of England and Wales **Britton and Brayley** London1803
The Day A Digger Ate Our Wall **Helen Greathead** University of Plymouth 2008
The Ingenious Mr Dummer **Celina Fox** eBLJ, article 10, 2007
The Storm **Daniel Defoe** 1704 Reprinted Penguin 2005
The Trams of Plymouth **Martin Langley and Edwina Small** Ex Libris Press1990
Turner's Rivers, Harbours and Coasts **Eric Shanes** Book Club 1981
Vanishing Plymouth **Brian Moseley** BS Moseley1982
Victorian Plymouth **Chris Robinson** Pen & Ink 1991
William Payne A Plymouth Experience **David Japes** 1992

Index

A

B

C

D

PRORSUM·SEMPER·HONESTE